Elements

The Novels of
James Dickey

For wonderful, smart Amy. A pleasure to meet you. Etowah Valley MFA 2018

Casey Howard Clabough

Casey Clabough

Mercer
University
Press
MMII

ISBN 0-86554-743-2
MUP/H558

© 2002 Mercer University Press
6316 Peake Road
Macon, Georgia 31210-3960
All rights reserved

First Edition.

∞The paper used in this publication meets the minimum
requirements of American National Standard for
Information Sciences—Permanence of Paper for Printed
Library Materials, ANSI Z39.48-1992.

Library of Congress Cataloging-in-Publication Data

Clabough, Casey Howard, 1974-
  Elements : the novels of James Dickey / by Casey Howard Clabough.—1st ed.
    p. cm.
Includes bibliographical references and index.
  ISBN 0-86554-743-2 (alk. paper)
  1. Dickey, James—Fictional works. 2. Dickey, James—Dramatic works.
I. Title.
  PS3554.I32 Z625 2002
  813'.54—dc21

                                                              2002004821

Contents

Abbreviations

Commonly cited works by Dickey are abbreviated in the following manner:

AL   *Alnilam*

DL   *Deliverance*

TS   *To the White Sea*

WM   *The Whole Motion*

Preface

This study considers Dickey's three published novels and the majority of his unpublished fiction. It does not address Dickey's (in)famous life and times, recorded in Henry Hart's biography, or his centrality in a battle of literary politics, discussed in Ernest Suarez's *Assessing the Savage Ideal.* It also gives little notice to the poetry, on which there are several book-length studies and for which he is most celebrated by scholars.

This book has two major goals: to articulate the fictive vision which spans Dickey's three published novels and to discuss both his unpublished fiction and the source material which fueled the published work. In regard to the latter two items, I do not mean to suggest a kind of manuscript history of the novels. Rather, I wish—while discussing the published work—to bring to light many of the hitherto undiscussed notes and unfinished fiction that Dickey left behind him. This not only provided me with a fuller understanding of the collective fiction, but also supplies scholars with new information they may wish to build upon or dispute.

Unless otherwise noted, all of Dickey's papers cited here are in the Woodruff Library, Emory University. Each unpublished source is footnoted in the following manner: series, box or cassette tape number, folder number (if identified), page number (if available).

Acknowledgments

Several individuals aided me in the writing, researching, and overall development of this project. Joyce Pair promptly read the manuscript at each stage of its development: I value her many suggestions. Jeanne Clabough, Dan Turner, and Dirk Goering also read and commented upon specific chapters during the composition process. My dissertation committee—chaired by Keen Butterworth and consisting of Pamela Barnett, Ashley Brown, and Thomas Brown—evaluated and corrected the work at an earlier stage. Matthew Bruccoli, Dickey's literary executor, gave me permission to quote from Dickey's unpublished papers, thereby increasing the project's scope and scholarly value. Steve Ennis and the fine special collections staff at Emory University answered my questions and copied masses of documents. Finally, but not least, Byron Campbell let me fly his vintage Stearman, an experience that helped me more than I expected in writing about *Alnilam* and *Crux.*

INTRODUCTION

THE PRACTICE OF MERGING

I think the degree to which you participate in a play or poem is
a very important factor. You have to help the writer, and the
poem.
    —*Dickey,* Self-Interviews, *66*

He combined the cunning of foxes with the feral grace of tigers,
always a shape-shifter and a threshold guardian.
    —*Pat Conroy on James Dickey*

I am pure space…
    —*Dickey, "Mexican Valley" in* The Whole Motion, *407*

Despite the existence of many fine articles on Dickey's fiction and several book-length studies of his poetry, there is no extended work of scholarship which seeks to establish his fictive vision in terms of his three novels. The *Texas Review* dedicated an entire issue to Dickey's novels around the time of his death,[1] yet every article save one focuses on a particular book. The single essay that takes account of all three novels—Joyce Pair's "Measuring the Fictive Motion: War in *Deliverance, Alnilam,* and

---

[1]*Texas Review* 17/3–4 (Fall/Winter 1996/1997).

To the White Sea"[2]—is important not only for addressing each novel, but also for its consideration of war and masculinity. Several years earlier, Gordon Van Ness's essay, "'The Whole Situation was Mine': James Dickey's Fictional Protagonists and the Ethic of Survival," considered Dickey's three novels in terms of their main characters. Van Ness investigates Ed Gentry's, Frank Cahill's, and Muldrow's "temporary physical mastery over the environment" as "Darwinian adaption."[3] These two essays, beyond their intuitive readings, are laudable in their attempts to consider a single important theme as it runs through each of Dickey's novel. Yet because they are journal-length essays—one a hefty thirty-seven pages, the other a brief seven—, it is not within their scope to consider Dickey's fictive vision in its entirety.

Where these essays made tentative headway this book takes a grand leap, developing a case for Dickey as a serious fiction writer and examining the common ideas informing the body of his work. Several factors have led me to believe in the importance of this study. One significant consideration is the bibliographical fact that, although Dickey is primarily known as a poet, there are over one hundred scholarly articles on the novel *Deliverance*—more than four times the number on any one of Dickey's poems. Such a huge and consistent outpouring of work points to the high critical regard in which the novel continues to be held.[4] Also of importance is the fact that Dickey invested massive amounts of time in *Alnilam*,[5] a commercial failure, though one of which Dickey claimed he would

---

[2]Joyce M. Pair, "Measuring the Fictive Motion: War in *Deliverance, Alnilam*, and *To the White Sea*," *Texas Review* 17/3–4 (Fall/Winter 1996/1997): 55–92.

[3]Gordon Van Ness, "'The Whole Situation was Mine': James Dickey's Fictional Protagonists and the Ethic of Survival," *James Dickey Newsletter* 10/1 (Fall 1993): 17.

[4]Scholarship on *Deliverance* has continued to flourish decades after the early 1970s, discounting the idea that much of the work's status is based on the initial popular success of the book and movie.

[5]Of the forty-one cassette tapes upon which Dickey recorded notes and ideas throughout his life, twenty-eight deal almost exclusively with the development of *Alnilam*.

not change a single word.[6] Dickey championed *Alnilam* as the attempted masterpiece of his career and, regardless of the largely disparaging receptions the book received, the immense quantities of time and energy he put into it bear him out.[7] It seems very significant that an artist celebrated for his poetry would point to a novel as his defining achievement. Furthermore, it has not helped matters that Dickey openly belittled his fiction, claiming on a number of occasions that his novels were only "spin-offs" from "Poetry...the center of my creative wheel"[8]; and scholars have not hesitated to share Dickey's categorization of the novels as secondary creations.

One problem the researcher faces when approaching scholarship on Dickey's work in general is the violently opposed reactions to it. To be sure, this situation exists to a greater or lesser extent in scholarship on all writers; yet in Dickey's case the phenomenon seems especially amplified. As Ernest Suarez comments in his study of Dickey's literary reputation, *Assessing the Savage Ideal*:

> Dickey's detractors claim that his bourgeois sensibility results in socially irresponsible poetry that advocates hedonism and violence. His emphasis on 'intuitive reaction' and on the poet as a maker of new realities is often construed as symptomatic of an unreflective, sensationalistic willingness to ignore social realities. To such critics, Dickey represents the reactionary escapism of the plantation novel, laminated with a myopic glorification of the self. Conversely his advocates hail him as a modern-day

---

[6]See "To Walter McDonald," in James Dickey, *Crux: The Letters of James Dickey*, ed. Bruccoli and Baughman (New York: Knopf, 1999) 467.

[7]The sheer bulk of source materials, notes, and manuscripts for *Alnilam*, easily dwarfs that of any other project—fiction or poetry—he ever worked on.

[8]Ronald C. Baughman, ed., *The Voiced Connections of James Dickey: Interviews and Conversations* (Columbia: University of South Carolina Press, 1989) 147.

transcendentalist, a poet who celebrates life-affirming instincts.[9]

As interesting as these opposing interpretations—Dickey as solopsistic amoralist or primal romantic—is the subjective manner in which they continue to be perpetuated. Considering Dickey's selected letters, *Crux*, one reviewer claims they "reveal a man consumed by a passion for language and life,"[10] while another explains Dickey's criticism of his contemporaries by stating, "Dickey is largely a sour novice."[11] Neither reviewer gives reasons or evidence for the claims he makes. The same can be said of J. D. McClatchey's hollow assessment of the fiction collected in the *James Dickey Reader*: "Better than serviceable though less than memorable."[12] Although the nature and format of the book review, to a certain extent, demands hyperbolic summaries, the repeated unsubstantiated celebration or dismissal of books pertaining to Dickey is worthy of note. Years after the publication of Suarez's study, critics—those who both praise and attack—continue to take extreme sides in a largely opinionated and adjectival debate.

Amid this turbulence one faces the difficult problem of selecting an avenue of critical inquiry, and, this being the first comprehensive examination of Dickey's novels, I neglect several potentially fruitful readings—those that would explore dynamics such as constructed "Southernness" and gender (or masculinity and its opposite)[13]—in arguing what I conceive to be Dickey's

---

[9]Ernest Suarez, *James Dickey and the Politics of Canon: Assessing the Savage Ideal* (Columbia: University of Missouri Press, 1993) 111.

[10]Henry L. Carrigan, Review of *Crux: The Letters of James Dickey, Library Journal* 124/17 (15 October 1999): 70.

[11]Review of *Crux: The Letters of James Dickey, Publishers Weekly* 246/43 (25 October 1999): 65.

[12] J. D. McClatchey, Review of *Crux: The Letters of James Dickey* and *The James Dickey Reader, New York Times on the Web* (19 December 1999) 1 January 2000 <www.nytimes.com/books/99/12/19/reviews/991219.19mcclact.html>.

[13]The following essays give varied attention to the issue of gender in Dickey's novels: Verónica Horenstein, "Phantom Lovers in *Deliverance, Alnilam,* and *To the White Sea,*" *James Dickey Newsletter* 17/2 (Spring 2001): 15–26; Jane

dominant fictive vision. Considering Dickey as a Southern novelist would seem at first glance an especially productive avenue for interpreting his fiction. However, while cultivating a Southern public persona, Dickey always maintained the universality of his art. A graduate of Vanderbilt and a literary apprentice for a time to Andrew Lytle, he nonetheless maintained, "The only way in which I am a Southern writer is that I am simply a writer who happens to come from the South. I don't have any doctrinaire feelings about this at all."[14] Dickey's independent approach to his art can also be traced to his interactions with his contemporaries. Unlike many other writers of his time who formed artistic and political alliances—the confessionals, the beats, and other lesser-known groups—Dickey remained an aesthetic loner, often making negative assessments of popular artists that earned him the censure of the literary establishment. With this in mind, I have resolved to confront his fiction largely on its own terms.

Dickey's art is irrevocably the product of an aesthetic sensibility which seeks to know the essence of things. In his acceptance speech for the National Book Award he asserted: "I find that I write poetry because I want to know something—to *come* to know it, even if I have to invent what I know—by living with it on as many levels as I can, by being intimate with it, severe with it, angry with it, baffled by it, in love with it. But what always emerges is the sense of its *importance*, or at least its importance to me, being quite literally all that I have."[15] Dickey's ambition to understand the bare bones of things on "as many levels" as possible naturally leads to his interest in animals and nature—fundamental aspects of existence: "When you live enough in the imagination, your loves

Hill, "Relinquishing Power and Light," *James Dickey Newsletter* 15/2 (Spring 1999): 2–13; Sandra B. Durham, "A Felt Absence: The Female in *To the White Sea*," *James Dickey Newsletter* 13/2 (Spring 1997): 2–7; and Joyce M. Pair, "Measuring the Fictive Motion: War in *Deliverance, Alnilam,* and *To the White Sea*," *Texas Review* 17/3–4 (Fall/Winter 1996/1997): 55–92.

[14]Baughman, *Voiced Connections,* 67.

[15]James Dickey, *Night Hurdling* (Columbia: Bruccoli Clark, 1983) 110.

get to be very deep and gentle; they seem not to be centered in islands of possessions, like most human loves, but to be diffused among people and animals and plants, and the shapes and colors and smells and sounds of things."[16] For Dickey, nature is the foundation of all reality—human and non-human—and thus, even in a postmodern era, is still the artistic subject most worthy of contemplation. Since his method calls for him to know things on all levels—or even from the inside out—, much of his art is marked by attempts at becoming the essence of nature itself—not contemplating the natural world but assuming or *being*, to the best of his artistic ability, some aspect of it: a tree, a rock, an animal waking up in heaven.

Dickey's affinity for assuming the identity of natural forms—human, animal, or otherwise—explains why many critics have classified him as a later romantic poet, possessing the gift for what Keats called the "Sympathetic Imagination": "If a sparrow come before my window, I take part in its existence and pick about the gravel."[17] In *James Dickey and the Gentle Ecstacy of Earth*, Robert Kirschten uses slightly different terminology to say as much: "[Dickey] heartily approves of Keats's conception of 'negative capability.'"[18] Likewise, Donald Greiner makes a clear argument for why Dickey's art is more romantic than modern: "Had Dickey maintained the modernists' intellectual contemplation of nature, had he, in effect, remained on his side of the wall, he might have assented to Frost's sense of fear and uncertainty in the face of nature's inexorable processes. But he does not.... The goal of Dickey's 'exchange,' of his embrace of the non-human life force, is not merely to see from a different perspective but to achieve a unified vision of life that is a composite of both the human and the

---

[16]James Dickey, "The Imagination as Glory," in *The Imagination as Glory: The Poetry of James Dickey*, ed. Weigl and Hummer, 166–73.

[17]John Keats, *The Complete Poetical Works and Letters of John Keats*, ed. Scudder (Boston: Houghton Mifflin, 1899) 275.

[18]Robert Kirschten, *James Dickey and the Gentle Ecstacy of Earth* (Baton Rouge: Louisiana State University Press, 1988) 144.

other."[19] There is explicit evidence for such a view in Dickey's poetry. In "The Three," Dickey uses Emersonian language to describe a natural union. The speaker contemplates a group of low-flying birds and feels himself "oversouling for an instant / With them..." (*WM*, 440). Like the romantic poet, Dickey assumes the existence of a natural form; however, the traditional Romantic may only participate up to a certain point—"oversouling for *an instant.*" As Ronald Baughman maintains, "After his initial celebration of the prospect of achieving union with nature, the writer realizes that he cannot acquire the union he desires without the loss of his own identity."[20] In the traditional romantic formula, loss of identity while bonding with the other results in the death of the self and—for those who identify him as a pure romantic—this is not something Dickey is willing to do.

My readings of the novels demonstrate that, although Dickey's art has romantic qualities, there is a more visceral and elemental sensibility at work. David Arnett claims, "The mind-link theme is uniquely Dickey's. It is related to the ability of the superior soul to rise and fall on the evolutionary scale and to taste the life experience of other beings,"[21] an evolutionary sentiment which corresponds to Van Ness's assessment of the novels' protagonists as experts in "Darwinian adaption." A dimension of scientific determinism, of animalistic survivalism, exists in Dickey's work which cannot be entirely accounted for by romanticism.[22] Such

---

[19]Donald J Greiner, "Robert Frost, James Dickey, and the Lure of Non-Human Otherness," in *His "Incalculable" Influence on Others: Essays on Robert Frost in Our Time*, ed. Wilcox, 69.

[20]Ronald C. Baughman, "The Poetry of James Dickey: Variations on Estrangement" (Ph.D. diss., University of South Carolina, 1975) 241.

[21]David L Arnett, "James Dickey: Poetry and Fiction" (Ph.D. diss., Tulane University, 1973) 146.

[22]Matthew Guinn articulates the shortcomings of a purely romantic reading in his discussion of naturalistic qualities in Dickey's poetry: "But counter to the romantic tradition, [Dickey] refuses to impose anthropocentric concepts on the natural world; nature in his poetry is too immediate and primal to be a reified incarnation of abstract principles" (Matthew Guinn, "The Neo-Romantic in the

existential fundamentalism—if such a term may be coined—is traceable to Dickey's interest in the pre-Socratic philosophers who believed that natural elements are the catalysts for existence. For example, Anaximander and Heraclitus, two of his favorites, interpret experience largely through manifestations of air and fire respectively.[23] In his identification with the other, there exists also an echo of Lucretius—the celebrated Roman poet with strong philosophical ties to the pre-Socratics—, whom Laurence Lieberman has referred to as Dickey's "mentor,"[24] and his fondness for Epicureanism: the attempt to explain all we perceive without inferring the existence of anything other than material objects and the space in which they move. Indeed, Dickey has expressed interest in resistant physical subjects as well as those whose identity he would attempt to assume. His admiration for the Japanese novelist Yukio Mishima is a result of this concern: "Mishima speaks of his personal cult of 'Sun and Steel': the pitting of the body against an obstacle, like the lifting of a weight. That kind of thing appeals to me."[25] In addition to using the ephemeral qualities of romanticism to lose his self in the essence of the other, Dickey employs Epicurean modes to contemplate the interstitial relationships among literal objects and imagine the physical reality of their being.

The archetypal significance of Epicureanism is not lost on Dickey, who had strong interests in anthropology and the reactions of primitive cultures to natural objects. In his reading of James Frazer's *The Golden Bough*, Dickey glimpsed another explanation for assuming the other's identity or employing, as I shall come to call it, the "practice of merging": "The idea that the soul may be deposited for a longer or shorter time in some place of security

---

Natural World: Naturalism in James Dickey's Poetry," *South Atlantic Review* 62/1 [Winter 1997]: 87–88).

[23]Phillip Wheelwright, *Heraclitus* (New York: Atheneum, 1974) 41.

[24]Laurence Lieberman, "Warrior, Visionary, Natural Philosopher: James Dickey's *To the White Sea*," *The Southern Review* 33/1 (Winter 1997): 164.

[25]Dickey, *Night Hurdling*, 172.

outside the body…is found in the popular tales of many races."[26] In weaving his own tales, Dickey saw similarities between himself and the people of ancient cultures, although artistic semantics, more than religious myth, was his tool for merging: "I would have made a great Bushman or an aborigine who believes that spirits inhabit all things…. The notion of reincarnation really appeals to me very much…. I'd like to be some sort of bird, a migratory sea bird like a tern or a wandering albatross. But until death, until this either happens or doesn't happen, I'll have to keep trying to do it, to die and fly, by words."[27] Whereas the purely romantic artist must eventually back away from union with the other in order to preserve the self, Dickey has no qualms about giving his artistic self over entirely to the spirit or essence of the thing he beholds. Like Hegel, he believes that the individual who truly contemplates a subject/object is "absorbed" entirely by it, sacrificing all consciousness of the "I,"[28] and, through his artistic method, Dickey hopes to arrive at what Heidegger calls the phenomenological world view: a position in which the observer shuns traditional interpretation in favor of having the world reveal itself to him as it truly is ("things themselves!").[29] Intellect, preconceived sensibility, and the self—or as much of it as possible—must be forgotten or repressed to the extent that reality becomes perceptible in its rawest form. Only in this way is the artist finally able to drift into the minds of animals.

---

[26]James Frazer, *The Golden Bough: A Study in Magic and Religion* (Hertfordshire: Wordsworth, 1993) 679. Dickey's merging practice also suggests Lucien Lévy-Bruhl's anthropological definition of "participation" in which animate and inanimate natural objects interact with and influence each other's existence. See Lucien Lévy-Bruhl, *How Natives Think*, trans. Lilian A. Clare (London: G. Allen and Unwin, 1926).

[27]James Dickey, *Self-Interviews*, ed. Barbara and James Reiss (New York: Doubleday, 1970) 79.

[28]See Alexandre Kojève, *Introduction to the Reading of Hegel* (New York: Basic Books, 1969) 37.

[29]Martin Heidegger, *Being and Time*, trans. Macquarrie and Robinson (New York: Harper & Row, 1962) 34.

Of course, all of this is more easily theorized than practiced, and to a substantial degree such an artistic approach is destined to repeated failures. The main danger is that portraying such events—which constitutes language's ultimate challenge—leads the artist to Kant's idea of the sublime: an inexpressible state or experience which is impossible to represent.[30] Such is probably the case when critics attack Dickey's language for failing to capture the experience it seeks to express.[31] Dickey strives, sometimes to the point of representational disintegration, for what Nietzsche says the pre-Socratic philosophers principally desired: "Something incommensurable...a certain deceptive directness and at the same time an enigmatic depth, indeed an infinitude, in the background."[32] Yet the almost inevitable failure in sublime representation is due more to the sheer impossibility of the attempt rather than any limitations or lack of talent on Dickey's part. Sartre perhaps makes this point best when he says, "Human reality is its own transcending toward what it lacks; it transcends itself toward the particular being which it would be if it were what it is."[33] A general human lacking, an inability to realize our potentials, stunts whatever gropings we make for our optimal selves. Since we are forever not what we are supposed to be, there is no way to attain what we lack; yet this is not to say that the attempt is not worth making, and—at the risk of utter failure—Dickey repeatedly makes the attempt.

What keeps Dickey from straying into the sublime too often is his aforementioned affinity for Epicureanism as demonstrated by his interest in space and the body. Dickey was constantly aware of

---

[30]Immanuel Kant, *Critique of Judgement* (London: Oxford University Press, 1978).

[31]See Leon Rooke, "Sergeant Muldrow finds Transcendence," *New York Times Book Review* (19 September 1993): 14. Rooke says of *To the White Sea*, "Dickey's language, which manages to be both airy and bloated, wobbles all over the place, especially when he attempts to balance the brutality of the action with his themes of transcendence."

[32]Friedrich Nietzsche, *Basic Writings of Nietzsche*, ed. Kaufman (New York: Modern Library, 1968) 80.

[33]Jean-Paul Sartre, *The Philosophy of Jean-Paul Sartre*, ed. Cumming (New York: Vintage, 1965) 170.

space both in his artistic themes and the composition process. His fondness for audio tapes as archives for unwritten ideas rested largely in their having nothing to do with the physical act of writing: "One must be careful, in putting something down on paper, for this occupies a *space* [Dickey's emphasis] on paper and also sets the direction of the writer's mind."[34] Whereas the filled space of an audio tape entry remains unwritten and auditory, and may be erased with the press of a button; writing on a white page represents a conceptual interpolation that is materially present, constituting a text existing in literate space. Dickey sought to avoid the existence of the written object until he had fully investigated the possibilities of its subject in the comparatively free medium of recorded ideas.

In a cryptic remark on one of his audio tapes Dickey says, "Instead of working with Orion like most poets have traditionally done, I work with space."[35] The declaration underscores his interest, not so much in symbolic objects themselves, but the dynamics of their existence in the space they occupy.[36] As we shall see in *Alnilam*, much of Orion's importance is, not the constellation itself, but the elements that make it up—the stars that exist in spatial relation to each other—and its ever-moving place and prominence in the winter sky, among the other stars. In entertaining this idea, Dickey's conception of space is similar to that of Hegel, who apprehends it as the defining quality of nature: "The first or immediate determination of Nature...is the abstract universality of its externality, its immediate indifference, i.e. Space. Space is the wholly ideal side-by-sideness (*Nebeneinander*) because it is externality, and it is absolutely continuous, because this mutual

---

[34]Series 11, tape 10.

[35]Series 11, tape 11.

[36]Dickey joins a philosophical tradition in his fascination with space. In his history of spatial physics, Max Jammer makes the claim, "From Descartes to Alexander and Whitehead almost every philosopher has made his theory of space one of the cornerstones of his system" (Max Jammer, *Concepts of Space: The History of Theories of Space in Physics* [Cambridge: Harvard University Press, 1954] 1).

outsideness is as yet entirely abstract, and involves no definite difference within itself."[37] Since Dickey believes in the importance of space as the invisible, yet significant and existing, background for nature and objects, it plays a central role in his art. Whereas other writers might overlook the presence of empty space, Dickey emphasizes its existence in the context of many of his characters' physical actions. In the introduction to one of his favorite books, Stanley Burnshaw's *The Seamless Web*, Dickey reveals his interest in the physical circumstances of fictional characters: "For me, the most fecundating of Burnshaw's researches are those dealing with the effects on the human body of the various environments in which it exists."[38] Although he has been both lauded and criticized as a "masculine" writer, Dickey joins feminists like Hélène Cixous in the belief that writing is often both created and apprehended in terms of the fictional and authorial body, and the conditions under which it exists. In 1976 one of Dickey's staunchest champions, Richard J. Calhoun, called for an examination of landscape in Dickey's poetry: "Enough has been said elsewhere about Dickey's use of exchanges of identities to make a rehash here unnecessary. The point I would add to the discussion of this concept is that more attention should be given to the landscape as the functional scene for Dickey's attempt to reestablish through his imagination 'a sense of intimacy with the natural processes.'"[39] Although articles have occasionally tackled Calhoun's suggestion—under various theoretical aegises—in terms of the poetry, none have sought to consider landscape and the elements of body and space, which are its underpinnings, in terms of the novels. The aim of my approach then is to demonstrate how Dickey, in his fiction, constitutes, as

---

[37]J. N. Findlay, *The Philosophy of Hegel* (New York: Collier, 1958) 276.

[38]James Dickey, "The Total Act," in Stanley Burnshaw, *The Seamless Web* (New York: George Braziller, 1991) viii.

[39]Richard J. Calhoun, "After a Long Silence: James Dickey as South Carolina Writer," *South Carolina Review* 9/1 (November 1976): 17.

Santayana says of Lucretius, "a poet of the landscape, a poet of matter."[40]

I have attempted to clarify, with the help of previous Dickey scholars and some important thinkers, my general observations on the idea of "merging" or assuming the existence of the other. However, the terminology of two theorists in particular—Michel de Certeau and Pierre Bourdieu—has aided me in specifying and applying the practice of merging to Dickey's novels. Certeau is a French ethnographic theorist whose most important ideas build upon Michel Foucault's writings concerning institutions. Foucault perceived existence as being shaped by procedural institutions that employ incredibly diverse techniques for the purpose of establishing "a certain mode of detailed political investment of the body, a new 'micro-physics' of power."[41] Certeau goes beyond Foucault's general observations to examine the social field in terms of "the clandestine forms taken by the dispersed, tactical, and make-shift creativity of groups or individuals already caught in the nets of 'discipline.'"[42] Concentrating his analysis on individuals entangled in the power of discursive authority, Certeau explores their ability to obtain agency despite the presence of pervasive and smothering institutions. Such an approach is not revolutionary in itself. For example, the influential hermeneutic thinker Jürgen Habermas uses a similar context of method in *The Theory of Communicative Action*, in which he develops "a theory of modernity that explains the types of social pathologies that are today becoming increasingly visible, by way of the assumption that communicatively structured domains of life are being subordinated to the imperatives of autonomous, formally organized systems of action"—the everyday social and psychological oppression of the

---

[40]George Santayana, *Three Philosophical Poets* (Cambridge: Harvard University Press, 1945) 57.

[41]Michel Foucault, *Discipline and Punish* (Harmondsworth: Penguin, 1991) 139.

[42]Michel de Certeau, *The Practice of Everyday Life*, trans. Rendall. (Berkeley: University of California Press, 1984) xiv–xv.

individual.[43] Thus, Certeau and Habermas, despite their divergent ideologies, are both concerned with the effects of institutional systems on aspects of autonomous human existence, such as language and physical space.

In *The Practice of Everyday Life* Certeau explores the significance of "immigrants," or people who do not belong—are alien—to the space they occupy. These are individuals who find themselves outside of what an earlier French philosopher and poet, Gaston Bachelard, called "felicitous space":

> The images I want to examine are the quite simple images of *felicitous space*. In this orientation, these investigations would deserve to be called topophilia. They seek to determine the human value of the sorts of space that may be grasped, that may be defended against adverse forces, the space we love. For diverse reasons, and with the differences entailed by poetic shadings, this is eulogized space.... Space that has been seized upon by the imagination cannot remain indifferent space subject to the measures and estimates of the surveyor. It has been lived in, not in its positivity, but with all the partiality of the imagination. Particularly, it nearly always exercises an attraction. For it concentrates being within limits that protect.[44]

Certeau's immigrants exist, not within limits that protect— "felicitous space"—, but rather those that oppress, and are defined in relation to what he identifies as "strategies"—the "force-relationship" which results from an isolated subject of power (a social system, an economy, etc.)—and "tactics"—the immigrants' use of a "practice" which has been transported into a space reserved for a static variable (x). As he explains, tactics are the means by which individual agency and imaginative acts may be obtained.

---

[43]Jürgen Habermas, *The Theory of Communicative Action*, vol. 1 (Boston: Beacon Press, 1984) xi.

[44]Gaston Bachelard, *The Poetics of Space* (New York: Orion, 1964) xxxi–xxxii.

Tactics, "[t]hrough their criteria and procedures, are supposed to make use of the institutional and symbolic organization in such an autonomous way that if it were to take them seriously the scientific representation of society would become lost in them, in every sense of the word. Its postulates and ambitions could not resist them. Norms, generalizations, and segmentations would yield to the transverse and 'metaphorizing' pullulation of these *differentiating* activities."[45] Tactics are *dif-ferentiating* in the sense that they "combine heterogeneous elements" in a manner remarkable for "the act and manner in which the opportunity is 'seized.'"[46] In short, a tactic "is a maneuver...within enemy territory.... It operates in isolated actions, blow by blow.... It must vigilantly make use of the cracks that particular conjunctions open in the surveillance of the pro-prietary powers"[47] Tactics disrupt the despotic force-relationship existing between immigrants and strategies. Of oppressive strategies, Certeau says: "I call a *strategy* the calculation (or manipulation) of power relationships that becomes possible as soon as a subject with will and power (a business, an army, a city, a scientific institution) can be isolated. It postulates a *place* that can be delimited as its *own* and serve as the base from which relations with an *exteriority* composed of targets or threats (customers or competitors, enemies...etc.) can be managed. "[48] Using disruptive tactics to establish an unorthodox practice in the presence of hostile and controlling strategies, Certeau's immigrants are able to maintain their individuality while functioning in an environment which seeks to make them subject to its rules.

In their resourceful ability to survive in a dominating setting, Certeau's immigrants resemble the protagonists of Dickey's novels who each have highly developed affinities for the hostile physical environments—natural fields instead of social ones—in which they

---

[45]Certeau, *Practice*, 59.
[46]Ibid., xix.
[47]Ibid., 37.
[48]Ibid., 35–36.

excel.[49] Furthermore, the idea of merging—as seen in our considerations of Romanticism and Epicureanism—is also important for the artist in contemplating his material. As Dickey says, the artist's "personality is fluid and becomes what it is most poetically profitable for it to become, in the specific poem in which it comes to exist."[50] Discussing the plight of the ethnologist rather than the artist, Pierre Bourdieu draws attention to the dangers inherent in attempting to assume the experience of the other: "One cannot *live* the belief associated with profoundly different systems of existence, that is, with other games and other stakes, still less give others the means of reliving it by the sheer power of discourse.... Those who want to believe with the beliefs of others grasp neither the objective truth nor the subjective experience of belief."[51] In answer to the ethnographer's plight, Bourdieu sees the ideal researcher as being capable of "participant comprehension," in which the individual projects the self within the existence and experiences of the contemplated other. Just as Certeau's immigrants use tactics in order to establish appropriate practices in a hostile terrain, Bourdieu's ethnographer employs "habitus" to form within himself the most objective observer for a given culture. A term originally appearing in the work of Hegel and a number of French sociologists, "habitus" is defined by Bourdieu as "an

---

[49]Citing the scientific findings of research biologist Hermann Schöne, I candidly translate the terminology of Certeau's theory of social space into environmental terms since its apparatus functions as effectively—or even better—with ecosystems as economies. This may conflict with the politics of Marxist-influenced spatial critics, many of whom believe, "As socially produced space, spatiality can be distinguished from the physical space of material nature and the menial space of cognition and representation, each of which is used and incorporated into the social construction of spatiality but cannot be conceptualized as its equivalent" (Edward W. Soja, *Postmodern Geographies: The Reassertion of Space in Critical Social Theory* [New York: Verso, 1989] 120). In Dickey's novels, the space of material nature is conceptualized as being much more important than socially produced space which, if anything, is derivative of or reliant upon natural environments.

[50]James Dickey, *Sorties* (New York: Doubleday, 1971) 160.

[51]Pierre Bourdieu, *The Logic of Practice* (Cambridge: Polity, 1990) 68.

acquired system of generative schemes objectively adjusted to the particular conditions in which it is constituted."[52] Whereas the anthropologist uses "habitus" to comprehend the observed subject, so the writer must employ a similar device to obtain the closest possible relationship with the material at hand.

The grounding for these somewhat dense social theories and the environmental manner in which I am appropriating them is not purely philosophical. Scientific studies have confirmed that natural environments can force animals to alter themselves significantly at the physiological level. Hermann Schöne explains in *Spatial Orientation* that:

> Developmentally determined differences, variability of orientation cues, compensation of perturbations, and tuning of the motor-sensory interaction appear at first glance to be quite heterogeneous topics. However, they are all concerned with changes in the orientation behavior. In particular, they deal with the effect of experience and environment on the form and operation of a system.... The basic structure of an orientation contains numerous junctures where environmental influences may be critical. They extend from the formation of central nervous structures during sensitive periods to the learning of special features of an orientation cue, and from idiothetic [a term referring to an animal's environmental location] storage of a movement sequence to continuous calibration of the motor-sensory interaction.[53]

The shifts that Dickey's characters undergo in relation to their environments are suggestive of such physiological changes, in addition to the intellectual and psychological transitions they

---

[52]Pierre Bourdieu, *Outline of a Theory of Practice* (Cambridge: Cambridge University Press, 1977) 29.

[53]Hermann Schöne, *Spatial Orientation: Spatial Control of Behavior in Animals and Man*, trans. Strausfeld (Princeton: Princeton University Press, 1984) 138.

experience. There may also be a physiological shift, brought on by actual experience or the imagining of experience, in the author's contemplation of certain subject matter. For example, a writer who has flown into a stiff headwind in a Stearman, or has the ability to powerfully imagine such a flight, may possess a physiologically-based imaginative advantage over an artist who has not or has little capacity or imagination for such an experience. Whether this particular argument is true or not, the theoretical explanations of merging with an environment are confirmed by biological research which identifies the physiological practice as "orientation process." As Schöne summarizes, "Orientation processes are the means by which an animal adjusts its behavior to the diverse spatial requirements of its environment."[54]

Dickey was extremely interested in the way an organism's biological composition affected mental awareness, crediting John Hall Wheelock with giving him the insight "that human consciousness is dependent on biological principles."[55] His protagonists—whether viewed as Certeau's immigrants, Bourdieu's ethnographers, or Schöne's biological test subjects—are able to employ appropriate tactics in order to establish practices within respective environments. As Chris Fitter maintains in his study, *Poetry, Space, Landscape*, no landscape is ever "'autotelic'—bearing a perennial and 'objective' appearance and significance independent of its 'reader,'"[56] and—as we shall see—Dickey's protagonists, drawing on their divergent backgrounds and personalities, each uses common tactics and practices to read, perceive, and interact with natural elements in different ways.

Dickey's favorite critic, Randall Jarrell, once wrote, "Everyone speaks of the 'negative capability' of the artist, of his ability to lose what self he has in the many selves, the great self of the world. Such a quality is, surely, the first that a critic should have; yet who speaks

---

[54]Ibid., 13.
[55]Series 2.4, box 92.
[56]Chris Fitter, *Poetry, Space, Landscape: Toward a New Theory* (Cambridge: Cambridge University Press, 1995) 9.

of the negative capability of the critic?"[57] In addition to the ideas of characters merging with environments and authors merging with their material, there is also the dynamic of readers merging with texts. At the conclusion of the same essay Jarrell summons Rilke's famous proclamation, "The work of art...says to us always: *You must change your life.*" [58] Yet the degree to which a text changes one's life is always contingent upon the reaction of the particular reader. As Certeau says of the reader, "Far from being writers—founders of their own place, heirs of the peasants of earlier ages now working on the soil of language, diggers of wells and builders of houses—readers are travelers; they move across lands belonging to someone else, like nomads poaching their way across fields they did not write...."[59] Dickey is more than willing to accommodate wandering readers and has spoken of their importance often in terms of "presentational immediacy," which he defines in the following terms: "I mean for words to come together in some kind of magical conjunction that will take the reader into a real experience of his own—not the poet's. I don't really believe what literary critics have believed from the beginning of time: that poetry is an attempt of the poet to create or recreate his own experience and to pass it on. I don't believe in that. I believe it's an awakening of the sensibilities of someone else."[60] Refusing to limit art as a closed-off forum for his own experiences, Dickey realizes that the success of a work depends on its ability to summon something in the reader which is the reader's own. Yet what is gained from a text is largely a result of how much, how completely, a reader is willing to enter into it. Looking at the same idea, not from the viewpoint of the creating artist, but the more detailed perspective of the reader, Dickey explains: "The first thing to understand about poetry is that it comes to you from outside you, in books or in words, but that for it to live, something from

---

[57]Randall Jarrell, "Poets, Critics, and Readers," in *Kipling, Auden & Co.: Essays and Reviews 1935–1964*, 305–18.

[58]Ibid., 318.

[59]Certeau, *Practice*, 174.

[60]Dickey, *Night Hurdling*, 302.

within you must come to it and meet it and complete it. Your response with your own mind and body and memory and emotions gives the poem its ability to work its magic; if you give to it, it will give to you, and give plenty."[61] Entering into the text allows readers to enrich their experiences but also, to a certain degree, guarantees the artist what kind of reader he/she will have. In other words, if the reader agrees to participate with the text on its terms, the artist is better able to determine the identity of the audience.

What Dickey has in mind for the reader is similar to Wolfgang Iser's idea of the "implied reader," which is a kind of creation of the text.[62] Like the actor in Jorge Luis Borges's parable, "Everything and Nothing,"[63] Dickey would have the reader assume the identity of the text through the persona of an ideal reader only to attain a more profound understanding of experience. Although this might seem to have the potential for a reverse-effect, in which a reader's individuality is dominated by the text, Dickey fights against the idea of the work being a kind of referendum to the reader. What he really has in mind is a more active role, reminiscent of Roland Barthes's familiar discussion of the reader's wish to be a producer rather than a passive consumer in the creative process:

> The goal of literary work (of literature as work) is to make the reader no longer a consumer, but a producer of the text. Our literature is characterized by the pitiless divorce which the literary institution maintains between the producer of the text and its user, between its owner and its consumer, between its author and its reader. This reader is thereby plunged into a kind of idleness—he is intransitive; he is, in short, serious: instead of functioning himself, instead of

---

[61]James Dickey, "How to Enjoy Poetry" (International Paper Company, 1982).

[62]See Wolfgang Iser, *The Implied Reader* (Baltimore: Johns Hopkins, 1974).

[63]Jorge Luis Borges, "Everything and Nothing" in *Labyrinths: Selected Stories & Other Writings*, ed. Yates and Irby (New York: New Directions, 1962): 248–49.

gaining access to the magic of the signifier, to the pleasure
of writing, he is left with no more than the poor freedom
either to accept or reject the text: reading is nothing more
than a referendum. Opposite the writerly text, then, is its
countervalue, its negative, reactive value: what can be read,
but not written: the readerly. We call any readerly text a
classic text.[64]

Imprisoned in the domain of the readerly the reader nonetheless
entertains the desire to take part in the production of the text.
Although this can never occur, Dickey at least attempts to persuade
the reader to enter into, with maximum participation, what is
already written in the hopes that this will evoke a new experience
for him.

The fact that so much depends on the reader in Dickey's
contemplation of other(s) is perhaps best articulated in a critical
comment by Mark Edmundson: "[Dickey] wants to be a dog: bang,
he's a dog. There's no intimation that a dog's sense of things might
be so far from a human's that a sudden metamorphosis results in
considerable complexity."[65] Feeling that Dickey does not
sufficiently, or convincingly, capture the essence of a dog,
Edmundson dismisses the poetic technique in its entirety.
Although Edmundson rejects Dickey's approach, the power of
Dickey's work and the reader's hoped-for surrender is a direct
result of Dickey's unique use of narrative voice. In fact, Fred
Chappell cites Dickey's narrative technique as perhaps his most
important aesthetic legacy: "An important part of this impetus
toward mannerism [the tendency of contemporary Southern
writers to establish distinctive voices] came, I believe, from James
Dickey, whom I will propose as the most important transitional
figure between Southern literature's modernism and its post-

---

[64]Roland Barthes, *S/Z*, trans. Miller (New York: Hill and Wang, 1974) 4.

[65]Mark Edmundson, "James Dickey: Learning from Others," *Raritan* 15/3
(Winter 1996): 54.

modernism."[66] The convincing quality of Dickey's narrative voice, its intimacy and total involvement, goes a long way in persuading the reader to give to the text. Joel Peckham likens Dickey's narrative attitude toward the reader to that of Bakhtin:

> [Dickey] seemed to understand with theorists like Bakhtin that a direct 'orientation toward the listener is usually considered the basic constitutive feature of rhetorical discourse.' For Dickey as for Bakhtin such a relationship implied an interactive approach to poetry, an approach that relies on 'an active understanding' between speaker and listener, 'one that assimilates the word under consideration into a new conceptual system, that of the one striving to understand, reestablishes a series of complex interrelationships, consonances and dissonances with the word and enriches it with new elements.'[67]

Containing, at least for many readers, the narrative power to energize words and convince readers to interact with them, Dickey's artistic technique is remarkable for its ability to seduce or persuade the reader—as a result of its rhetorical intimacy—to enter the world of the text on its own terms.

Beyond the role of narrative in the melting relationship between reader and text exists a strong psychological dimension which Jung defines as *participation mystique*. For Jung, the deepest and most complete artistic meaning is achieved

> [w]hen we are able to let the work of art act upon us as it acted upon the artist. To grasp its meaning, we must allow it to shape us as it once shaped him. Then we understand the nature of his experience. We see that he has drawn upon

---

[66]Fred Chappell, "'Not as a Leaf': Southern Poetry and the Innovations of Tradition," *Georgia Review* 51/3 (Fall 1997): 482.

[67]Joel B. Peckham, Jr., "James Dickey and the Narrative Mode of Transmission: The Sheep Child's Other Realm," *The Mississippi Quarterly* 52/2 (Spring 1999): 242–43.

the healing and redeeming forces of the collective psyche that underlies consciousness with its isolations and its painful errors; that he has penetrated to that matrix of life in which all men are embedded, which imparts a common rhythm to all human existence, and allows the individual to communicate his feeling and his striving to mankind as a whole.[68]

Robert Penn Warren, who possessed a strong Jungian sensibility, says in his essay "Why Do We Read Fiction?", "You will have to surrender something of your own identity to him [the protagonist], have to let it be absorbed in him."[69] Implied here is the idea that psychological merging between reader and writer or fictional character—assuming the consciousness of the implied reader—gives the reader access to whatever timeless archetype or element of the "collective psyche" the work seeks to portray. However, this may not always be a smooth relationship, particularly when contemplated in psychological terms. On one occasion Dickey speaks of drawing the reader into the text at all costs: "I feel that what I really want the poem to do is to devour the reader. I want it to engulf him. I want him to become entangled with it inextricably, and, in order to do that, you can't use just a line or two, you have to draw him in and then throw your lassos."[70] In this context, it may seem necessary for the reader to struggle with the author in order, as Blanchot thought, to give the work back to itself.[71] A certain amount of tension and conflict may therefore be necessary between the reader and author in order to produce meaning. As Sartre summarizes: "If the author existed

---

[68]C. G. Jung, "Psychology and Literature," in *Modern Man in Search of a Soul*, trans. Dell and Baynes (New York: Harcourt, Brace, and Company, 1933) 172.

[69]Robert Penn Warren, "Why Do We Read Fiction?," in *New and Selected Essays*, 58.

[70]Baughman, *Voiced Connections*, 12.

[71]See Maurice Blanchot, *The Blanchot Reader*, ed. Holland (Cambridge: Blackwell, 1995).

alone he would be able to write as much as he liked, the work as *object* would never see the light of day and he would either have to put down his pen or his despair. But the operation of writing implies that of reading as its dialectical correlative and these two connected acts necessitate two distinct agents. It is the conjoint effort of author and reader which brings upon the scene that concrete and imaginary object which is the work of the mind." For, he continues, "There is no art except for and by others...."[72]

Just as Dickey's protagonists merge with their environments and the reader interacts with/combats the author in becoming part of the text, so it finally follows that the work of art may give us a representation of the artist, whose essence is perhaps present in the work.[73] As Rilke says of the landscape artist, "The painter depicted landscape, and yet in doing so was not concerned with *it* but with himself"[74] Rilke's observation anticipates James Applewhite's findings concerning landscape; in *Seas and Inland Journeys: Landscape and Consciousness from Wordsworth to Roethke* he cites romantic and modernist writers' use of landscape (the relation of external topography to the self) as a vehicle for exploring the unconscious portions of the psyche.[75] Dickey agrees with Applewhite in this interpretation when he asserts, "I'm like Malcolm Lowry—a great, great favorite of mine—who is really interested in the work because it leads him to the man. I think

---

[72]Sartre, *Philosophy*, 375.

[73]Many deconstructionists hold that authors do not serve as harbingers of "true" meaning for their texts, asserting that texts exist only in reference to each other—a condition that perpetually defers meaning. Although I do not reject this valuable form of reading, I question its accountability for the practice of merging, in which the terms "self," "text," and "author" become more fluid than definitive—each exchanging parts with aspects of the others, depending on the circumstances.

[74]Rainer Maria Rilke, "Concerning Landscape," in *Where Silence Reigns*, trans. Houston (New York: New Directions, 1978) 3.

[75]See James Applewhite, *Seas and Inland Journeys: Landscape and Consciousness from Wordsworth to Roethke* (Athens: University of Georgia Press, 1985) vii, 16.

they're absolutely incapable of being disassociated from each other"[76] Later in his career he would be even more explicit: "Perhaps in the end the whole possibility of words being able to contain one's identity is illusory; opinions, yes; identity, maybe. Perhaps the whole question of identity itself is illusory. But one must work with such misconceptions for whatever hint of insight—the making of a truth—they may contain: that fragment of existence which could not be seen in any other way and may with great good luck, as in the best poetry, be better than the truth."[77] Whether or not authorial identity may come to exist in a work of art, thereby giving the reader the artist, Dickey feels that the artist must work with the assumption that it does. In proceeding from such a premise, the artist may not arrive at the truth of himself—the reader at the essence of the artist—but perhaps an artistic truth, or maybe even something beyond that—a Kantian sublime more enriching to artist and reader than the artist's true self ever could be.

As I demonstrated earlier, Dickey did not really think of himself as a Southern writer, nor do his novels collectively betray his assertion. Yet, he saw himself as part of a literary tradition, though an eclectic one, that is scarcely recognized. As early as 1952—before his literary career had begun—Dickey had scrawled in a notebook the determination: "To write 'out of' the brute and animal nature of reality, to deal with essences, entelechies (Rilke, (Graham), Roethke) *as if I were* a stone, frond, tiger, kiss. There is too much clever, 'judged' poetry, 'judged and rendered' verse. I would like a poetry which proceeds naturally (or *is*) from the situation or encounter, which is the *essence* of its make-up, its being, which is the situation as it utters itself through me."[78] In his quest for an art of essence, Dickey sought the "company of the great empathizers," a curious group of writers reflecting Dickey's

---

[76]Dickey, *Self-Interviews*, 24.

[77]Dickey, *Night Hurdling*, xi.

[78]James Dickey, *Striking In: The Early Notebooks of James Dickey*, ed. Gordon Van Ness (Columbia: University of Missouri Press, 1996) 118.

wide-ranging and voracious reading. Not surprisingly, the leader of the group is Dickey's great American poet, Theodore Roethke, who appears with more frequency than any other artist in his journals, notes, and interviews:

> Now we don't live in Wordsworth's age, or Pater's, but an attitude of mind—a kind of *being*—like Wordsworth's is no more impossible to us than it was to him. Theodore Roethke, the greatest poet we have ever had in this country, is a marvelous proof of this. 'I, who came back from the depths laughing too loudly, / Become another thing; / My eyes extend beyond the farthest bloom of the waves; / I lose and find myself in the long water; / I am gathered together once more; / I embrace the world.' That is what we want: to be gathered together once more, to be able to enter in, to participate in experience, to possess our lives.[79]

Here, Dickey connects Wordsworth and Roethke in their gift, which is essentially a Romantic gift, for entering experience—for exploring objects of the exterior world from within. In the first poem of "North American Sequence" Roethke writes of the quest for the "imperishable quiet at the heart of form,"[80] form being his word for internal coalescence. Roethke's approach to experience is what Dickey admires—in various manifestations—in other writers and serves as the defining qualification for the "company of the great empathizers":

> I had long been disturbed by a strange and doubtless indefensible distinction between poets who *merely* tell you of their experiences ('My grandmother's walking-stick had a brass knob') and those who are able to relate *you*, the unknown but potentially human Other, to the world that all of us exist in. If you have heard wind, you have heard

---

[79]Dickey, *Sorties*, 204.

[80]Theodore Roethke, "The Longing," in *The Collected Poems of Theodore Roethke* (New York: Doubleday, 1966) 182.

Roethke's wind; the wind of your experience comes doubly to life. If you have touched the bark of a tree, you have touched one of Roethke's trees, and understand through the words of the poem what you felt years before, standing there in the pine grove speechless. Roethke is of the company of the great Empathizers, like Rilke and D. H. Lawrence, and in this association none of those present need feel embarrassment. They are all the Awakeners, and can change your life not by telling but by showing, not from the outside but from within, by the lively and persistently mysterious means of inducing you to believe that you were *meant* to perceive and know things as Rilke, as Lawrence, as Roethke present them.[81]

The empathizers, not all of them Romantics, are the masters of merging, whom Dickey uses as models in his own art. In a letter to Peter F. Neumeyer,[82] Dickey even uses the expression "merging" while discussing his appreciation of Rilke:

> [Rilke] seems to have such a strong identification with other forms of life—even with inanimate matter—that it is often difficult for a person like myself, who is always so conscious of his *own* identity to understand exactly what is going on. I guess the difference between his attitude and mine is that we *merge* with things differently. He seems to be able to *become* the other thing, while I am very conscious of the fact that *I am also involved in the merging* [Dickey's emphasis], and that I am giving something to the thing I am merging with as well as getting something back from it.[83]

Indeed, Rilke, like Dickey, was very fond of entering the existence of landscapes and animals in his work. One recalls his aesthetic

---

[81]James Dickey, *Babel to Byzantium: Poets & Poetry Now* (New York: Farrar, Straus and Giroux, 1968) 149.

[82]The letter is dated 16 March 1970.

[83]Matthew J. Bruccoli and Judith S. Baughman, eds., *Crux: The Letters of James Dickey* (New York: Knopf, 1999) 321.

reflections on the rolling plains of Russia and the marshy environment of Worpswede, along with his various descriptions of European cities. Among the animals, Rilke repeatedly captures the existence of cats (lions, panthers, and the domestic variety) and, especially, dogs. In *Die neun Gedichte* he expresses a dog's experience of dwelling on the threshold between man and beast: "Neither excluded, or incorporate, / ...so close to comprehension, nearly reaching,/ and yet renouncing: for he wouldn't *be*."[84] Yet, while Dickey admires Rilke's technique for merging, he is bothered by the total loss of all self, which does not carry over into his own work. Although Dickey often seeks to become completely the thing he contemplates, he still uses his powerful narrative voice to maintain and reflect the aesthetic consciousness which produces the speaker's impressions.

Whereas Dickey admired Rilke's ability to assume natural objects in their entirety, he was drawn to D. H. Lawrence just as much for the way he lived his life as the manner in which his art participated with nature:

> I was reading Aldous Huxley's introduction to the letters of D. H. Lawrence, where he talks about the profound influence his friendship with Lawrence had. Huxley thought that it was a put-on at first, that Lawrence should react to things in such an unusual and individual way, but he goes on to say that it wasn't long before he felt that he really *was* in the presence of someone who could tell him what it felt like to be a flower, or a tree, or a breaking wave, or the moon. This struck me as being very closely akin to my attitude toward things. It seems to me that a writer, at least one kind of writer, is very well served by being able to project himself into things that are foreign to him: that he have an encompassing and at the same time penetrating

---

[84] *New Poems*, trans. Leishman (New York: New Directions, 1964) 293.

ability to feel what it must be like for some one or something else.[85]

The most powerful example of Lawrence's reaction to the natural other is probably his poem "Fish," where at times Lawrence and even poetry seem to fall away from the page, leaving the reader with the most approximate experience of an unthinking fish that language can offer. However, fascinated by Lawrence's ability to convince others, through the medium of conversation, of the nature of natural objects, it is clear that Dickey admired his personality or personal mysticism—his penchant for assuming the other in his everyday life—as much as, or more than, his work.

Although I have mentioned Dickey's abjuration of the Southern writer label, two Southern novelists are present in the company of the great empathizers. In Thomas Wolfe Dickey beheld both a tragic biographical figure and a poetic application similar to his own: "*This* is what you read Thomas Wolfe for: complete immersion in a scene, imaginative surrender to whatever a situation or a memory evokes; quite simply, the sense of life submitted to and entered.... Wolfe stands us in good stead here, in these stories as elsewhere, which tell us in bewildering and heartening plenty to open up entirely to our own experience, to possess it, to go the whole way into it and with it, to keep nothing back, to be cast on the flood."[86] What most attracted Dickey to Wolfe was the latter's rendering of prose through a poetic sensibility—something Dickey practiced himself. Often accused of sensationalistic "over-writing," Wolfe felt the traditional prose method of rendering experience in relatively impersonal terms was inadequate for expressing the situational and emotional truths he wished to convey. The romantic yearnings of Eugene and the roaring oratory of Gant in Look Homeward, Angel[87] exhibit Wolfe's lyrical prose writing at its finest. The same poetic dynamic exists

---

[85]Dickey, *Night Hurdling*, 193.

[86]James Dickey, foreword, in *The Complete Short Stories of Thomas Wolfe*, ed. Skipp, xiv–xv.

[87]Thomas Wolfe, *Look Homeward, Angel* (Charles Scribner's Sons, 1929).

for James Agee, whom Dickey thought, "For all he drank, and despite the shambles of his emotional life, did have this quality of complete participation, of commitment of the self to whatever it was he contemplated."[88] Like Wolfe before him, Agee used lyrical prose and a poetic spontaneity of emotion at the expense of rendering his art in a subjective manner. Yet, believing that words could only go so far in embodying experience, Agee explored photography and screenplay writing—as Dickey himself did—, thinking that visual images might better capture what words could not. Dickey, who read Agee's screenplays and wrote some of his own, may have come to believe this to an extent, although—as for Faulkner and others—money was undoubtedly the main consideration in his Hollywood exploits.

Money was also the motivating factor in Dickey's production of four big coffee-table books: *Jericho*,[89] *God's Images*,[90] *Wayfarer*, and *Southern Light*. Yet these commercial books, publicized in places like *Southern Living*, also underscore Dickey's interest—traceable to James Agee—in the relationship between language and the visual arts. Although the collective writing in these books perhaps is not worthy of a full-length consideration, it is significant for Dickey's explicit instructions to the reader in regard to the practice of merging. Before the publication of the first coffee-table book, *Jericho*, an excerpt from it appeared in *Playboy* as "Small Visions from a Timeless Place: The South as One Poet has Known It." Prefacing the excerpt was an introduction not included in the book-length publication, in which Dickey establishes his expectations for the reader: "The general plan of these pieces demands a good deal of the reader. I ask him, first of all, to give up his external identity—that is, his body—but to keep his senses preternaturally alive. I ask him to become invisible and to be able

[88]Dickey, *Self-Interviews*, 75.

[89]James Dickey and Herbert Shuptrine (illustrator), *Jericho: The South Beheld* (Birmingham: Oxmoor House, 1974).

[90]James Dickey and Marvin Hayes (illustrator), *God's Images: The Bible: A New Vision* (Birmingham: Oxmoor House, 1977).

to take any shape that gets him deeper into some aspect of the South, or Jericho, as I, with the help of the King James Bible, have renamed it."[91] Working with the medium of artistic images as well as words, Dickey realizes the increased importance of the beholder's willingness or unwillingness to be drawn into the words and pictures before him. To further entice the reader or beholder Dickey issues a kind of challenge for him to make the personal idea of self so invisible that he becomes the essence of what is seen:

> The idea of the reader's becoming invisible and omniscient, ranging unsystematically over the Southern land and through many types of Southern people, is fundamental here. I should like the reader to be able to become a horse, a pine tree, a house, a church, a stock car, a hen, a rattlesnake, a human prisoner, a blues player at night in his cell listening to a freight train, a racoon in a tree, a revivalist in a tent in midsummer. I should like the reader to help me *behold* the South and not simply see it. And I should like him to behold with such intensity, with whatever help these paragraphs are capable of giving, that he will look into the nearest mirror and half-believe that if he concentrates strongly and imaginatively enough, in his individual way—one known only to him, and from birth—he will see himself fade out before his own eyes and become what these paragraphs most want him to be: a Spirit, the essence of himself, a Beholder of Jericho.[92]

Dickey challenges the reader, not only to view the art and words on the page, but to somehow become the subjects they convey. Beyond giving the beholder a "sense" of the South, Dickey wants him to experience the being of different aspects of the region. The same idea exists in *Wayfarer* in which the traveling narrator—who wanders through the Southern mountains—is sent away by a local

---

[91]James Dickey, "Small Visions from a Timeless Place: The South as One Poet has Known It," *Playboy* 21/10 (October 1974): 152.
[92]Ibid.

farmer with a promise of his having bonded with the land: "You done reached down through the ferns. You done drunk lonesome water. You're bound to the hills. It's already workin' on you, right where you're standin.' It'll walk on out of here with you. You got it, and you'll come back with it."[93] One of the pleasures of Dickey's practice of merging is the idea that the assumed thing stays with the beholder—fictional character or reader—forever. As in *Deliverance*, in which Ed Gentry realizes he has internalized the river upon returning to Atlanta, the protagonist of *Wayfarer* takes some part of the mountain landscape with him when he departs. Yet such merging internalizations are not limited to solid physical phenomena. In *Southern Light* Dickey asks the reader to become light—the essence of the physical phenomena—itself:

> One thing is certain: wherever you look, and any scene or vision is possible, light is part of it, and it *makes* it possible. You not only see by light, you dream by it, and of it: of its coming of its falling as it does, when and where it does, on what it falls and of the way in which it falls... Where you stand, where you sit or lie, even with your eyes closed, even asleep, you have a relation to light, for the light in dreams is still light. What this book wants is for you to have *more* of a relation to it, to possess it more than you did before you opened the pages. Jim Valentine [the book's photographer] and I want you to enter light as though you were part of it, as though you were pure spirit—or pure beholding human creature, which is the same thing—to become part of light in many places and intensities, to make it something like a dream of itself with you in it....[94]

When Dickey writes of "a dream of itself with you in it" he gets at the core of the entire merging process. For though we cannot enter the essence of a rock, we may enter the essence of our idea—our

---

[93]James Dickey, *Wayfarer: A Voice from the Southern Mountains* (Birmingham: Oxmoor House, 1988) 96.

[94]James Dickey, *Southern Light* (Birmingham: Oxmoor House, 1991) 8–9.

dream—of it; and, while in it, we may still maintain our conscious thought while being completely given over to the thing we contemplate from its own perspective. Running through Dickey's poetry, novels, and even the commercial coffee-table books, this idea constitutes a large portion of his artistic vision and even his approach to personal existence. As his older son recalls, "When he'd been drinking…he lumbered dangerously through the fragile auras of strangers in small spaces,"[95] and Dickey's commencement addresses—his advice to the young—often evoke the practice of merging as a more involved way of living: "The external world will be what it is. What can change is not it but us. We can both enter more deeply than we do into those activities we have chosen to undertake—our particular specialties—and at the same time we can refuse to be limited by them; we can transcend them; we can perch *with* the bird on the wire."[96] The artist with the bird, the reader with the art, and the individual with existence, the practice of merging ultimately goes beyond aesthetics to constitute a way of living as well.

Discussing the published novels chronologically, each of the first three chapters begins with an examination of the practice of merging, using the terminology of Michel de Certeau and others in relation to a character or characters in each work. Employing my consideration of merging—which is central to each text—as a base, I discuss other important dynamics and bring in source materials where they seem especially illuminating and appropriate. Chapter 1 considers *Deliverance* in terms of the disparate practices employed by the four Atlantans on their canoe trip, and how Ed Gentry's tactics are the most successful because they come closest to assuming the strategic essence of the wild river environment.

Chapter 2 addresses *Alnilam* and *Crux*. Although Dickey was working on *Crux* at the time of his death, technically making it a

---

[95]Christopher Dickey, *Summer of Deliverance: A Memoir of Father and Son* (New York: Simon and Schuster, 1998) 165.

[96]James Dickey, "Vale of Soul-making," Commencement Address, *USC Magazine* (Winter 1968): 9.

later chronological work than *To the White Sea*, I examine *Alnilam* and *Crux* together since they employ the same characters and ideas, and because the general plot of *Crux* had already been established by the time Dickey completed *Alnilam*. Initially tracing Joel Cahill's flying practices—his relationship with an environment of air—, I go on to demonstrate how his air tactics also shape his philosophical and utopian ideas. I also identify numerous source materials and quote from unpublished portions of *Crux* in order to strengthen my reading of *Alnilam* and for the purpose of making previously unknown information available to scholars.

Chapter 3 considers the practice of merging in terms of the tactics Muldrow employs in *To the White Sea*. Whereas Ed Gentry merges with water and Joel Cahill with the air, Muldrow repeatedly attempts to assume the distinctive colored essences of the various landscapes and animals he encounters. His merging practices train and prepare him for the spiritual and/or visceral transformation he undergoes at the book's conclusion. As in the first two chapters, this discussion is informed by important source materials and notes.

Chapter 4 is entirely different from the first three chapters since it aspires to assess Dickey's unpublished fiction. Because these pieces have never appeared in print and remain only marginally discussed, I give detailed summaries of each work before providing relatively brief critical evaluations. Part of my purpose here is simply to make these works known for future scholarship and to establish connections between them and the published fiction. Evaluating a novel manuscript and stories from the 1950s and screenplays from the 1970s—all dealing with diverse subjects and themes—, the chapter does not seek to artificially pigeonhole the material into the thesis which fuels my readings of the published novels. In conclusion I return to the book's thesis and consider very briefly the implications of my findings concerning Dickey's fiction.

CHAPTER 1

WATER: *DELIVERANCE*

The more one meditates on the river, the more completely the subject erodes the distinctions between and definitions of time and space, until finally these basic concepts are flooded by a chaotic sea of confusion in which all things seem one, and in which there is no time and there are no spaces, only space unfolding.
—*Wyman Herendeen,* From Landscape to Literature, *3*

Put on the river/Like a fleeing coat,/A garment of motion,/Tremendous, immortal./Find a still root/To hold you in it/Let flowing create/A new, inner being...
—*Dickey, "Inside the River" in* The Whole Motion, *128–29*

Who shall deliver me from the body of this death?
—*Dickey, epigraph for* The Deliverer[1]

Not long after the publication of *Deliverance*, Dickey told an interviewer that "with the automobile there is this strange kind of schizophrenic existence, where you are in a white shirt and a tie in an office one day, and then late that afternoon you can be in a canoe in an almost untouched kind of wilderness."[2] In

---

[1]Series 2, box 91h. *The Deliverer*, a ninety-page manuscript, is the initial manifestation of the novel that would become *Deliverance*.

addition to explaining the impetus for the book's adventure—four "office men" driving out to the wilderness—, Dickey's words point to the novel's preoccupation with space and the idea of spatial "aliens" moving through physical areas—previously "untouched" ones—that are radically unfamiliar. This distinction suggests the spatial underpinnings of Michel de Certeau's book, *The Practice of Everyday Life*, in which he explores the significance and "practices"—or actions—of "immigrants," or people who do not belong to the space they find themselves occupying. Using Certeau's terminology for my interpretive vocabulary, I will be exploring the novel in terms of its "strategies"—the influence of its diverse environments—on the one hand and its "immigrants" and "practices" on the other, establishing a new reading of the book's narrative action and the reader's relationship to it.

From the novel's beginning, we are presented with the existence of the systems which enforce "strategies." The book's action initiates in Atlanta, a social system to which all the characters have varying degrees of social, economic, and familial ties. Even the aspiring *ubermensch* Lewis—who would like to think he is freer than the others—is subject to its "force- relationship": "He talked continuously of resettling in New Zealand or South Africa or Uruguay, but he had to be near the rental property he had inherited..." (*DL*, 6). Removed from Atlanta is the intermediary strategic system—quite different from the urban and suburban city—of Oree and Aintry or, more generally, the system of the hill people. This system is intermediary because it straddles the fence between Atlanta (or "industrialized civilization") and raw nature, and it inhabits almost the same physical space as the latter. Most importantly, its "force-relationship" with the four Atlanta men is something each of them has trouble accepting and understanding. In fact, they can hardly even acknowledge its existence—for Ed, "Oree was sleepy and hookwormy and ugly, and most of all, inconsequential" (*DL*, 55); for Lewis it is merely "a little nothing

---

[2]Ronald C. Baughman, ed., *The Voiced Connections of James Dickey: Interviews and Conversations* (Columbia: University of South Carolina Press, 1989) 71.

town" (*DL*, 7). Yet, simultaneously, Lewis admits, while describing the hill people, "There may be something important in the hills" (*DL*, 40). Perhaps the best description of the men's relationship to the social system of the hill people and the hills themselves is articulated by the man who fills their tanks at the Oree gas station: "You don't know nothin'" (*DL*, 57).

One of the many things the Atlantans do not know is the implied history of the social system they are entering. In one of the early corrected typescripts of *Deliverance*, Lewis recounts to Ed, during their drive, the post-Civil War story of a black factory worker who is told to leave town (presumably Oree or Aintry, although the name is not mentioned) and refuses to do so. The sheriff kills him and "surrounding the action was a maniacal howl [from the sheriff], an abandoned animal cry of neither pain nor ecstacy, but a sound of release beyond all justice, all law." Lewis explains that the mountain county has had few black residents since this incident.[3] In addition to its foreshadowing of the rape scene, the sheriff's lawless howl underscores the peculiar justice which is Aintry's own, independent of both Atlanta's system and nature's. The superiority of "hill justice" to that of the state or federal government stems mainly from the clannish quality of the hill people, accompanied by a suspicion of anything or anyone that is foreign. Ed seems conscious of his portrayal of the hill people as a collective system rather than as individuals, for he barely makes any character distinctions between the Griner brothers—they are merely the "first" brother and the "second"—or the rapists, who are described mostly in terms of their physical characteristics, and he constantly emphasizes the biological reality of the hill people's widespread kinship.

---

[3]Series 2, box 91h, 112. Dickey's friend Al Braselton claims to have heard a similar story from some bootleggers during one of his North Georgia canoe trips with Dickey and Lewis King (Henry Hart, *James Dickey: The World as a Lie* [New York: Picador USA, 2000] 251).

Dickey has been criticized at length for Ed's non-bucolic portrayal of the hill people[4] and in early manuscripts of the novel Ed stereotypes their culture to an even greater extent.[5] Yet Dickey is quick to point out that his depiction of the two rapists often has been cited erroneously as his representative attitude toward Appalachian culture in general. Eighteen years after the book's publication Dickey lamented: "I'm afraid somebody is going to shoot me because they said I portrayed all mountain people as degenerate sodomists.... But that's taking the short view. What about the people at the inn who try to help Jon Voight and Ned Beatty, who try to get them to eat something? Those are hill people, too. Hill people are not subject to anything less than the rest of us are. There are good ones and bad ones."[6] Dickey's point is that good and evil are universal constructions, applicable to human beings regardless of the different cultures in which they manifest themselves. The idea that the rapists would be "bad men" in any society is reflected by the fact that in *The Deliverer* Dickey nearly decided to identify them as at-large criminals. In the scene where Ed and Bobby encounter the hillmen, Dickey wrote in the margins, "Perhaps escaped convicts."[7] In any event, the reader should remember that it is Ed—a fictional displaced suburbanite—and not Dickey himself—a product of the Atlanta suburbs but a descendant of Georgia hill people—who makes disparaging remarks about hill culture. And it is fitting that Dickey has him do so, for it underscores his ignorance of the environment he is entering.

---

[4]See Daniel R. Schwartz, "Reconfiguring *Deliverance*: James Dickey, the Modern Tradition, and the Resistant Reader," *Texas Review* 17/3–4 (Fall/Winter 1996/1997): 93–111; and Don Johnson, "Balancing Negative Stereotypes in *Deliverance*," *James Dickey Newsletter* 2/2 (Spring 1986): 17–22.

[5]He says, for example, "There's a saying that there's nothing to do in the country besides hunt and drink and fuck." Series 2, box 91h, 35.

[6]Ronald Baughman, ed., "James Dickey at Drury College," *James Dickey Newsletter* 5/1 (Fall 1988): 21.

[7]Series 2, box 91h, 35.

The inability of the men to "know" the strategy of the system in which they function[8] increases when they find their way beyond Oree and into the book's most important system: nature.[9] Although Rosemary Sullivan's consideration of the novel labels nature as a violently chaotic *non*system,[10] it is, after all, an *eco*system possessing specific environmental—rather than social—functions and interactions with the life-forms that enter its space. Furthermore, its "force-relationship" is almost imperceptible since it operates naturally and so far removed from the experience of the Atlanta men. For example, when the party has finished constructing their first camp, Ed remarks, "We had colonized the place" (*DL*, 83). In an early manuscript of *Deliverance*, Dickey has Ed tell us on the first night, "I went to sleep quickly, but part of my mind did not, but lay waiting for some awful—or strange—sound to come out of the night."[11] Bothered by its presence in an alien environment, part of Ed's mind—presumably an area of his subconscious—anticipates disturbing phenomena in order to

---

[8]The simple device of having the city men enter an unknown environment is suggestive of traditional *bildungsroman* narratives. For a reading that considers the novel in terms of literary initiation themes see Michael Moorhead, "Dickey's *Deliverance*," *The Explicator* 51/4 (Summer 1993): 247–49.

[9]In labeling the book's natural system "most important" I conflict with readers like Frederic Jameson who interpret the socio-economic status of the Atlanta men as the central dynamic of the book. Although Jameson's reading contains several penetrating observations—one of which is quoted later in this essay—, I agree with Heinz Tschachler's evaluation of his general approach: "Frederic Jameson's interpretation of *Deliverance* as 'political fable,' persuasive as it is, cannot fully do justice to the novel precisely because the allegation of 'political wishfulfillment' implies that there is very little at stake beside the material interests of a ruling class" (Heinz Tschachler, "'Un principe d'insuffisance': Dickey's Dialogue with Bataille,"*Mosaic* 20/3 [Summer 1987]: 91).

[10]"Each novelist [Dickey and Margaret Atwood] feels that self-definition can be achieved through a return to nature in a test of survival. In flight from the 'world of systems,' each feels a need for submergence in a concept of the primal that verges on violence or madness" (Rosemary Sullivan, "Surfacing and Deliverance," *Canadian Literature* 8 [1976]: 6).

[11]Series 2, box 91h, 27.

remain alert. However, the sound that eventually wakes him is, not a scream, but that of his tent fabric tearing: "The canvas was punctured there, and through it came one knuckle of a deformed fist, a long curving of claws that turned on themselves. Those are called talons, I said out loud" (*DL*, 88). Yet, Ed does not interpret the owl's penetration as a recolonization of its natural space and a kind of colonization *of him*; rather, he dreams comfortably of hunting with the animal and gazing through the night from its "man-made" perch. But Dickey is not finished with this theme and the idea of nature's recolonization is reiterated the following morning when Ed is consumed by the fog: "I looked at my legs and they were gone, and my hands at my sides also; I stood with the fog *eating* me alive" (*DL*, 94). Unfortunately, Ed still cannot grasp the reality of nature's colonizing "force-relationship" to himself, nor its non-human quality. He is searching for the conclusion articulated by one of Dickey's favorite writers, Richard Jefferies: "On the contrary, a great part, perhaps the whole, of nature and of the universe is distinctly anti-human. The term inhuman does not express my meaning, anti-human is better; outre-human, in the sense of beyond, outside, almost grotesque in its attitude towards, would nearly convey it."[12] Ironically, Ed says of the woods, "There was nothing in them that knew me" (*DL*, 87), when, more accurately, there is nothing in him—at least at this point in the novel—that knows *it* and recognizes its non-human power.

Elsewhere, Dickey has described nature and especially rivers as systems which defy human order and are "unknowable": "Here is the other river: not the Mississippi, but something best observed from the position of a butterfly on a stone. The water is too dangerous for you not to have given yourself a way out that has nothing to do with the water...[it] falls out of the mountains with such fury that all systems of thought are made impossible...on each side of the river are deep woods, and through the haze of water is a bobcat, who understands why this place is like it is."[13] Although

---

[12]Richard Jefferies, *The Story of My Heart* (Portland ME: Mosher, 1900) 45.

[13]James Dickey, "Small Visions from a Timeless Place: The South as One Poet has Known It," *Playboy* 21/10 (October 1974): 220.

Dickey's river description seems to constitute a negation of intellect in nature, elsewhere he has compared rivers to the ideas of his favorite Greek philosopher, Heraclitus, arguing that both are irrefutable and sublime, and that something other than conventional human logic and rationality—but something nonetheless perceptive—is needed to interpret their deep, all-encompassing qualities.[14] Wyman Herendeen supports this archetypal idea in his study, *From Landscape to Literature: The River and the Myth of Geography*, describing the archetypal significance of rivers: "Whatever the period and whatever the culture, the river retains its fundamental identification with the material world and its more divine potential: it is the thread joining the body and mind. It is in such beginnings, where history and myth, geography and cosmography, science and magic are all but indistinguishable, that one must first look for the river, and it is there that our cultured responses to landscape are formed."[15] Like the pre-Socratic philosophers, the river's symbolic implications bring together body and mind and math and mysticism in establishing a paradoxically—at least in human terms—sublime vision. Using mind and body, thought and instinct, the Atlanta men must come to know the river in order to function effectively in its alien environment.

Having summarized the strategic systems—that of the hill people and nature itself—against which the immigrants must define themselves and their practices, we must consider how the characters go about doing this—their "tactics." As I explain in the

---

[14]"I suppose I am drawn to a philosopher like Heraclitus because of my interest in rivers and the way he uses them as illustrations. He is probably my favorite philosopher because he's so mysterious. You can't *refute* him, because he speaks in parables, in images, 'The way up and the way down are the same.' The way up to *what*? The way *down* to what? Well, it doesn't matter. What makes it marvelous to me is that it's so evocative. It could apply to anything: it could apply to life; it could apply to the exercise of a craft" (James Dickey, *Self-Interviews*, ed. Barbara and James Reiss [New York: Doubleday, 1970] 69).

[15]Wyman Herendeen, *From Landscape to Literature: The River and the Myth of Geography* (Pittsburgh: Duquesne University Press, 1986) 8.

introduction, while strategies are roughly consistent with poststructuralist notions of a reality constituted by separate hegemonic systems (with the exception of nature itself), tactics make allowances for the otherness inherent in the practice of the immigrant—with the immigrant becoming an agency-possessing imposter in the space of a static variable. In the afterward of the screenplay version of *Deliverance*, Dickey maintains that the ontological essences of the characters—the practices, the separate variables, which defined their beings—were never fully explored in the film: "The psychological orientation—the *being*—of the characters, their interrelations, their talk with each other, the true dramatic progression, are only hinted at here and there. If these things were to be realized in another version of *Deliverance*, my later, true ghost—not the one that wandered apologetically and impotently through the thickets and over the clifftops of the sets of the movie—would be pleased."[16] In addition to disclosing the importance Dickey placed on his characters' various functions and differences, his statement is particularly helpful in terms of thinking about the novel, in that it provides an effective avenue for investigating the various "tactics"—by considering them through characters.

Perhaps the best way to begin a discussion of "tactics" is to examine those that are the most ill-suited to the book's main environment, nature. In regard to the novel's characters, this immediately suggests Bobby Trippe. In a spatial system which calls for a decisive brand of "tactics" or action, Bobby's are wholly inadequate, and Dickey goes to great lengths to underscore his physical and symbolic unsuitability. In addition to being obese—the flabby opposite of Lewis (the athletic man of action)—Bobby is described as "dead weight," incapable of "moving" himself and, all the while, burdening others: "Lew and I hauled and shoved, with Bobby sitting in the bow with his face absolutely perfect as an expression of dead weight" (*DL*, 74).

---

[16]James Dickey, *Deliverance*, Screenplay (Carbondale: Southern Illinois University Press, 1982) 157.

Physically, he is, in effect, a "bad immigrant," lacking the ability to move through a space which demands physical prowess and is inimical to his athletic shortcomings—a space without escalators, air-conditioning, and cars.

In his inability to either let go of his tactics or compensate them for the purposes of his environment, Bobby resembles, to some degree, Dickey's generic rural Southerner (not the clannish hill people but the basic country Southerner who frequents the landscape beyond Atlanta): "From such a trip you would think that the South did nothing but dose itself and sing gospel songs; you would think that the bowels of the southerner were forever clamped shut; that he could not open and let natural process flow through him, but needed one purgative after another in order to make it to church" (*DL*, 38). Like Bobby, Dickey's imagined country Southerners have developed practices incongruous to their environment. Although the implications of their tactical error are less serious than Bobby's, they are unable to fully comprehend existence because of their mind-numbing and "unnatural" dependence on drugs and religion. Furthermore, Bobby and the rural Southerners are drawn together symbolically through Dickey's attention to their bowels. Whereas the "shut bowels" of the Southerners reflect the unsuitability of their interdependent religious and narcotic practices, the invasion of Bobby's anus by the hill man exhibits the inadequacy of his tactics in a tragically foreign environment.

Even before the rape sequence Dickey uses "bowel imagery" to underscore the futile and frustrated effects of Bobby's actions: "'Fuck it,' he said. 'Let's get on with it. I'm tired of this woods scene; I'm tired of shitting in a hole in the ground. This is for the Indians'" (*DL*, 100). Unlike the Native Americans of the past, Bobby is unable to adapt to the system in which he finds himself and instead of "shitting" in a hole—his disrupting the space of nature with both the digging of the hole and his excrement—he soon finds his own inner space violently colonized, disrupted, and filled. Exercised on a soft figure who celebrates the sterile luxuries of civilization, Bobby's brutal rape is all the more powerful.[17] Even during his traumatic experience Bobby cannot let go of his Atlanta-style tactics—taking off his pants, he looks "for a place [a dresser perhaps] to put them" (*DL*, 113). Ultimately, the appropriation of his inner space—the subordination of his tactics to those of the deviant hill men—defiles him in Ed's eyes ("None of this was his fault, but he felt tainted to me" [*DL*, 128]) and reinforces Bobby as a figure of barely ambulatory "dead weight": "He would always look like dead weight and like screaming, and that was no good to me" (*DL*, 276). His tactics being weak, useless, and ultimately "no good," Ed shuns him even when they return to Atlanta, the environment to which Bobby's fragile practices are best suited.

Whereas Bobby's tactics fail through their subordination to the practices of others, Lewis Medlock's are foiled because they seek to conquer—not only other practices—but nature's very strategic system. At least two critics have associated Lewis with the frontiersmen of R. W. B. Lewis's *The American Adam* in his attempt to tame and overcome nature through a colonizing mentality and personal willpower.[18] Although this distinction is important, especially in terms of considering the novel's place in the American literary tradition, it does not fully account for the singular complexities that accompany his character. Like Bobby, Lewis is largely defined by his body. As Dickey explained in an interview, "Lewis is the college athlete who can still outdo almost any college athlete at the age of thirty-eight. You see he intellectualizes about it, which gives him even more authority. And then he says somewhere in *Deliverance* that the body can't be faked—it's either there or it's

---

[17]In *The Deliverer* the rape scene is even more graphic with additional detailed descriptions of the hillman's penis and Bobby's anal blood.

[18]R. W. B. Lewis, *The American Adam* (Chicago: Chicago University Press, 1955). Rosemary Sullivan, for example, argues that the male party "as a whole" and the novel itself "give powerful embodiment" (Sullivan, "Surfacing," 7) to Lewis's book, whereas Susan Spencer narrows her focus to Lewis as Adam, with Ed as a foiling "American Cain" figure (Susan A. Spencer, "James Dickey's American Cain," *College Language Association Journal* 36/3 [March 1993]: 306).

not! And his is."[19] Dickey's explanation is important in that it stresses the potent existence and power of Lewis's body: it *is there*, possessing all the necessary tools for carrying out hegemonic physical practices and appropriating space. Furthermore, the comment links Lewis's physical authority to that of his intellect—at times he is able to "push" or influence Ed, morally and mentally, the same way he "pushes" weight when bench-pressing. In fact, after giving a description of the different manifestations of Lewis's physical prowess early in the novel, Ed concludes, "So I usually went with him whenever he asked me" (*DL*, 6). In the *Deliverer*, Lewis's last name is Followill,[20] suggesting both his determined willpower and Ed's willingness to follow him anywhere. We are also told in the *Deliverer* that Lewis's father committed suicide,[21] a fact that goes a long way in explaining Lewis's general insecurity, vanity, recklessness, and desire to mold himself into an immortal super-male. In his own mind, Lewis does not experience life and people, they experience Lewis; and given the choice he would likely deign to *become* Atlas and heave the world upon his own bulging shoulders, influencing an entire planet with his practices.

Although Lewis's tactics of dominance are relatively successful with Ed and even the hill people,[22] he errs when attempting to apply them to nature—in this he echoes not only a fallen Adam, but a whole range of heroes stretching into antiquity. The initial evidence of Lewis's tactical war with nature appears at the beginning of the book in Ed's description of the map: "The whole land was very tense until we put our four steins on its corners and laid the river out to run for us through the mountains 150 miles

---

[19]Baughman, *Voiced Connections*, 73.

[20]Prior to Followill, Lewis's last name had been Queen, a play upon the name of Dickey's canoeing buddy Lewis King. Queen appears in the published version as the name of Sheriff Bullard's skeptical deputy, Arthel Queen. In *Alnilam*, Followill is listed among the names of Joel Cahill's cadet sycophants.

[21]Series 2, box 91h, 2.

[22]Lewis's aggressive exchange with one of the Griner brothers over driving their cars to Aintry (*DL*, 64) and his murder of the "taller" hillman—the deadly disruption of the man's inner space with an arrow—are examples of his assertive "force-relationship" with the hill people.

north. Lewis' hand took a pencil and marked out a strong X in a place where some green bled away and the paper changed with high ground, and began to work downstream, northeast to southwest through the printed woods. I watched the hand rather than the location, for it seemed to have power over the terrain." (*DL*, 3) From the start, Lewis is portrayed as having an authoritative rapport with nature—one in which he, not the strategic system (nature), initiates the "force-relationship"—which Ed readily buys into. Although Lewis feels it presents a respectable challenge to his authority, ultimately nature must roll over and submit to his will to power—the practices he performs in its space. Yet, the map itself is a kind of colonized representation—a model based on the finite principles of human knowledge. Although Ed does not appear to grasp this idea in its entirety, he does notice the map's attempt to impose order: "Yet the eye could not leave the whole; there was a harmony of some kind. Maybe, I thought, it's because this tries to show what exists" (*DL*, 11). As a fallible representation of imposed human order, the map seduces Lewis into asserting his authority over an illustration, the true essence of which he clearly "does not *know*." Because Lewis is a risk-taker he is all the more easily deceived, counting on his natural prowess to get him out of any unforeseen dangerous situations. In fact, Ed describes him as "the first to take a chance" (*DL*, 9) and Lewis recounts a previous outing in which he injures his ankle. Furthermore, he is not above jeopardizing the lives of those who go with him. When Lewis relates his hunting trip with Shad Mackey, in which Mackey breaks his leg, Ed makes the foreshadowing comment, "Lewis was forever getting himself and other people into situations like this" (*DL*, 47). Clearly, Lewis makes a habit of getting himself and his associates into scenarios where their collective lack of knowledge leads to genuine peril. Too often he depends on his personal abilities and rational constructions, like maps and multiple-step methods, to rescue him from folly.[23] Both the fallibility of the map and the

---

[23]At the beginning of *The Deliverer* Lewis and Ed discuss mounting animals and Lewis flippantly recalls, "I took a correspondence course in all that stuff one time," as if that automatically makes him an expert. Series 2, box 91h, 5.

"unknowing" of Lewis become evident when he initially fails to find the river after leaving Oree. Yet, he does not amend his world view until, in a clear case of irony, his body—the instrument which makes his forceful tactics possible—is "broken" by the very ungovernable power he wishes to "break" and tame beneath the yoke of his will.

Whereas Bobby and Lewis are identified largely in terms of their bodies, Drew Ballinger—the least developed and most short-lived character of the quartet—is defined mostly by his close association with the idealistic principles of industrialized civilization. Of the four men Drew is clearly the most contented with his life and work in Atlanta. Describing Drew's job with a soft-drink company, Ed says he "believed in it and the things it said it stood for with his very soul" (*DL*, 9). Just as Lewis idealizes and romanticizes the body, so Drew develops an almost religious faith in his employment which goes beyond the simple economic value of having a job. Drew is content with industrialized civilization but his idealization of it has potentially destructive consequences. When Ed comments on some littered plastic containers, Dickey records Drew's response in the following terms: "'[It] doesn't go back to its elements,' he said, as though that were all right" (*DL*, 76). The unnatural[24] synthetic quality of urban society, about which Ed feels ambivalent, does not pose any problems for Drew, which invites Ed's derision. For him, Drew remains largely a naive idealist—admirable for his honesty ("You were the best of us" [*DL*, 220]) but little else—whose identity is summed up succinctly and somewhat backhandedly as a "decent city-man, the minor civic leader and hedge-clipper" (*DL*, 60).

One of a countless mass of transparent city-types, Drew is the industrialized everyman and, as such, entertains the most reservations about the canoeing endeavor: "There's not one of us knows a damned thing about the woods, or about rivers" (*DL*, 7). Although Drew is thrilled by the canoe trip once it is underway, the

---

[24]Drew's symbolic unnaturalness is further underscored by the disgusting growth on his son's face, which Ed attributes to the horrors of biology (*DL*, 9).

adventure remains an undertaking for which—though he may develop aptitude—he has no real feeling or talent. Drew's abilities, like his guitar-playing, appear to stem more from acquired technical proficiency than any inherent gift, which explains why he is awed and confused by the brilliant yet "mindless" musical improvisations of the idiot Lonnie.[25] Stubbornly clinging to societal justice after the rape scene, even when his own life is threatened in a non-human environment, Drew's economy-based idealism and rational methodology are symbolically obliterated by the rifle shot to the head—the seat of intellect and morality—which pitches him into the river.[26] A human manifestation of industrialized ideals, his body is cast into the unforgiving waters only to reappear later twisted, broken, and lifeless—crushed by a system in which it had no place.

Whereas Drew's societal ideals make him inadequate for the river environment, Bobby's and Lewis's tactics are defined through their bodies and both suffer regardless of their diverging tactical approaches—one marred by his lack of action, the other in his attempt to dictate action to a violent, strategic system. In Ed Gentry we glimpse something altogether different. Like Lewis, Ed possesses a certain authority in regard to the people with whom he interacts; although, unlike Lewis—who forcibly deals with the hill men—, Ed's dominance initially is limited to the strategic system of Atlanta. In regard to his business he feels an unmistakable

---

[25]In an early manuscript Drew suggests he and Lonnie play "Buckdancer's Choice," a reference to Dickey's third book of poetry, instead of "Wildwood Flower," a well-known country traditional. Both of these tunes lost out to the now-famous "Dueling Banjos" in the movie version. Series 2, box 91h, 22.

[26]Dickey was much more explicit in describing Drew's death early on, avoiding any mystery as to its cause. In *The Deliverer* his injury is described in the following terms: "The back of Drew's head blew off. It looked at first—and I can see it as though I were still sitting in the canoe—as if something, a puff of wind, but something stronger and more unnatural than that, snatched at his hair, and I looked to see what it was, but he was going over the right side of the canoe into the water, and I saw the eaten away pinkish matter of his brain lolling backward, loosening." Series 2, box 91h, 48.

satisfaction in its creation in economic and physical space, and the power it affords him over the practices of others: "I may not have had everything to do with this—with creating this—I said to myself in a silent voice that was different from my usual silent voice, but I have had something to do with it. Never before had I had such a powerful sense of being in a place I had created.... These people would probably be working for somebody else, but they would not be here. They are in some ways my captives; their lives—part of some, most of some—are being spent here" (*DL*, 17). Although Ed takes pride in his existence as a kind of "mini-system" of economic authority in the hegemonic system of Atlanta, it is a voice *other* than his "usual silent voice" which controls the narrative and expresses his thoughts. This lends credence to the idea that he recognizes—whether consciously or unconsciously—the arbitrary nature of his authority: it is linked to a constructed system, one other than nature. In addition, Ed's mastery is portrayed as a decidedly masculine one amid a space inhabited almost entirely by women[27]:

I was halfway up [to the office] when I noticed how many women there were around me. Since I had passed the Gulf station on the corner I hadn't seen another man anywhere. I began to look for one in the cars going by, but for the few more minutes it took me to get to the building, I didn't see a one. The women were almost all secretaries and file clerks, young and semi-young and middle-aged, and their hair styles, piled and shellacked and swirled and horned, and almost everyone stiff, filled me with desolation. I kept looking for a decent ass and spotted one in a beige skirt, but when the girl turned her barren, gum-chewing face toward me it was all over. (*DL*, 15)

---

[27]Keen Butterworth makes a similar observation in his essay, "The Savage Mind: James Dickey's *Deliverance*": "When Ed returns to his office from lunch, he realizes there is not a man, save himself, on the street, only a bevy of women" (Keen Butterworth, "The Savage Mind: James Dickey's *Deliverance*," *Southern Literary Journal* 28/2 [Spring 1996]: 6).

Populating Ed's business district with stiff, physically unattractive women, Dickey seeks to feminize Atlanta while simultaneously emphasizing the dull, unnatural and unsatisfactory quality of that femininity,[28] as opposed to its powerful manifestations in nature.[29] He accomplishes this in Ed's domestic sphere as well when he cites Ed's wife as a major catalyst in his desire to leave, "just as it's any woman's fault who represents normalcy" (*DL*, 27). Furthermore, Ed's physical interpretation of women—his observance of their hair styles and his quest for a "decent ass"—serves as the impetus for the merging of his business and domestic spheres—both of which he feels he is master—while having sex with his wife: "It was the heat of another person around me, the moving heat, that brought the image up. The girl from the studio threw back her hair and clasped her breast, and in the center of Martha's heaving and expertly working back, the gold eye shone, not with the practicality of sex, so necessary to its survival, but the promise of it that promised other things, another life, deliverance." (*DL*, 28). Ed's joining of these two spheres (that of the employed model and domestic mate) against the physical practice of sex makes him envision the gold eye, which reflects—not upon the physical action of his love-making—but promised *other* things, things of which he is not master: the *deliverance* he may find in an untamed, natural system.

Ed is in the throes of a struggle that Dickey identified elsewhere as the "rape of sensibility": "For the tragedy of modern man, the tragedy of his productive specialization, is not so much

---

[28]In *The Deliverer* Dickey is even more unflattering in his description of the city women's unattractive qualities: "The last part is a hill, and to climb it I have to enter into a large company of returning secretaries, dozens of them, cheap-looking girls with tooth-picks and wrong-styled hair, blocky waists and uninteresting shoulders." Series 2, box 91h, 7.

[29]Lewis refers to the river as "she" (*DL*, 70) and Ed experiences a kind of sexualized relationship with the gorge while scaling it. These natural feminine phenomena—the river and the gorge—are anything but dull, having the capacity for both deliverance and death.

the environment he has created by means of it, but is what might be called the rape of his sensibility: the dreadful mental and physical laziness that has descended on him: that he feels entitled to."[30] Ed's rejection of the boredom and despair that accompany his professional and domestic spheres is evident in his decision to accompany Lewis on the trip. As the book's epigraph reads, "There exists at the base of human life an element of incompleteness," and Ed hopes to recapture the value of existence by forsaking his unchallenging lifestyle in favor of an heretofore unknown experience. In the novel's typescript version with corrections by Dickey and Jacques de Spoelberch we learn, near the end of the book, that Ed's newly-energized imagination has enabled him and Martha to discover a hidden and necessary sexual desire for bondage and role-playing.[31] Although the sequence has a large line

---

[30]James Dickey, "Vale of Soul-making," Commencement Address, *USC Magazine* (Winter 1968): 9.

[31]I include the entire sequence here—which would appear following the paragraph ending "She is not" (*DL*, 277) in the published novel—so that readers might experience its full effect and be free to form their own conclusions regarding its implications:

We have been working out of the coalyards, and her fantasies have the reality of her; she lives them truly, and therefore they have the dimension of the flesh. We found out, without going to a psychiatrist, that what she really wants is punishment, and she wants to deserve it. She wants it at a particular time and place—all history opened to us when we discovered this—and for a particular act, or for the failure to perform a particular act.

She wanted it to change her, and make her better. I read history books a good deal, and my good dependable Martha becomes a Carthaginian slave girl, a Spanish heretic, and English princess, an American slave. Sometimes we sent Dean off to spend the night, and Martha can then scream discreetly, though once, during the Time of Punishment, the phone rang and a strange voice almost scared me to death. But the voice was not country, and when it was nothing but a neighbor who had never called before, one who asked if anything was wrong, I knew we didn't need anything except more pillows.

Martha also likes to go back to the hospital in her mind. She has a very strong thing about medicine and morality, and about discipline. She also has a very strong thing about tape:

drawn through it, indicating its exclusion from the next draft, it seems significant that Dickey ever imagined—even as a joke to his editor—such a bizarre interpolation in the tight, flowing plot of his

---

They brought Nurse Martha Gentry down to the sub-basement in the service elevator. Six of the older heavier nurses held her, though she was struggling madly. Head Nurse Cartwright was there, and Doctor Coleman.

—Well, Gentry, said Nurse Cartwright. —You've done it this time. You knew that patient was diabetic. You knew his dosage and his time and his diet. And he very nearly died. You know that. Don't you?

—Yes but... O I'm sorry. I'll never...

—You certainly won't. Peel, Gentry.

—You mean...?

—I mean strip bare-assed. Peel, or we'll help you.

Dr. Coleman went into the other room and sat reading the Journal of the American Medical Association. Sounds came to him from the outer room.

—Stop it Stop it *Stop* it. I'll scream.

—Shriek would probably be a better word, also came in. —You're going to shriek and scream and bellow and howl and beg and plead and roar. You surely are, Gentry. But you'll never do what you did again. Not ever.

They brought Nurse Gentry in, naked. Without looking up, Dr. Coleman said, Put her down, and tape her down tight. By main strength they laid her over the narrow surgical table. Holding her arms down along the gleaming tubular steel legs of the table, they taped them to the legs, beginning at the armpits and spiraling the tape down (Martha likes this part very much) to the wrists and then back up, doing it very quickly and efficiently.

—Do you want her legs spread? Nurse Cartwright asked.

—No, just tape them together at the knee, and tape them to the leg. Let her kick.

One nurse said to another, as they stood on the other side of the little room after having taped Nurse Gentry's arms,

—She needs it, the little bitch.

—Well, she's going to get it.

Dr. Coleman got up and took off his belt. —Nurse Gentry, hospital routine is inflexible. Routine is what makes us a hospital. If you can't learn it one way, you're going to learn it another. But after tonight you're going to be a good nurse. The best on the third floor.

He doubled the belt and popped the sides together. He went over to the weeping, struggling, helpless girl and rolled up his right sleeve.

[Dickey's note to his editor:] We are working on this. Dr. Coleman is a very interesting character.

Series 2, box 91j, 270–71.

promising manuscript. Yet Dickey was completely serious about the scene, explaining to Spoelberch: "I wanted to implant in the reader's mind a couple of things. First, that the narrator without his knowing it, has been a monster all his life, a born killer as well as an 'ordinary suburbanite,' and this one chance episode which *gave* him a chance to energize this hidden part of his personality has, in a sense, freed him of it. His monstrousness may now take other forms: ones that are imaginary and harmless. That's why I've added the final sexual scene with the wife."[32] Ed's experiences then in the alien environment of the river are meant to bring into the forefront of his consciousness the golden-eyed "other life" he imagined while fantasizing about the model and having sex with Martha before the trip. Discovering it was there all along, struggling for expression, he and Martha may now act on it through the relatively harmless medium of imaginative play.

Once he is out of Atlanta and on the river, Ed, like Bobby, initially struggles with the unsuitability of his tactics. When confronted by the two hill men, Ed—the man who constantly penetrates a feminine business district to enjoy his practice of economic mastery—finds his own space in danger of being oppressed: "They came on, and were ridiculously close for some reason. I tried not to give ground; some principle may have been involved" (*DL*, 108). The "principle" being Ed's inadequate Atlanta tactics of dominance, the hill men continue to distort Ed's and Bobby's perceptions of space, calling into question the certainty of their very geographical location: "This-here river don't go nowhere near Aintry" (*DL*, 109). By contrast, the hillmen are comfortably functioning in an environment familiar to them; in an early manuscript Ed describes the shorter man during the encounter as having the "relaxed, enjoying look of belonging anywhere he happened to be, and particularly in the woods."[33] Insouciant in their own familiar space, the hillmen's undermining of the Atlantan's geographical space is accompanied by a psychological

---

[32]Hart, *James Dickey*, 441.
[33]Series 2, box 91h, 113.

reduction of Ed's physical size—"I shrank to my own true size" (*DL*, 108)—and an emasculating turn in the hill men's language: "'Boy,' said the whorl-faced man, 'you don't know *where* you are'" (*DL*, 109). Small, lost and deprived of his masculinity, Ed describes his language as "clinging to the city" (*DL*, 112)—wholly unable to adjust his tactics to the situation in which he finds himself.

The first few pages of *The Deliverer* are written in the first person, present tense, Dickey ostensibly having started the novel this way for the purpose of dramatic effect, reducing in the reader's mind the probability of Ed's survival. However, even though the published novel projects Ed's thoughts in the past tense, Dickey still convinces us that his life is repeatedly endangered. Although Ed's practice is incapable of dealing with the hill men—Lewis's forceful tactics are needed to liberate him and Bobby—he, unlike the other characters, eventually adjusts his actions to nature's system: a transition that results in his literal deliverance. The first traces of this appears when the men capsize on the rapids and Ed finds himself being swept among the rocks: "I turned over and over. I rolled, I tried to crawl along the flying bottom. Nothing worked. I was dead. I felt myself fading out into the unbelievable violence and brutality of the river, joining it" (*DL*, 144). Attempting a number of his own practices against the river and discovering that "nothing worked," Ed resorts to "joining" with it—a decision which spares him from injury: "Body-surfing and skidding along.... Everything told me that the way I was doing it was the only way, and I was doing it" (*DL*, 144–45). Ed's "joining"—his submission, or rather his parasitic affixing, to the "force-relationship" of the river—stands in direct contrast to Lewis's futile struggle to enforce his own tactics: "He was writhing and twisting uselessly, caught by something that didn't have hold of me, something that seemed not present" (*DL*, 146-147). Even in his broken state, Lewis struggles *against* nature's invisible force—a power which has disrupted his bodily space because he resisted its power. Mentally and physically, Ed has successfully changed space and, in doing so, has departed from his typical pattern of existence and formed an association with a space that is "psychically innovating." As Gaston Bachelard says, "This change of *concrete space* can no longer be a mere mental operation that could be compared with consciousness of geometrical relativity. For we do not change place, we change our nature"[34] While Lewis flails against nature ineffectually, Ed, rather than combating the force, attempts to *become* it, changing his nature and acting as a sort of hitchhiker on it or within it, until it is safe to embrace his own tactics again.

Ed's practice of merging occurs again when he makes his decision to climb out of the gorge. Standing at the base of the rock wall, he describes himself as "not thinking of anything, with a deep feeling of nakedness and helplessness and intimacy" (*DL*, 161). Ed's lack of mental activity brings us back to Dickey's portrayal of nature as a system beyond human rationalization, requiring a certain *non*rational medium, other than intellect, of understanding. Devoid of thought, Ed must "sense" his way up the gorge, joining with the wall and, in fact, becoming the wall when he must. Comparing himself to blind musicians, he reflects, "I have got something like that.... I have got up here mostly by the sense of touch, and in the dark" (*DL*, 172). The musical analogy for his merging suggests that Ed—a graphic designer who makes collages on the side—may be employing his artistic sensibility in order to carry out his practice.[35] In any event, Ed's technique is clearly more instinctual than rationally intellectual—he says early in the novel, "I was not much on theories, myself" (*DL*, 6)—which is probably a good thing since, as Bourdieu says of his subjects, "It is because they do not, strictly speaking, know what they are doing that what they do has more meaning than they know."[36] Regardless of what resources he draws on, Ed—not unlike the speaker in "On the Coosawatee"—finds himself "drifting deeper into the forest" (*WM*,

---

[34]Gaston Bachelard, *The Poetics of Space* (New York: Orion, 1964) 206.

[35]For an interpretation of Ed as artist see Mia Anderson, "A Portrait of the Artist as a White-Water Canoeist," *James Dickey Newsletter* 2/1 (Spring 1986): 11–16.

[36]Pierre Bourdieu, *Outline of a Theory of Practice* (Cambridge: Cambridge University Press, 1977) 79.

141), or, in this case, the wall of the gorge. Ed's "sensing" of the rock becomes more intensely emotional as the gorge becomes steeper near the top and Dickey begins to sexualize his motions: "Then I would begin to inch upward again, moving with the most intimate motions of my body, motions I had never dared use with Martha, or with any other human woman. Fear and a kind of enormous moon-blazing sexuality lifted me, millimeter by millimeter" (*DL*, 176). As the most intimate form of human union, sex provides the best vehicle for describing Ed's practice of joining and it is this fusion, not his colonizing mastery of the cliff's spatial crevices, which "lifts" him to its crest. At the steepest point his senses reach an orgasmic crescendo and he weeps once it becomes easier to climb again, expressing his emotional relief at no longer having to "fuck it for an extra inch or two in the moonlight" (*DL*, 177).

Ed's ability to match his tactics to the strategies of nature results in his survival of both the river and the gorge. However, he must apply his "joining" practice in a different manner when killing Stovall, matching his tactics to those of another human mind from a different strategic system: "For me to kill him under these conditions, he would have to be thinking as I had thought for him, and not approximately but exactly. The minds would have to merge" (*DL*, 185). Quite detached from his interaction with nature, Ed believes he must join with the mind of a man from a different system in order to make his practice prevail over that of his companion/enemy.[37] David Arnett summarizes Ed's dilemma in terms of a "mind-link motif": "The mind-link motif plays an important role in *Deliverance*. Dickey was faced with the problem of plausibly explaining the means by which an untrained

---

[37]For two psychological readings of this sequence see George L. Alexander, "A Psychoanalytic Observation on the Scopophilic Imagery in James Dickey's *Deliverance*," *James Dickey Newsletter* 11/1 (Fall 1994): 2–11; and Harold Schecter, "The Eye and the Nerve: A Psychological Reading of James Dickey's *Deliverance*," in *Seasoned Authors for a New Season: The Search for Standards in Popular Writing*, ed. Louis Filler (Bowling Green: Bowling Green University Popular Press, 1980).

suburbanite lost in the wilderness could stalk (at night) and kill a mountain man probably born and raised in the wilderness. It was a difficult proposition, and Dickey resorted to ESP—the mind-link of his poetry."[38] Although Arnett captures the fundamental problem of an alien suburbanite besting an almost indigenous hill man, ESP hardly explains Ed's tactics. Leonard Butts perhaps comes closer to the process Ed undergoes when he asserts, "The method of his achievement is through the ritual of the hunt, and Dickey draws upon the ages-old belief that the accomplished hunter is able to transcend the restricted bonds of his senses and can actually lock minds with his prey."[39] Butts's reference to the archetypal relationship between predator and prey echoes the work of early anthropologists like James Frazer that Dickey so admired. In the *Deliverer* Dickey emphasizes the mystical aspect of Ed's readiness for a predatory undertaking upon nearing the top of the gorge: "I felt better—I felt wonderful, in fact,—like somebody's secret enemy with the power of life and death over him, having the assistance of a god or of invisibility."[40] The nature of the god-like power—or rather "technique"—Ed utilizes becomes apparent when he hones in on the man while preparing to shoot: "We were closed together, and the feeling of a peculiar kind of intimacy increased, for he was shut within a frame within a frame, all of my making" (*DL*, 191). It is important to make the distinction here that, unlike Ed's "nature joining"—in which he merges his practice with the strategy of nature—, Ed closes with the mind of the hill man in order to "encase" him within his own practice: an authoritative yet mutual relationship of his *own* making.

Following Ed's construction of a dominant mental joining, the merging of the men is made physical after Ed lets loose his arrow and falls from the tree, landing upon a broadhead. The men share common wounds, each penetrated by arrows, and as Ed tracks

---

[38]David L Arnett, "James Dickey: Poetry and Fiction" (Ph.D. diss., Tulane University, 1973) 154.

[39]Leonard C. Butts, "Nature in the Selected Works of Four Contemporary American Novelists" (Ph.D. diss., University of Tennessee, 1979) 49.

[40]Series 2, box 91h, 58.

Stovall even their blood becomes intermingled: "I was on my knees, bleeding wherever I looked for his blood" (*DL*, 196). The fact that Ed's merging temporarily decenters his own identity is reflected in his violent desire to mutilate the hill man's body in some way.[41] In the *Deliverer* Dickey has Ed smile at Stovall after shooting him, before he cuts his throat, and wonders, "My God, what am I?"[42] Uncertain of his actions and even his identity, Ed may only separate himself from Stovall once he accepts the fact that he is dead: "His brain and mine fell apart" (*DL*, 199). Despite his anxieties regarding the loss of self, Ed's is the dominant practice throughout the sequence and it is he who practices the role of killer and pursuer, ultimately dictating—as the cliff and river had determined his tactics—when to conclude their peculiar union. As opposed to his earlier failure to act against the hill men on the river, Ed's merging allows him to know the practice of the other in order to make his own similar for the purpose of the other's subordination and ultimate annihilation.

At the beginning of the novel's "After" section, Ed describes himself as "the survivor of some kind of explosion" (*DL*, 244). To be sure, on both a literal and symbolic level, he emerges the most "unscathed" of his companions—Bobby's rape and the mangled bodies of Drew and Lewis—one dead, one not—loom more ghastly than Ed's broadhead puncture. Like Stevie—the idiot whose blown apart body symbolizes a fractured narrative—in Joseph Conrad's *The Secret Agent*,[43] the abused and violated bodies of the men mark the inadequacy of their practices against the strategy of nature. In

---

[41]For readings that derive their meanings largely from the novel's images of violence and savagery—the suburbanites' and the hill men's—see Heinz Tschachler, "'Un principe d'insuffisance': Dickey's Dialogue with Bataille," *Mosaic* 20/3 (Summer 1987): 81–93; Mark Royden Winchell, "The River Within: Primitivism in James Dickey's *Deliverance*," *West Virginia University Philological Papers* 23 (1977): 106–14; and Donald J. Greiner, "The Harmony of Bestiality in James Dickey's *Deliverance*," *The South Carolina Review* 5/1 (1972): 43–49.

[42]Series 2, box 91h, 67.

[43]Joseph Conrad, *The Secret Agent: A Simple Tale* (Garden City: Doubleday/Page, 1921).

addition, Ed is now symbolically *apart* again and his ability to merge, which seems to have been linked to the immediate possibility of death, has become dormant. He has regained the static, autonomous nature of his body and in response to the doctor's inquiry on the condition of his stitches replies, "[They are] holding me together, like you said. There ain't *nothing* getting in or out" (*DL*, 250). However, there is something that has lodged itself inside him. Once he immerses himself back into Atlanta's system he remarks: "The river and everything I remembered about it became a possession, as nothing else in my life ever had. Now it ran nowhere but in my head, but there it ran as though immortally. I could feel it—I can feel it—on different places on my body. It pleases me in some curious way that the river does not exist, and that I have it" (*DL*, 275). As Frederic Jameson and Dickey himself have noted, part of what appeals to the characters about the adventure is the terminal nature of the river,[44] something to which Dickey is sympathetic both in fiction and life.[45] Its space no longer existing as a system—or rather existing as a drastically different

---

[44]Jameson has pointed out that the expedition "was organized in the knowledge that this partially unexplored wilderness area would soon be flooded in order to make an artificial lake. In this perspective, we rejoin the old theme of the imminent destruction of the wilderness which Cooper sounded in the earliest volume of the Leatherstocking series, and which has in our own time received its strongest mythical expression in Faulkner's *Go Down, Moses*" (Frederic Jameson, "The Great American Hunter, or Ideological Contents in the Novel." *College English* 34 [November 1972]: 183). For his own part, Dickey describes the men's rationale for the adventure in the following terms: "Well, why not? If this guy [Lewis] thinks that there's something for us up there in those woods, damn! we ought to go. What else have we got? And it might be fun, too. We'll take some whiskey, and they're going to destroy the wilderness, anyway. The river is going to be damned up. Why don't we have a little contact with the primitive? And that's essentially the motivation for the trip" (Baughman, *Voiced Connections*, 76–77).

[45]In his foreword to Adrien Stoutenburg's *Land of Superior Mirages*, Dickey praises the harsh portrayal of real estate developers: "Love for these destroyed mysteries is matched by the poet's hatred of the destroyers—agencies, hardly people—who swap life for money" (foreword, in Adrien Stoutenburg, *Land of Superior Mirages* [Baltimore: Johns Hopkins Press, 1986] iii).

system (a lake) with new strategies—the extinct river now runs within Ed, still informing his practices ("The river underlies...everything I do" [*DL,* 276]) even though he has returned to Atlanta and is no longer a physical prisoner within its manifested system.[46] In the river's coming to exist only as it is constructed in Ed, it has become a kind of "merging" immigrant in Ed, while simultaneously retaining its "force-relationship," to which he must still react.

In terms of the reader's consideration of the novel, it becomes conspicuous that the "merging" Ed practices in the book is something Dickey wishes the reader to experience with his text. This is made apparent largely through the changes we perceive in Lewis at the book's conclusion. The idea of joining surfaces, not in Ed, but Lewis at the very end of *Deliverance*: "'I think my release is passing over into Zen,' he said once. 'Those gooks are right. You shouldn't fight it. Better to cooperate with it. Then it'll take you there'" (*DL,* 278). Although many scholars point to Ed as the character who has been revitalized by his ordeal, Lewis appears to have gained just as much, if not more.[47] Having gleaned the error

---

[46]Many critics have interpreted the novel as a mythical and transformational cycle with Atlanta as the point of departure and return. See Ronald Schmitt, "Transformations of the Hero in James Dickey's *Deliverance,*" *James Dickey Newsletter* 8/1 (Fall 1991): 9–16; Angelin P. Brewer, "'To Rise Above Time': The Mythic Hero in Dickey's *Deliverance* and *Alnilam,*" *James Dickey Newsletter* 7/1 (Fall 1990): 9–14; and Gary Kerley, "Unifying the Energy and Balancing the Vision: Nature, Man, and Quest in James Dickey's *Deliverance* and *Alnilam,*" *James Dickey Newsletter* 5/2 (1989): 17–26.

[47]For readings that interpret Ed's journey as a quest which results in some kind of revitalization or completion of the self see Daniel R. Schwartz, "Reconfiguring *Deliverance*: James Dickey, the Modern Tradition, and the Resistant Reader," *Texas Review* 17/3–4 (Fall/Winter 1996/1997): 93–111; Ronald T. Curran, "Biology and Culture: Hollywood and the Deliverance of Dickey's Weekend Backwoodsmen," *Southern Quarterly* 18/4 (1980): 81–90; Barnett Guttenberg, "The Pattern of Redemption in Dickey's *Deliverance,*" *Critique* 18/3 (1977): 83–91; Linda Tate Holley, "Design and Focus in James Dickey's *Deliverance,*" *South Carolina Review* 10 (1978): 90–98; Rosemary Sullivan, "Surfacing and Deliverance," *Canadian Literature* 8 (1976): 6–20; Henry J. Lindborg, "James Dickey's *Deliverance*: The Ritual of Art," *Southern*

of his dominant practices, he now comprehends the advantages of applying one's tactics to the system in which he finds himself—working with it rather than against it. At the beginning of the *Deliverer* Ed and Lewis discuss the nature of archery: "You've got the control, I said. Or maybe the luck. Or maybe something else, he said, grinning more. Or maybe something else. That mystical something. Yeah, man. That's where we going: up yonder where that mystical something stays."[48] Even at the inception of the *Deliverer* Lewis instinctively recognizes the connection between his formidable shooting accuracy and the mystical qualities of remote natural environments. Humbled and broken at the book's conclusion, only then does he realize that true mastery lies, not in total control, but close association and Zen-like transcendence. Having realized the value of merging, Lewis serves as a model for the reader, who—through Ed's tactics and Lewis's transformation—hopefully has learned, or at least recognized, it himself. Yet the book does not claim that the practice of merging should be applied to all aspects of existence. Although it is useful in regard to nature and archery, it remains either unproductive or unnecessary to exert it upon human systems, which Dickey classifies as catalysts for "the rape of sensibility." As opposed to nature and Dickey's art, which call for a kind of worthwhile suspension of resistance in order to be experienced more fully, modern systems—which divest humans of their "sensibility"—ostensibly call for active resistance and the necessary dominance that Ed exhibits in his Atlanta tactics.

The typescript version of the novel with corrections by Dickey and Jacques de Spoelberch contains an epigraph from Sartre: "If we are to believe in an enterprise we need in the first place to be pitched into it; we have to ask ourselves what is the best method of bringing it to a successful conclusion; we must not ask ourselves

---

Literary Journal 6 (1974): 83–90; Daniel B. Martin, "James Dickey's *Deliverance*: Darkness Visible," *South Carolina Review* 3 (1970): 49–59; and Donald W. Markos, "Art and Immediacy: James Dickey's *Deliverance*," *Southern Review* 7 (1971): 947–53.
    [48]Series 2, box 91h, 14.

what its object is."[49] The passage applies not only to the book's plot—four city men cast onto a wilderness river—but also the reader's plight. Just as the Atlantans struggle to find the best method of survival, so the reader must establish the avenue of interpretation which best reveals the complexities of the text. In other words, the reader should be concerned with appropriating the practice best suited to produce meaning, rather than coming to the book with a preconceived object in mind—to do so is to allow the text to shape one's reactions rather than imposing a prescribed order or preconceived response upon it. An even earlier epigraph for the novel was, "Who shall deliver me from the body of this death?",[50] which is answered in the salvation Ed achieves on his own by forsaking his body and assuming the essence of natural phenomena. Since death is manifested in a physical form, life must be that which either has no form or—like Ed—can physically or psychologically change form (be delivered from the body). This translates into the reader's deliverance as well. Whereas the reader is ultimately responsible for establishing meaning, the methods for attaining it are there in the text. In using the book's implements, in playing by its rules, in changing one's form from page to page, the reader experiences the deliverance of reading in its entirety and avoids the death of meaning, exemplified by a body of ideas forced upon the written word.

---

[49]Series 2, box 91j.
[50]Series 2, box 91h.

CHAPTER 2

AIR: *ALNILAM* AND *CRUX*

*The beginning is yet to be. It does not lie behind us as
something long past, but on the contrary stands before us....
The beginning has fallen into our future, it stands there as the
distant decree over us, to bring again its greatness.*
    —*Heidegger,* Die Selbstbehauptung der deutschen
Universistät, *11*

*He who will one day teach men to fly will have moved all
boundary stones; the boundary stones themselves will fly up
into the air before him, and he will rebaptize the earth—'the
light one.'*
    —*Nietzsche,* Thus Spoke Zarathustra *in* The Portable
Nietzsche, *804*

*The syne of Oryon rendreth the watres to be proud and
cruelle.*
    —*Caxton,* Eneydos XII[1]

In *Deliverance,* Ed Gentry's practice of merging goes beyond the
book's narrative action to serve as a kind of model for reading.
Despite the otherwise formidable differences between Dickey's

---

[1]Both the quotation and citation are from Dickey's notes on *Alnilam.* Series
2.3, box 84.

first two novels, a similar dynamic exists in *Alnilam* in the character of PFC Aviation Cadet Joel Wesley Cahill (A/C 2027858),[2] even though he never fully appears in the book. However, as in Daphne du Maurier's *Rebecca*,[3] the main character is absent yet somehow omnipresent. Like the star from which his group takes its name, Joel is vague and mysterious yet central—pervading the minds of the base personnel and the air in which they fly. As he toiled through the arduous development of *Alnilam*, Dickey resolved that his background reading would fall into four main categories: flying, codes and communication, utopias, and warfare.[4] Although most every critic has considered the novel through the experience of Joel's father, Frank Cahill, the four topics apply almost exclusively to Joel and the shrouded group he forms.

Following a brief overview of the book, I will be investigating *Alnilam* largely in terms of the categories Dickey identifies. Since these facets of the Alnilam group stem from Joel, I initially will examine Joel's flying—his merging relationship with and mastery of the air—and the dynamics of his personality which allow him to capitalize on his mystical talent. I also will seek to demonstrate how Joel's practices are reflected and magnified through the actions of his father, Frank. These talents or actions serve as the basis for the philosophy of the Alnilam group in that Joel develops a complex theory of existence which ostensibly explains his prodigious flying ability and personality. After considering the arguments of characters and critics who denounce or ignore Alnilam's philosophy, I go on to illustrate how Joel's air tactics and principles serve as the basis for the utopia he imagines once Alnilam becomes a national or global movement. I then venture into the unpublished sequel *Crux*[5] in order to trace the group's failure as a

---

[2]Joel's middle name was originally "Hamilton" instead of "Wesley"; his last name (and Frank's) was originally "Mitchell."

[3]Daphne du Maurier, *Rebecca* (Garden City: Doubleday, 1938).

[4]Series 2, box 91g, 43.

[5]This chapter considers *Crux*, not as an autonomous work, but as a continuation of *Alnilam*. Among the many notes, source books, cassette tapes,

result of the brutality and dehumanization it champions under the auspices of Joel's successor, Malcolm Shears.[6] Finally, I examine the central character in *Crux*, Stathis Harbelis, in order to illustrate how the positive aspects of Joel's philosophy ultimately are redeemed through him.

Both in its sales[7] and the critical attention it garnered, *Alnilam* generally was considered a disappointing book, especially when compared to the extraordinarily profitable success of *Deliverance*. Although Dickey was bothered by the novel's reception, he had expressed doubts about it during its composition: "What I'm trying to do with *Alnilam* is to go for some kind of enormous multifaceted, multilayered type of book, a Nobel Prize type of book, and it'll fail. Because I'm talking about a big, big book; it's rather like *Ulysses*, lots of layers to it. I want to see if I can do it. I know I can't do it, but I want to try."[8] Dickey's fear that the novel would falter on the grounds of its intricate structure would be confirmed by reviewers who found the book too fragmented and overly detailed.[9] During the composition process, Dickey's

---

and folders Dickey assembled in preparation for *Alnilam* is a single sheet of paper with the sentence, "This novel [*Alnilam*] is conceived as the first of two, the whole to be called The Spreading God." Series 2, box 91g.

[6]Malcolm Shears's name was originally "Joe Riley."

[7]Doubleday associate publisher David Gernert called sales "absolutely less than we expected" (Review of *Alnilam*, *Publishers Weekly* 233/10 [11 March 1988]: 51) in regard to the initial 100,000 copies published.

[8]Ronald C. Baughman, ed., *The Voiced Connections of James Dickey: Interviews and Conversations* (Columbia: University of South Carolina Press, 1989) 148.

[9]See Ronald T. Curran, Review of *Alnilam*, *World Literature Today* 62/4 (Autumn 1988): 656–57; and Campbell Geeslin, Review of *Alnilam*, *People Weekly* 28 (6 July 1987): 16. Indeed, the novel is extraordinarily detailed in its attempt to do for flying what Melville did for ocean voyages. Dickey's data on the specifications of aircraft like the PT-17 Stearman and Colonel Hoccelve's advanced single-engine trainer, the AT-6, are derived from James C. Fahey, *U.S. Army Aircraft* (New York: Ships and Aircraft, 1946); and Leonard Bridgeman, ed., *Jane's All the World's Aircraft* (New York: MacMillan, 1941). The novel's extensive information on military flying procedures and equipment like the sextant and E6B is drawn largely from *Air Navigation*. Air Force Manual 51-40

struggles with *Alnilam*'s organization and technicalities became all too evident when he decided to consult Fitzgerald's organizational chart in *The Last Tycoon*[10] as a possible format for working out the complexities of the book's massive plot.[11]

Beyond the challenges in sorting out specific details and organizing sophisticated themes, *Alnilam*—like some of Dickey's poetry—also flirts with the sublime in a manner that sometimes threatens to inhibit meaning. Dickey even encouraged such an ethereal condition in provocative, yet potentially vacuous, comments like, "Really the book is about the air...about flight, about the stars."[12] On one of his tapes Dickey also made a personal note to investigate the Faust legend in relation to *Alnilam*.[13] More than any other aspect of Goethe's monumental work, *Alnilam* inherits the theme of ultimate and sublime "unknowability"—the deep human fear that some things are not meant to be known. The obvious danger in tampering with such a trope is that the author and the text may remain too "unknowing" to convey meaning. In a letter to Walter McDonald, Dickey explained: [14] "There were many times I thought I would never finish *Alnilam*, and not only that I didn't have the key to it, but that there was *not* any key. But I went on, down one false trail after another, and ended up with what you read. I also ended up with the one book of mine of which I can truthfully say that I would not change a word. For better or worse,

---

(Washington: Department of the Air Force, [1 June] 1951); and *Air Navigation: Students' Manual*. AFTRC Manual No. 53-O-2 (rev.) ([1 September] 1946). Dickey also made a personal note to himself to consult James Gould Cozzens in regard to air base procedures. Series 11, tape 19. Cozzens served in the Army Air Corps under General H. H. Arnold during World War II and his novel *Guard of Honor* (New York: Harcourt, Brace, 1948) incorporates important documents he read during the war. Dickey never contacted him.

[10]F. Scott Fitzgerald, *The Last Tycoon* (New York: Charles Scribner's Sons, 1941): 166–67.

[11]Series 11, tape 15.

[12]Charles Truehart, "James Dickey's Celestial Navigations," *Washington Post*, 24 May 1987, F1.

[13]Series 11, tape 15.

[14]The letter is dated 26 June 1989.

Alnilam is what I want to say, put in the way I want to say it."[15] Despite the objections of reviewers, Dickey maintained that he could not have crafted the novel any more effectively, and the false trails he explored were both numerous and long during the more than thirty years he struggled with the book.

Seventeen years rest between the publications of *Deliverance* and *Alnilam*; however, Dickey had worked on his second published novel long before he ever conceived of the first. The basic plot of *Alnilam* originally was entitled *The Romantic* and started appearing in Dickey's notebooks in the early 1950s. As he began charting out and tweaking the nature of Joel's group, the project went through a number of different working titles. One of these, *The Table of the Sun*, is a reference to a line by the French poet, Emmanuel Looten: "J'installerai mes faims à la table du Soleil." In this manifestation of the story, the Table of the Sun is the name of Joel's group, "where we would plan everything openly, in the fullest light...."[16] Another early title was *Trouble Deaf Heaven*, part of a line from Shakespeare's Sonnet 29.[17] Dickey also used as a working epithet *The Field of Dogs*, which gave way to the heading he used through much of the 1970s: *Death's Baby Machine*. He explained, "The machine, in cadet parlance, was the washing machine, the machine that you were in when you were on the way to being washed out of pilot training."[18] As the speaker confesses in "Two Poems of Flight-Sleep," "I was in Death's baby machine, that led to the fighters and bombers..." (*WM*, 386). As he became increasingly interested in the mysterious role celestial navigation would play in the book, Dickey finally decided on *Alnilam*, the name of the center star in the belt of the constellation Orion.

---

[15]James Dickey, *Crux: The Letters of James Dickey*, ed. Bruccoli and Baughman (New York: Knopf, 1999) 467.

[16]Series 2, box 91k.

[17]Series 2.3, box 91o.

[18]Henry Hart, "James Dickey and World War II—History into Story," *James Dickey Newsletter* 14/2 (Spring 1998): 4.

Although the title of the book suggests Joel and his group, most critics have interpreted the novel in terms of Frank Cahill.[19] Yet Dickey's ambitions for *Alnilam* indicate that he was more interested in the implications of Joel and his followers than the personal discoveries of the blind temperamental father: "I hope...that the book will say something about the connection between political power and personal mystery, and between religion, cultism, exhilaration, and cruelty."[20] These ideas—among the most important in the novel, according to Dickey—apply to Joel and his cadets much more than Frank. Serving as the catalyst for Joel's relationship to these concepts is his strong affinity for the air. Apart from his brilliant intellect and charisma, what most fascinates the cadets and administrators about Joel is his literal mastery of the air through flying: the way he can take a standard PT-17 Stearman and make it do seemingly impossible things.[21]

As a natural ace in the vein of prodigious fliers like the Red Baron and Chuck Yeager, Joel is the envy of everyone at the base, including the cadets—who idolize him—and the staff—some of whom resent him. A maverick pilot, Joel dominates the element of air itself, which embodies one of the most central themes in the book. Dickey asserted, "What I really want to try to do in *Alnilam* is to write about the air itself. That's the element that we're in, you know, and it's maybe more dramatic to write about than water and the mysterious creatures that live in it, even *Moby-Dick*. Air is more fundamental than water. When we fly in it, we enter a new

---

[19]For essays that explore the book with respect to Frank Cahill's mythic quest for knowledge of his son and his personal rebirth, see Ronald Baughman, "James Dickey's *Alnilam*: Toward a True Center Point," *South Carolina Review* 26/2 (Spring 1994): 173–79; Angelin P. Brewer, "'To Rise Above Time': The Mythic Hero in Dickey's *Deliverance* and *Alnilam*," *James Dickey Newsletter* 7/1 (Fall 1990): 9–14; and Gary Kerley, "Unifying the Energy and Balancing the Vision: Nature, Man, and Quest in James Dickey's *Deliverance* and *Alnilam*," *James Dickey Newsletter* 5/2 (1989): 17–26.

[20]Series 6, box 123, folder 15, 2.

[21]McCaig tells Frank he once saw Joel perform a falling leaf *upside-down*, a risky maneuver even for experienced stunt pilots. Joel accomplishes the feat without any preparatory training and after logging only a few hours in the air.

kind of existence."[22] A difficult fact for "frequent-flying" twenty-first century readers to imagine is that in 1943 air propulsion was still "a new kind of experience," especially for boys in their late teens who had only been driving cars a short time. Placed in the open cockpits of frail, small-engine trainers, many of these young men found themselves overwhelmed by the pure sensation of being in the air with so little separating them from the act of bodily flight. In a letter to William Wallisch, Dickey explained,[23] "One of the things I wanted most to do in *Alnilam* was to restore the sense of *bodily* flight to people: the feeling of being *carried* in the element they breathe, which is a sensation full of uncertainty, precarious balance, exhilaration, and above all, transgression."[24] For anyone who has ever piloted or flown in an open, old-style propeller-driven aircraft the sensation is unforgettable, and Dickey does an extraordinary job of capturing and mythologizing that "exhilarating" and "transgressing" experience. Joel's success in the air, like Ed's survival on the river, is the result of a practice which seeks to approximate the individual as closely as possible to the essence of his immediate natural element. Harbelis recounts to Frank:

He [Joel] used to talk about the air, and the huge way that it was…that it's…that it's alive all around you. You'd have to go up in an airplane to understand what he meant. But as soon as you understand what that feeling is all about, what your body has to do with it, this being, well, lifted up on this enormous *body* that's sensitive from hundreds of miles up, and down to the smallest, the very smallest grass blade, and you're *in* it, don't you see, and you understand how you relate to it, and what you can do not against it but with it, not what it'll do to you but what it'll do for you, that's when you can fly. (*AL*, 339)

---

[22]Baughman, *Voiced Connections*, 199.
[23]The letter is dated 13 January 1988.
[24]Bruccoli and Baughman, *Crux*, 446.

In his scientific study of environmental adaption, Hermann Schöne asserts that "objects [animals] can...be oriented with respect to magnetic fields."[25] Whether or not Joel's gift for identifying with the air is magnetically biological—like that of the great migrating sea birds in Dickey's poetry[26]—or arduously acquired, it seems to have tapped into an unorthodox vein of knowledge where, as Santayana put it, "The machinery of nature is too fine for us to trace or eludes us by involving agencies that we lack the sense to perceive."[27] Thinking he possesses a special undetectable perception of the air, Joel preaches to his followers that, as one critic summarizes, "they become a part of it as it becomes a part of them."[28]

The circumstances surrounding Joel's death suggest that he may have practiced what he preached. Crashing his plane into a blazing forest fire, Joel is pulled from the wreck by Luther Bledsoe, a local farmer who witnesses the impact while bulldozing dirt in an effort to protect his house and family from the gusting flames.[29] Turning Joel over to his wife Adel, Luther returns to his bulldozer and continues his desperate battle against the raging fire. Despite Adel's attempts to stop him, Joel—even though he is suffering from bad facial wounds—pushes past her and vanishes into the wind and smoke. Although McCaig later finds a piece of Joel's boot near the river (half-a-mile from the house), the Bledsoes, airbase search team, and river sweepers fail to discover any trace of Joel's body; it has disappeared entirely. As one of the novel's epigraphs implies, Joel—at least symbolically, if not literally—has, in Lucretius's words, "dissolved and changed into air."

---

[25]Hermann Schöne, *Spatial Orientation: Spatial Control of Behavior in Animals and Man*, trans. Strausfeld (Princeton: Princeton University Press, 1984) 190.

[26]See, for example, "Reincarnation (II)" (*WM* 50–58).

[27]George Santayana, *The Life of Reason* (New York: Scribner's, 1932) 158.

[28]Robert Covel, "'A Starry Place': The Energized Man in Dickey's *Alnilam*," *The James Dickey Newsletter* 5/2 (1989): 7.

[29]Over the course of *Alnilam*'s composition, the farmer's last name changed from "Dallon" to "Rabun" to "Bledsoe."

Although Joel is gone, it seems unwise simply to pronounce him dead and departed. In the scene where a figure appears in Frank's room while he bathes, the apparition implores his help before departing with the sound of an airplane engine starting (*AL*, 604).[30] On a tape, Dickey identifies this sequence as "a variation on the *Hamlet* theme," a reference to Hamlet's dialogue with his father's ghost, who disappears at the crowing of the cock.[31] Although the book leaves open the unlikely possibility that the ghost could be a cadet or an hallucination (Frank is drinking whiskey), it is significant that Zack, Frank's enormous mongrel dog, senses the presence as well and even lunges at it, succeeding only in jarring himself against the wall. In any event, Dickey's compositional intention is clear: it is Joel's ghost. Thus, the possibility that Joel, or a projection of him, could reappear at any time is meant to be very real in the novel. Near the end of the book, Private Parris Gilbeau and Cadet Frank Spain[32] both claim to have seen him although no one can confirm their stories. In fact, Dickey had proposed using an epigraph from Wittgenstein's *On Certainty*[33] that would have hinted at Joel's imminent and miraculous return: "Such a proposition might be e.g. 'My body never disappeared and reappeared again after an interval.'"[34] Whether or not Joel has actually dissolved into air while maintaining a spiritual presence, the idea certainly fascinates everyone in the novel, including Frank. Despite his stubborn realism, Frank describes himself and Zack as "a blind man and a dog lookin' for somebody

---

[30]As I will point out in my discussion of Alnilam's philosophy, Dickey hints that Joel may have succeeded in becoming the "man-in-the-machine" the group theorizes about and who served as Dickey's visual catalyst for the novel. Bearing this in mind, the sound of the airplane engine signaling the disappearance of Joel's ghost is not accidental.

[31]Series 11, tape 18.

[32]The real Frank Spain was a friend of Dickey's in the Air Cadet Corps (Henry Hart, *James Dickey: The World as a Lie* [New York: Picador USA, 2000] 68).

[33]Ludwig Wittgenstein, *On Certainty*, ed. G. E. M. Anscombe and G. H. von Wright, trans. Denis Paul and G. E. M. Anscombe (Oxford: Blackwell, 1969).

[34]Series 2, box 91g, 60.

in the air" (*AL*, 160), and, even though he vacillates in his opinions, he quietly says to Vernon Hoccleve, the commanding officer of the base—either because he believes it or simply to disturb the colonel—, "He's out there somewhere" (*AL*, 527).

While Joel's whereabouts remain unknown, specific location plays a very important role in the air practices he uses and teaches. By location, Joel meant one's position in relation to the universe as determined through celestial calculation. As Dickey says of the sextant, the device used in determining one's place: "[It gives one] certain proof of the relationship of human bodies to celestial: the complex star-angled keys to everything."[35] Joel uses celestial position as a metaphor for a cosmic frame of mind—one that understands the body's relation to air and the universe. Without this understanding nothing else matters. The navigator, Captain Lennox Whitehall, says of Joel, "He said that precision leads to impulse, I remember. He was all for impulse. But the utmost precision first. That locates you. Then, wherever that puts you, you can sing, dance, eat, fuck. Whatever. He was for abandon" (*AL*, 153). Possessing the right universal location and understanding, one is free to function in a manner that appears spontaneous but is really determined by a calculated location/mental predisposition. According to Joel, the situational precision must come first: from that all else follows.

Whereas Whitehall, a professional navigator, is interested in the practical and mathematical applications of celestial, Joel is fascinated more by its unique association of the human body to the cosmos, and how one might potentially exchange places with, or overlap into, the other. Dickey explains:

As Whitehall, the navigator, says, it's a fundamental mystery, but it works. Joel was concerned with what was behind it, but for Whitehall it's enough that it just works. As he tells Cahill right at the end, it's great to know that if you've got the key in your hand to unlock these particular

---

[35]Baughman, *Voiced Connections*, 208.

secrets of the stars and mathematics that these celestial bodies *have* to tell you where you are if you know how to ask them. They *have* to tell you. That there is a place in the universe that the universe cannot deny you.[36]

During the part of the novel in which Captains Whitehall and Faulstick tell Frank their war stories,[37] Whitehall recounts how, after hours of flying in heavy clouds, he is finally able to get a fix on a single star, thereby setting a course to base and saving his flight group from running out of fuel over the Pacific ocean. Dickey based this story largely on Antoine de Saint Exupéry's *Night Flight*, in which the protagonist is caught flying in a bad storm and glimpses the stars only to perish later: "He climbed and it grew easier to correct the plunges for the stars gave him his bearings. Their pale magnet drew him up; after that long and bitter quest for light, for nothing in the world would he forgo the frailest gleam."[38] In both narratives the stars themselves function as guides with the potential of delivering their beholders from death. With Joel's desire to know what lies "behind it," Dickey, at one point, had thought to make the navigator—like Fedallah in *Moby-Dick*—a demonic Faustian figure, whose knowledge comes to hold a strange and evil power over Joel. Although Dickey eventually decided on the affable and aristocratic Whitehall instead, later manuscripts still exhibit traces of the diabolical aura associated with the original navigator.[39] Furthermore, some of the early navigator's sinister mastery of knowledge beyond limits was infused into Joel himself, whom Private Gilbeau calls "a demon from the pit" (*AL*, 609).

---

[36]Ibid., 266.

[37]This portion of the novel appeared in the April 1987 issue of *Esquire* under the title "The Captains." Dickey was especially fond of this section of the book, frequently presenting it at public readings.

[38]Antoine de Saint Exupéry, *Night Flight* (New York: Harcourt Brace Jovanovich, 1932).

[39]In a relatively late manuscript of *Alnilam*, Whitehall remarks, "My star is Algol. The Ghoul, the Demon Star: that's what saved us. The Blinking Demon. My star is Algol, from now on and for good." Series 2, box 91, 392. In the published version the redeeming star is Vega, the "falling buzzard."

Although Joel fascinates the cadets with his charismatic and mysterious personality, his celestial and air practices are the necessary proofs of his genius, from which everything else follows. Shears explains to Frank how the cadets came to heed Joel:

> I can't speak for the others—only sort of—but when Joel got us together and started talking to us, there was some doubt about what he was trying to get across. He told us that all that would be taken care of, as soon as we got back into the air: back into the air from this barracks. As soon as *he* got into the air, word got around fast, not only from the boys but from the instructors. The more he flew, the more we believed him; the more pressure his flying put on the instructors, the more they talked him up, the more behind him we were. The more tours he walked, according to Lieutenant Spigner's orders and the colonel's, the more we went with *his* orders. (*AL*, 426)

Through his unorthodox air practices, Joel demonstrates how easy it is to fly, thereby awing his peers and undermining the au-thority of the check riders, Colonel Hoccleve, and—ultimately— the military. Since Joel can "out-fly" his superiors, he attains a measure of natural authority, oblivious to rank, which he passes on to his followers through his teachings. On one of his tapes Dickey says, "you'd think the guy in charge was the cadet" when he went up with an NCO.[40] Check riders like the sour Lieutenant Foy, who is jealous of Joel and uncertain of his own flying ability, were never good enough for combat, so they waited the war out and got their kicks washing out cadets. Suddenly, they are stripped of what little worth they possess when Joel proves he can both practice and teach flying better than they.

Because his air practices are so extraordinary, the cadets begin to take seriously Joel's ideas on other matters. Dickey explained:

---

[40]Series 11, tape 8.

Joel Cahill speaks in parables. He talks about precision mysticism. What the hell does that mean? You don't know what it means, and in the novel it's not explained. Yet I intended to implant that in the reader's mind. Precision mysticism. When you relate that to an airplane engine and to Joel's relationship to flight, it takes on another meaning, but you're never able to understand exactly what. The Alnilam plotters think it's something that may be beyond anything they have ever been able to perceive. That's the fascination of Joel Cahill. He's able to formulate these weird, strange, provocative, evocative notions. And he can get up there in an airplane and prove them—or what he does in an aircraft seems, to the Alnilam fliers, to bear out everything he talks about.[41]

In addition to his flying ability, Joel has the intelligence and charisma to turn his techniques into engaging gospels that may be applied to different arenas of experience. Both in his flying and his attitude, he takes the right pose coming off the air, creating a persona and matching theories to accompany his very substantial gifts. On this basis, Joel founds a flight club which plays upon his own masculine mystique and the insecurities of young men not so talented as himself. As McClintock McCaig tells Frank, "Everybody who knew him could tell there was somethin' not real about him, and there was. Not real, but better" (*AL*, 139). Witnessing his ability and his explanation of it, the cadets hasten to join him in the hopes of improving their own flying, but also to escape the mundane mediocrity of constituting just another flier. Dickey asserted, "The reason that people join the Alnilam conspiracy, that the plotters join up with Joel Cahill, is that they believe that he is initiating them into an elite which everyone wants to be in. It is like a college fraternity. A college fraternity is not based on what the word 'fraternity' suggests; it is not based on brotherhood and

---

[41]Ernest Suarez, "An Interview with James Dickey," *Contemporary Literature* 31/2 (Summer 1990): 130.

inclusion but exclusion."[42] Using his practices and charisma to draw in followers and further his more ambitious ideas, Joel begins building Alnilam into the powerful organization of which he dreams.

Beyond the practices and persona Joel establishes for the purpose of constructing Alnilam, his personality possesses a natural proclivity for mystery and imagination. This is best seen through Hannah Pelham, "the wild mountain flower of the cotton mills," whom Dickey identified as his favorite character from all his fiction.[43] Whereas the cadets all admire Joel for his air prowess and manner, Hannah is the only character who makes any headway understanding him on an intimate, personal level. More than a lover, Hannah possesses a sharp, albeit uneducated, wit and imagination which enable her to recognize Joel's needs. Dickey's appreciation of and affection for Hannah's significance was obvious during the composition process: "In the creation of the character of Sara,[44] I want a magnificent, sick, foul-mouthed, vital girl."[45] Hannah's unpolished charm and crass wordplay are summarized in Dickey's assertion, "She talks a strange kind of country surrealism."[46] Despite their divergent backgrounds and purposes, she shares with Joel a command of language and astuteness which is arresting yet unconventional.

Although Joel, like all prophets and demagogues, is a masterful human manipulator, his feelings for Hannah are genuine and are probably amplified by the fact that she is dying.[47] As a result of their bond, her comments about him are among the most

---

[42]*Ibid.*, 128.

[43]See Ernest Suarez, "An Interview with James Dickey: Poet and Novelist," *Texas Review* 17/3–4 (Fall/Winter 1996/1997): 137.

[44]Hannah's first name was originally "Sara" and her last name was "Culclashure"—the maiden name of Dickey's longtime literary assistant, Paula Goff—instead of "Pelham."

[45]Series 11, tape 13.

[46]Ibid.

[47]In an early manuscript, Hannah describes her illness and says she has only eight months to live. Series 2, box 91k. Her symptoms suggest she is suffering from an advanced case of terminal leukemia.

insightful, particularly in terms of his mysterious personality. On one of Dickey's tapes, she says of Joel, "He said he would rather people didn't understand him. That gave him a power over them that nothing else could."[48] The overall mysterious quality of *Alnilam*—fueled by Joel's personality, as well as Frank's ignorance of his son and the cryptic nature of the group—is derived largely from Jocelyn Brooke's *The Image of a Drawn Sword*, which Dickey cites as a source text.[49] The novel follows Reynard Langrish, a sensitive-natured English veteran of World War II, who enters into a strange friendship with Roy Archer—a predatory, militaristic figure who "held authority; what kind of authority he [Reynard] could not guess...."[50] Roy Archer, who resembles Joel in his mysterious charismatic appeal and the vague hints he gives about preparations for an obscure "emergency" and the new order to follow, attempts to recruit Reynard into a secret group—the members of which have a sword with a snake coiled about it tattooed on their forearms—that will fight an enemy known only as the "other" during the time of "emergency." Most of the novel is spent with Reynard, like Frank Cahill, trying to establish the purpose of the group and the nature of the conflict, which he never fully succeeds in doing. Like Roy Archer, Joel Cahill takes advantage of his personal appeal in winning people for a cause that is either vague to begin with or will involve a significant amount of personal sacrifice. By hinting at unrealistic potentials and emphasizing their own formidable gifts, men like Joel and Roy Archer are able to gain power over people while withholding information that could jeopardize their hegemony. In this practice they endorse Montesquieu's belief that power without knowledge is power lost. To disseminate knowledge to followers is to compromise one's dominance over them; and Joel's secretive personality effectively obscures—both from other characters and readers—the roots of his arcane erudition.

---

[48]Series 2, box 91k, 117.

[49]Series 11, tape 27.

[50]Jocelyn Brooke, *The Image of a Drawn Sword* (New York: Knopf, 1951) 14.

Accompanying Joel's use of personal mystery is his interest in the applications of the imagination. Hannah says of him, "He seemed to like imaginary situations better than real ones. He said he had a theory of power, based on imagination."[51] The book's use of imagination makes its most powerful manifestation during Frank's and Hannah's love scene,[52] in which she acts out the detailed sexual fantasy she had created with Joel's help.[53] Whereas Hannah uses her imagination at Joel's urging for the purpose of shared sexual pleasure, Joel matches his creative powers with his mysterious persona in coordinating Alnilam. Dickey summarized: "Joel says to his followers, we're going to make it like it should have been at the beginning. But you don't know what that is. He talks about existence as seen from an aircraft, the great blue field and the purple haze and so on. My point here is, that if you have somebody as charismatic as Joel Cahill, his followers follow him toward his ultimate goal not *despite* the fact its vague, but *because* it's vague."[54] Using imaginative terminology[55] to describe an uncertain condition, Joel captivates the cadets more effectively than he ever could with logical ideas or statistics. Another reason Joel never relates his blueprint for change stems from his conceptual belief,

---

[51]Series 2, box 91k, 88.

[52]This section of the book appeared as "Broomstraws" in *Helicon Nine: The Journal of Women's Arts and Letters* 17/18 (1987): 112–34. Another section of the book involving Frank, entitled "Blind Snow, Warm Water," was solicited in a letter of 15 December 1983 by William Phillips for the fifty-year anniversary issue of *Esquire.* The excerpt was never published.

[53]On one of his tapes, Dickey had Sara remark on Joel's spanking her with his slide rule: "There were numbers all over my ass!" Series 11, tape 13. Dickey was interested in the way Joel's sexual imagination interacted with his creative use of numbers and codes. In this episode, the spheres blend together through the numbers imprinted on Hannah's rear.

[54]Suarez, "An Interview with James Dickey," 130–31.

[55]Dickey examined Stephen Spender's early poems for the idealization of young men and the presence of airplanes. Much of Spender's work contains images of flying and in one of his untitled poems he urges young men to "advance to rebel" (Stephen Spender, *Collected Poems, 1928-1953* [New York: Random House, 1955] 31).

not in war, but freedom.[56] Thus, an involved schemata of means would run the risk of contradicting the imaginative ends it seeks to achieve. As Dickey pointed out, ultimately, "all Joel Cahill has to do is appear and all that loose, wandering emotion in the young people focuses on him, and he becomes their channel."[57] The imaginative means of the man and the man himself, rather than the concepts for which he stands, fuel Joel's appeal.

Discussing Joel's use of mystery and imagination in building Alnilam leads to the entrancing tactics by which the actual process takes place. On one of his tapes, Dickey describes Joel as "attractive" and "dangerous," but "perhaps right, too."[58] "Attraction" and "danger" are inherent in Joel's ability to effect a kind of hypnosis on the people around him. On another tape, Dickey has Colonel Riker[59] characterize Joel as "very peculiar...almost hypnotic."[60] Private Gilbeau—whose obsession with Joel runs deeper and more violently than anyone else's—says of him:

> I never saw such an intense expression on anybody's face as there was on his. He always seemed about to say just one word that would...would, I'm not sure, would resolve something, would get somebody to do something that had maybe been set up: like he was always ready to say something like 'Go. All right. Go on. Do it. Get on with it. *Now.*' He seemed always getting ready to say *now*, and if you knew what it was he wanted you to do, you would do it, and you wouldn't fool around. (*AL*, 307)

Although Gilbeau is not a member of Alnilam, there is evidence that Joel may have used a form of hypnosis on the cadets who join his group. Vaughn Blazek, the "Jewish Eagle," recounts that Joel's eye color did not matter, but rather "what was comin' through 'em,

---

[56]Series 11, tape 7.
[57]Suarez, "An Interview with James Dickey," 127.
[58]Series 11, tape 9.
[59]Riker would evolve into Colonel Vernon Hoccleve.
[60]Series 11, tape 7.

out of him. You could look straight at 'em, if he wanted you to, if he didn't mind, but if he did mind, you couldn't. They would tighten down, and light up. That was when you were comin' in to where he was. That was when you knew you could do anything. You didn't need to look at him anymore" (*AL*, 587). Blazek's description is important since it focuses, not on what Joel says, but the suggestive and controlling effect of his gaze.

Another cadet, Billy Crider, insinuates both hypnosis and ESP[61] when he describes how being with Joel puts one on the other side of verbal communication (*AL*, 299). In fact, Dickey experimented with the possibility of having Joel use ESP to coordinate the members of Alnilam as a kind of single organism. According to him, this is something that Shears would have suggested by subtle means throughout the two books, until in *Crux*—during a long nocturnal, aerial chase-sequence at high altitude—Shears actually hears a voice.[62] As Dickey explains in his notes, Shears loses the enemy plane and "is as close as it is possible for him to get to panic, because he has been within firing range, and he's afraid he might run into the Japanese aircraft. Then a voice speaks to *him*, giving him turn instructions; the target comes back on the scope, and Shears makes the kill."[63] ESP also may play a part in both the aforementioned "ghost scene" and Gilbeau's story of hearing Joel's voice in the wind tunnel where the infirmary stores its files. Although Frank Cahill discounts Gilbeau's claims—he thinks Private Gilbeau is sexually obsessed with Joel—, Frank Spain claims to have seen Joel—the ghost in the machine—through the whirring propellers on graduation day (*AL*, 639). Whether or not these

---

[61]Dickey cited Arthur Koestler as his source in applying the principles of ESP to *Alnilam*. See Koestler's essay on ESP, "Science and Reality," in *The Heel of Achilles: Essays 1968–1973*, 155–57; and his book on parapsychology, *The Roots of Coincidence* (London: Hutchinson, 1972).

[62]In the first chapter of *Crux*, Harbelis is fascinated by the instinctually choreographed movements of flying fish (James Dickey, "Journey to the War," in *The James Dickey Reader*, ed. Henry Hart [New York: Touchstone, 1999] 212). Furthermore, one of the Alnilam aphorisms describes the group as a single muscle which each member feels as his own.

[63]Series 2, box 91g, 65.

events are attributable to ESP, the overly fervent imaginations of mesmerized young men, or something else, Joel's powerful spellbinding effect is undeniable.

Serving as a coda in this consideration of Joel's practices and personality is a brief account of the sources Dickey used in creating him. Although Dickey was fond of saying that Joel was based on his older son, Christopher, more of Joel's personality comes from Dickey's own experience as a cadet in World War II. Whereas Colonel Hoccleve repeatedly mentions that he considered dismissing Joel on the grounds of "attitude," Dickey maintained that his "washing out" of Primary Flight Training at Camden, South Carolina, was largely a result of repeated insubordination and a quota system that allowed only a certain number of cadets to pass.[64] Joel, however, is not a fictionalized Cadet Dickey and many of his specific characteristics and interests come directly from the young Englishman Julian Bell in the double-biography, *Journey to the Frontier* by Peter Stansky and William Abraham.[65] Dickey was an ardent admirer of *Journey to the Frontier* and for a time even contemplated translating it into a screenplay. Although, like most of Dickey's cinematic projects, it never materialized, the work is still notable for the attributes Dickey took from Julian Bell in the creation of Joel Cahill. Bell, a Cambridge graduate and the nephew of Virginia Woolf, had a strong interest in utopias and even developed "plans and ideas for a model town."[66] Giving advice to his friend, John Lehmann, Bell suggested "a settled and orderly life in which certainty and precision rule."[67] Furthermore, at Cam-

---

[64]Also of biographical interest, Hart notes that one of Dickey's friends, Cadet Peck, crashed while "hedge-hopping" and died several days later as the doctors continued to extract shards of glass from of his face (Hart, "James Dickey," 2–3). Dickey used Peck's name as the impetus for christening *Alnilam*'s air base Peckover, and the details of the glass shards embedded in his face are used in describing Joel's appearance after his violent crash.

[65]The book recounts the lives of Bell and John Cornford, two young and talented Englishmen who both died in the Spanish Civil War.

[66]Peter Stansky and William Abraham, *Journey to the Frontier* (Boston: Little, Brown and Company, 1966) 33.

[67]Ibid., 72.

bridge he was an important member of the Apostles, a prestigious philosophical organization. As Stansky and Abraham explain, the Apostle group, like Alnilam, functioned under the pretext "that any problem could be dealt with without too much difficulty and with no special qualification beyond being an apostle."[68] Although Julian was serious about this organization, he conceptualized him-self politically as a "party of one," aspiring to be—like his grand-father, Sir Leslie Stephen, and Joel Cahill—"a partisan of the ideas struggling to remould the ancient order and raise the aspirations of mankind." He said of himself, "I am proposing to turn myself into a man of action, cultivate my tastes for war and intrigue, conceivably even for town-planning and machines, and generally for organizing things and running the world."[69] However overly ambitious and unrealistic Bell's goals may have been, Joel Cahill would have been hard-pressed to describe his own aspirations any better.

One dynamic that does not come from Julian Bell's biography is the relationship between Joel and his father. Among his many ambitions for *Alnilam*, Dickey wanted to write the "ultimate novel of fathers and sons"[70] and, in addition to his other functions in the book, Frank subtly reinforces Joel's practices and personality. This takes place on both a literal and symbolic level when Frank has sex with Hannah, acting out Joel's fantasy role and probably contracting gonorrhea in the process—an STD Joel had transmitted to her. More importantly, Frank seems to possess the same merging sensibility that makes Joel's air practices so brilliantly effective. On more than one occasion in the novel Frank is powerfully moved when he remembers his experience of standing in a waterfall, in "a mixture of water and air," where he "had no body" (*AL*, 129). The experience suggests the same sensibility as Joel's concept of dissolution in air and is similar to that of the speaker in Dickey's

---

[68]Ibid., 91.
[69]Ibid., 114.
[70]Series 11, tape 18.

poem "The Twin Falls," who feels water streaming by him "in the shape of [his] shoulders" (*WM*, 118).

Joel's and Frank's characteristics also overlap in the way they create things. Joel arranges Alnilam in the same manner that Frank assembles his fun house, the Honeycomb, using intuition and instinct more than rational methodology. Frank says of his construction, "I guess I had some kind of a plan when I started out, but it kept changin' around, you see. I didn't draw no plans, because I didn't want to be locked into 'em" (*AL*, 358). Just as the Honeycomb is a work of improvisation and intuition, Joel appropriates Orion for his group because it constitutes a free and non-static "moving center" (*AL*, 154), a shifting symbol, sweeping slowly across the winter sky.[71] Furthermore, in an early manuscript Frank describes the Honeycomb in terms that suggest Alnilam: a "spread" "with an atmosphere of freshness, openness, and uniqueness, secrecy."[72]

The most important manner in which Joel's and Frank's shared sensibility is reflected centers, not surprisingly, around the practice of flying. Dickey begins this association subtly through some of Frank's flashback experiences, identified in early manuscripts as "The Air-Frame."[73] In the first of these flashbacks Frank remembers helping a young boy fly a model plane in an Atlanta park. Later, "The Air-Frame" is evoked right before McCaig and Frank arrive at a principles of flight class. Frank's early experience with a toy aircraft functions as a determinant in uncovering his buried interest in flying as he attempts to imagine what is going on around him at the base. Still later, it becomes apparent that Frank's reminiscences on flight underscore a natural talent for the practice. Shears genuinely is surprised by the speed with which Frank picks up on Joel's flight simulation technique. He exclaims, "You've got

---

[71]As Frank runs his hand over the Stearman's engine before going up with McCaig, he associates it with a honeycomb (*AL*, 475). Frank's metaphor links his own creative imagination to Joel's, which uses the engine for different symbolic purposes.

[72]Series 2.3, box 91c, 142.

[73]Series 2, box 91.

it, quicker than anybody I ever saw" (*AL*, 417). Frank's aeronautical instincts are confirmed when he performs exceptionally in the Link Trainer and then flies with McCaig during the section of the novel Dickey called "A Wheedling of Knives."[74] Throughout these episodes, Dickey hints that Frank's affinity for the air is strengthened by his blindness, and Frank repeatedly mentions his use of an imaginary level in order to feel the air and trim the aircraft.[75] Drawing upon his lack of sight and heightened senses as powerful attributes, Frank forms a connection with his son through flight, echoing Joel's merging mastery of the air.

Frank's sensibility and its more refined manifestation in Joel, serves as the basis for the latter's incomparable practices in the air. These practices, in turn, function as the foundation for the development of Alnilam and the philosophy it champions.[76] Shears says as much when he explains to Cahill, "The basis of what Joel was on to, and what we think we're on to, is the air itself, and the way we take it, and the way we fly in it, and the organization we've arrived at, based on this kind of understanding that we have" (*AL*,

---

[74]Dickey used this title to differentiate this part of the book, beginning on page 464, in early manuscripts. It is a reference to the musical whine of a Stearman's engine.

[75]Early on, Dickey had contemplated having Frank encounter a blind street musician so that he might learn something about the aesthetics of touch-based perception. Incidentally, he compared the jerky motions of Frank's eyes to the twitching leg muscle of Will Barrett in Walker Percy's *The Last Gentleman* (New York: Farrar, Straus and Giroux, 1966). Series 11, tape 4. Dickey contacted a number of blind men as sources for Frank's condition and his perceptions. Merril A. Maynard, a wood-worker specializing in furniture restoration, wrote to Dickey on 19 June 1972, giving a brief account of his life. Dickey also consulted Gary Ackerman at the University of Illinois about going blind from diabetes. In addition, Robert Russell, a professor at Franklin and Marshall College, sent him general information on blindness.

[76]For essays that address the philosophical underpinnings of the novel see Robert C. Covel, "'A Starry Place': The Energized Man in Dickey's *Alnilam*." *The James Dickey Newsletter* 5/2 (1989): 5–17; and Gary Kerley, "Understanding 'This Hunter Made Out of Stars': The Myth of Orion in James Dickey's *Alnilam*, *James Dickey Newsletter* 4/1 (Fall 1987): 15–22.

406). The name of the organization alone provides a certain degree of insight into its nature. Alnilam is a dim star, sputtering in the middle of Orion's belt. Although it is part of the most visible constellation in the winter sky, it is difficult to get a fix on and generally is regarded as a bad star for navigation. However, because it constitutes the middle part of Orion's belt, it is—like Joel—secretive yet central and its centrality was especially important to Dickey:

> If I wanted to be pretentious, which sometimes I do, I would say that the notion of centrality of [Alnilam] in that huge, spectacular constellation was suggested to me, at least in part, by the philosopher Heidegger's notions about the mystical properties of centrality. I wouldn't insist on that at all. I would say that it was suggested to me by something I was reading of Heidegger's where he was discussing at great length what it means to be the center of something. And it occurred to me that the centrality of the constellation Orion was marked by that star, Alnilam, and the notion from there that seemed to radiate out into the whole notion of the group of young fliers, the cadets that are led by Joel Cahill, the young pilot, who calls it the Alnilam Group—he himself being the center of them.[77]

Just as Joel serves as the creative and literal center of the group, ancient cultures associated Orion with national heroes, warriors, and demigods—their own mythological and self-defining "centers." In Greek mythology, the god Orion is usually described as having "a somewhat boastful disposition, as he is said to have claimed dominion over every living creature."[78] Correspondingly, Joel writes in his literature book that "whosoever masters the air

---

[77]Ira Broughton, "James Dickey," in *The Writer's Mind: Interviews with American Authors Volume II*, ed. Ira Broughton, (Fayetteville: University of Arkansas Press, 1990) 175.

[78]Robert Burnham, Jr., *Burnham's Celestial Handbook*, vol. 2 (New York: Dover, 1966) 1283.

masters the breath of every creature living, every other man, and masters him from the inside" (*AL*, 406). In addition to its connotation of mastery, Orion appears in the writings of Virgil, Pliny, and Horace as a harbinger of destructive events, sometimes associated with the ocean. Furthermore, in Babylonian and Hindu legends Orion often was identified with vicious winter storms, and Alnilam certainly succeeds in wreaking a wintry tempest of destruction upon Peckover.

Alnilam's concern with the stars and the cosmos as philosophical symbols also corresponds to Dickey's long poem, *The Zodiac*. Like the protagonist of that work, Hendrick Marsman, Joel is concerned "With *Einfühling*, with connecting things that lay their meanings" (*WM*, 346). In his keen ability to link seemingly disparate ideas and disciplines—such as math, poetry, freedom, precision, magic, and technology—together, Joel gives each thing a new meaning while arriving at a unique definition of reality which he identifies with a single star: a fundamental aspect of the universe. Furthermore, just as Marsman wishes "to relate himself, by means of the stars, to the universe" (*WM*, 345), Joel's interest in celestial navigation—his desire to get behind and beyond the practicalities of the discipline—lies mainly in the imagined possibility of an exchange or consolidation between himself and the cosmos. Finally, Joel, like Marsman, endorses the premise, "The stars are mine, and so is / the imagination to work them—" (*WM*, 352), suggesting that the symbolic potentials of celestial bodies are limited only by the creative powers of the beholder. Succeeding in arriving at what Dickey hopes to achieve in his poem, Joel draws the stars into their myths, making Alnilam his own through the imaginative manner in which he establishes a new mythology and philosophy.

The gift Joel possesses and Marsman seeks in his poem is a truly rare one. As Dickey said of Joel's philosophy, "Whether it's Alexander the Great, Caesar, Frederick II, Napoleon, Hitler, John F. Kennedy, or Joel Cahill, it satisfies some deep hunger in people that somebody has got hold of a truth and a way of life that they themselves cannot command."[79] Joel's masterful command of a unique philosophical outlook is a result of a sensibility—a distinctly artistic one—that takes its deep ideas from the air; in an interview Dickey even called him "the Rimbaud of the air."[80] Chief among Joel's aesthetic practices is his heavy and unorthodox use of metaphor. Gilbeau says of him, "He had sure read a lot, and he had just an amazing memory. Everything meant something it didn't, or didn't know it meant, everything stood for something else; there was a secret behind it. Some of what he talked about sounded like religion, and some of it like psychology" (*AL*, 308). Whitehall makes a similar point in a more articulate manner:

> He was always talking about what was beyond: what was beyond this and what was beyond that; what was underneath this surface, what was hidden by this, that, or the other thing. Air was not really air, water was not really water. An engine was doing some other thing than it was supposed to be doing. Navigation was really a form of poetry. So was mathematics in general .... [He] seemed to believe that there's some kind of freedom that's beyond all discipline, beyond all skill..." (*AL*, 442–43).

In his unusual use of metaphors, Joel makes associations between seemingly disparate things in an effort to arrive at fresh new meanings. The freedom "beyond all discipline" that Whitehall mentions is partly a simple, yet artistic, open-mindedness in confronting the problem of existence, which allows one to make connections between things in an original, seemingly apriori manner.

Although Joel's approach seeks to resolve ideas in new ways, his metaphors are rarely clean-cut, as if a certain amount of mystery, paradox, and even contradiction is necessary to make them possess the desired connotation and effect. This practice

---

[79]Suarez, "An Interview with James Dickey," 128.
[80]Truehart, "James Dickey's Celestial Navigations," F6.

resembles Heraclitus's conception of reality, in which the unity of things: "Is a subtle and hidden kind of unity, not at all such as could be expressed by either a monistic or a dualistic philosophy. The oneness of things, or rather their mutual attunement, cannot exist or even be conceived apart from their manyness and discord. The wisdom that steers all things through all things...is something that cannot be expressed without paradox."[81] This world-view is revealed in Joel's philosophy through seemingly contradictory terms like "precision mysticism," which suggests both mathematical exactness and sorcery. Like Anaximander, the pre-Socratic philosopher of the air, Joel is "very strongly caught in the mystic and poetic enchantment"[82] of interpreting experience—an enchantment that identifies things, not as they should be organized, but as they truly are. Joel calls mathematics and astronomy "precision mysticism" because of a perceived mystical dimension in his understanding of spherical trigonometry. As Captain White-hall says, the mystery of universal location "comes out of the numbers, which are kind of like a spell, you might say" (AL, 153). Contradicting conventional Western thought, Joel views math as a highly-ritualized language, in which the numbers, somewhat like the lettered variables of higher theoretical math, take on complex symbolic meanings. Galileo tells us as much: "The Universe, which stands continually open to our gaze, cannot be understood unless one first learns to comprehend the language and read the letters in which it is composed. It is written in the language of mathematics...."[83] Thus, in its inclusive use of traditionally autonomous disciplines, *Alnilam* may be viewed as a "cosmogonical" work in the same manner that Paul Valéry applied the term to Poe's scientific poem, *Eureka*: "The reader of *Eureka* will see how Poe has extended the application both of the nebular hypothesis and the law of gravity. On these mathematical foundations he has built an

[81]Phillip Wheelwright, *Heraclitus* (New York: Atheneum, 1974) 105.

[82]Charles H. Kahn, *Anaximander and the Origins of Greek Cosmology* (Philadelphia: Centrum Philadelphia, 1982) 94.

[83]Galileo Galilei, *Discoveries and Opinions of Galileo*, trans. Stillman Drake (New York: Doubleday, 1957) 237–38.

abstract poem, one of the rare modern examples of a total explanation of the material and spiritual universe, a *cosmogony*. It belongs to a department of literature remarkable for its persistence and astonishing in its variety; cosmogony is one of the oldest of all literary forms."[84] Like Poe and the pre-Socratics, Joel combines elements of the arts, mysticism, and numbers in building his compelling interpretations of the universe. Using flight, astronomy, and celestial navigation as his mathematical foundations, he assembles the poetic philosophy by which he hopes to change the world.

Although Joel's thinking is wide-ranging, sometimes to the point of sublime opacity, Dickey was very specific about the kinds of philosophical statements Joel made. Among the most important categories he identified as Alnilam aphorisms, Dickey listed statements on machinery, the characteristics of the iron (or steel) men, and the man-machine connection.[85] These aphorisms are among the most notable in the book since they are directly related to Dickey's inspirational guiding vision in the composition of *Alnilam*. In an interview he explained:

There used to be a sort of legend in the Air Force that—this was in the days of propeller-driven aircraft—that if you were, say, on the flight line and there was an aircraft where you could look through the propellers, and see what was behind them, if there was another aircraft behind the first with the propellers going and you looked through both propellers at the same time it would form an image of a

---

[84]Paul Valéry, "On Poe's 'Eureka,'" in *Variety*, trans. Malcolm Cowley (New York: Harcourt, Brace and Company, 1927) 137.

[85]Dickey identified the other aphorisms as Shelley quotes, the philosophical aims of the group, the practical modus of the plot, general cryptic comments, characterizations of flight, characteristics of the future state, and the characteristics of the father. Series 2.3, box 84. All of these are discussed at various places in this chapter.

man, sort of like a shadow of a man. The idea of the ghost in the machine appealed to me.[86]

Fascinated by the figure in the propellers, Dickey expanded upon his application of this captivating idea in an essay he wrote after *Alnilam*'s publication: "As a result of the shadowy figure in the twin propellers, I began to feel that there might be some kind of spirit in the machines that men have made, and that this might be both indifferent to them and superior to them; in short, not so much a ghost in the machine but a God. From this there stemmed a kind of religion, and its inevitable prophet and martyr...."[87] The concept of the ghost/god in the machine reaches its apotheosis in the novel when Joel appears to Frank Spain amid the whirring propellers on graduation day. As Spain recounts to Frank Cahill:

> Just before I went in on that second pass, I saw a plane that hadn't been hit. I was standing on the brake and turning, and through two props, mine and somebody else's that was there just for a second, just when they came together, one over, one behind the other one, when they...when they kind of intersected with each other, overlapped...there was one blur made out of two blurs, and that was when I saw who was in the plane.... He was in that blur, but his face was right there, coming out like...like a negative in the hypo. Like in that film. I saw it, as plain as I can see you. He had on a helmet and goggles, like the rest of us, but it was him. He had that expression on his mouth, and it was him. (*AL*, 639)

Although Spain's vision could easily be attributed to the propellers, the chaos of the event, or his ardent worship of Joel, his story is strengthened—or at least complicated—by the fact that the plane

---

[86]Donald J. Greiner, "'The Iron of English': An Interview with James Dickey." *South Carolina Review* 25/2 (Spring 1994): 13.

[87]James Dickey, "Lightnings: Or *Visuals*," *James Dickey Newsletter* 8/2 (Spring 1992): 8.

with Joel in it—the very one Frank and McCaig had gone up
in—disappears from the runway during the carnage.

Dickey's fascination with man's relationship to machinery is
traceable to his experience with and interest in modern warfare and
its aesthetic implications. In a statement in a catalogue for a World
War I exhibition he wrote:

> Here [in World War I], human creatures were brought
> abruptly face-to-face with the misery and degradation that
> they and their own inventions had created. The machine
> had turned on its inventors, with a cold and callous fury
> quite literally beyond words, as men struggled desperately
> to live among the high-speed metals, the rats and the slime.
> The human sensibility changed permanently toward its
> darker, more pessimistic side, and this was reflected in its
> art in such startling ways that art was given, in a grim sense,
> a new release, a new beginning....[88]

The artistic relationship between man and machine, so central to
Alnilam's vision, Dickey based on the early work of the German
writer Ernst Jünger. In *Der Arbeiter*[89] Jünger explores the
advantages of humans identifying themselves with machines. He
describes a condition of "organische Konstruktion," in which
people literally assimilate technology so as to become organic
mechanisms. This bears a strong resemblance to Shear's
descriptions of the "steel phase" of Alnilam and the necessity of its
members having hard edges. He explains to Frank that Alnilam
wants "to get rid of all of the usual human characteristics, the
things that slow you down, that get in the way, like too much
sympathy, too much analysis, too much mind-complication....
Precision steel...that's what the Alnilam men are made out of. And
what we practice is precision mysticism. We not only make the

---

[88]James Dickey, World War I Statement, Joseph M. Bruccoli Great War
Collection #10875-s, Special Collections Department, University of Virginia.

[89]Ernst Jünger, *Der Arbeiter: Herrschaft and Gestalt* (Hamburg:
Hanseatische Verlagsanstalt, 1932).

engine, but we *are* the engine, and beyond the engine" (*AL*, 408). Shears specifies that steel is a metaphor for Alnilam's chief weapon: "Indifference. Indifference and austerity: to let nothing give us an emotion. That's the basis of Alnilam. Or of this phase of it, anyway: the steel phase, the metal phase. The sleep phase" (*AL*, 433). Beyond its symbolic associations with inhuman perfection and the airplane engine, steel is also a clever psycho-rhetorical device for hardening the cadets to the inevitable death and sacrifice that must accompany Alnilam's growth. By reacting to war and adversity as robotic somnambulists, Alnilam members will be able to continue their metal-phase functions, paving the way for the stages to follow.

In addition to the connotations of steel and organic machines, Dickey also read Jünger's work for the concept of mechanical spiritualization. In *An der Zeitmauer*, Jünger explores technology in spiritual terms, as "the form and beginning of a new spiritualization of the earth in the final stages of historical temporality."[90] Captain Whitehall explains to Frank that Joel thought of the airplane's engine as being "different from the parts: as being somethin' completely beyond the parts" (*AL*, 161). Joel interprets the sum of a machine's components as a kind of soul, which can be used as a mimetic pattern for humans to achieve a given end, at which time it might be conveniently discarded. Heidegger's views on new technology help clarify this point:

> We can affirm the unavoidable use of technological devices, and also deny them the right to dominate us, and so to warp, confuse, and lay waste our nature. But will not saying both yes and no in this way to technical devices make our relation to technology ambivalent and insecure? On the contrary! Our relation to technology will become wonderfully simple and relaxed. We let technical devices enter our daily life, and at the same time leave them outside, that is, let them alone, as things which are nothing absolute but remain dependent on something higher. I would call this

---

[90]Ernst Jünger, *An der Zeitmauer* (Stuttgart: Klett, 1959) 502.

comportment toward technology which expresses 'yes' and at the same time 'no,' by an old word, releasement toward things.[91]

Like Heidegger, Joel sees the use of machines as a kind of beneficial paradox. He wishes to idealize and maximize their function for a specific purpose while also avowing their ultimate disposal. With this in mind, Shears identifies the ultimate goal of Alnilam as "[a] place, a kind of place where human beings have got on through to the other side of the machine. The aircraft engine is what we use. We have become the machine, like a kind of ghost, and gone on out through to the other side, to a place where no machine can ever touch us again. We can leave it. We will be human full time and all the time. Only human, but completely. That's all we want, and it's everything. We won't lose it, once we have it" (*AL*, 412). Although the machine is romanticized, it is viewed simultaneously as an expendable necessity. Like a cocoon or an afterbirth, it fulfills its function and then dies out of the cycle of creation. In this sense, Alnilam utilizes machine-like inhumanity as an imperative step in a perceived evolution toward a more promising, complete, and fully realized human awareness.

Matched with the technological metaphors of Alnilam is an archetypal sense of promised fulfillment following the various stages of development. In its unusual archetypal aims, accompanied by cutting-edge machinery, Alnilam has some unfortunate historical precedents. In a memorable description of Adolph Hitler and fascism, Arthur Koestler declares: "Half of Hitler's genius consisted in hitting the right unconscious chords. The other half was his alert eclecticism, his flair for hyper-modern *avant-garde* methods in Economy, Architecture, Technique, Propaganda and Warfare. The secret of Fascism is the revival of archaic beliefs in an ultra-modern setting. The Nazi edifice was a skyscraper fitted with hot water pipes which drew on underground springs of volcanic

---

[91]Martin Heidegger, *Discourse on Thinking*, trans. John M. Anderson and E. Hans Freund (New York: Harper & Row, 1966) 54.

origin."[92] In its dual application of technology and timeless human tendencies, Alnilam's practices are similar to those that gave Germany to the Nazis. However, the ideals behind Alnilam are more visionary and profound, not to mention less racist and didactic, than those which motivated the Reich. Whitehall unknowingly articulates an archetypal reading of the group when he says, "There's a deep bottom on this thing. Real deep. It comes out of the caves, and it'll go on out beyond the planet, when it comes to that" (AL, 660). In its focus on new experience and the deep penetration of human consciousness, Alnilam promises what Koestler calls our "lost half": "To recover the lost half of our personalities, man's wholeness and holiness, the art and science of contemplation has to be learned; and in order to be learned, it has to be taught. But this teaching should not be left to the hacks of Yogi-journalese, nor to crank-philosophers who dispense a minimum of information about breathing-technique wrapped in a maximum of obscurantist bombast."[93] Joel's balance between "obscurantist crank-philosopher" and true teacher is part of the tension that fuels Alnilam, yet he instinctively understood that archetypal myths are necessary in the success of political movements and the establishment of governments—whether they resemble Nazi Germany or the United States. As Nietzsche asserts in The Birth of Tragedy, "It is the fate of every myth to creep by degrees into the narrow limits of some alleged historical reality, and to be treated by some later generation as a unique fact with historical claims."[94] Manipulating archetypes and establishing provocative myths and philosophies, Alnilam seeks to authenticate a compelling spirit which promises to translate itself into history in the ages to come.

While he taps the chords of archetypal tendencies, Joel also disparages traditional methods of thought. Dickey cites Carl Sagan

---

[92]Arthur Koestler, The Yogi and the Commissar (New York: Macmillan, 1945) 123.

[93]Ibid., 246.

[94]Friedrich Nietzsche, Basic Writings of Nietzsche, ed. Walter Kaufman (New York: Modern Library, 1968) 75.

as providing material for Joel's concept of the "old brain."[95] Just as Joel uses the expression to abjure traditional ways of thinking while furthering his own cosmic philosophy, Sagan was interested in the changing relationship between human civilization and the universe: "We live in an extraordinary age. These are times of stunning changes in social organization, economic well-being, moral and ethical precepts, philosophical and religious perspectives, and human self-knowledge, as well as in our understanding of the vast universe in which we are imbedded like a grain of sand in a cosmic ocean."[96] Joel, like Sagan, is interested in the intersection of politics and the universe—albeit for very different reasons—and both men believed that the secrets of the cosmos would come to change civilization in unforseen ways. When Sagan recounts holding the jar-encased mind of the nineteenth-century brain anatomist Paul Broca, he claims that the "lesson which he has inadvertently provided us is to challenge, deeply and seriously, our own most strongly held beliefs."[97] Dickey maintains, "Joel's system is in some way like Ezra Pound's elite," in that it seeks to create a "new order'" by "new means" which are difficult for traditionally-minded people to comprehend.[98] Dismissing the world as it is and putting forth an alternative philosophy, Alnilam convinces its converts that they must not be afraid to throw away the "old brain" in favor of new and radical ideas.

One of the heretofore unmentioned traits of the new order, which coincides with the mythology of the Jüngeresque steel men, is the idealization and application of nihilism. Shears explains that World War II is only a spring-board for Alnilam: "There is only one victory, and the main thing about it is that when we get it we'll throw it away, and live in a world of nihilism and music. We'll be weightless, in the Second Body, the Old Brain, but still control the ground under our feet" (*AL*, 409). Shears's post-war vision echoes

---

[95]Series 2.3, box 84.
[96]Carl Sagan, *Broca's Brain: Reflections on the Romance of Science* (New York:Random House, 1979) xi.
[97]Ibid., 12.
[98]Series 11, tape 8.

the final two lines of Gottfried Benn's[99] poem, "Hier ist Kein Trost" or "No Consolation," which, at one point, Dickey used as an epigraph for the novel: "Eden und Adam und ein Erde / aus Nihilismus und Musik" ("Eden and Adam and an earth/of nihilism and music").[100] In connecting a paradisal state and music with nihilism, the poem exemplifies Joel's use of provocative, though seemingly irreconcilable, paradoxical statements. In fact, for *Crux* Dickey played with the idea of inscribing upon Joel's goggles "the final coded message," which would be deciphered by Harbelis, the last surviving member of Alnilam, at the end of the book. The message, ostensibly an explanation of everything for which Alnilam stood, would consist of a single word: "nothing."[101] Although this epitaph may be read as a cry of despair or a cruel joke, it also corresponds to Joel's air-driven philosophy and the doctrine, shared by Lucretius, that "empty space was no less real [or important] than matter,"[102] and that "Everything comes from nothing and falls back into nothing if we consider things."[103] Not accidentally, the abstract idea of nihilism and the empty essence of air, upon which Joel bases his philosophy, come together in his final written word.

In addition to idealizing an edenic existence and/or final condition, nihilism also serves as an applicable tool in Alinalm's functions. When Frank asks where Alnilam's state of nihilism and music will occur, Shears replies, "Partly in the mind, partly outside. We'll make the outside come to us; it has certain things we need. The rest we'll bring. Nobody else has ever had it" (*AL*, 409). Paramount in Shears's explanation is his emphasis on Alnilam actively making the internal condition an external reality. Joel had emphasized the importance of a nihilistic brand of action in his

---

[99]German poet (1886–1956).

[100]Gottfried Benn, *Primal Vision*, ed. E. B. Ashton (New York: New Directions, 1971) 224.

[101]Series 11, tape 13.

[102]George Santayana, *Three Philosophical Poets* (Cambridge: Harvard University Press, 1945) 26.

[103]Ibid., 45.

literature book: "It is better for our purposes to be inhuman than superhuman. It is also harder, for our actions must contain as little cruelty as possible" (*AL*, 436). Although Joel cautions his followers about abuses of the nihilistic outlook, which unfortunately become all too evident during Shears's inimical reign, he still believes it to be the most effective practice for the achievement of Alnilam's larger goals. As Spain says, "Panic is the strongest force in the world. If you're not on the other side of it, if it hasn't turned into the greatest calm in the world, where you don't even have to think, it will do you in every time" (*AL*, 396). The other side of panic is a form of applicable nihilism, which Joel calls the "Second Body." Corporal Phillipson recounts that Joel walked his tours with "the Second Body" (*AL*, 295), an unthinking state of effective action, and Cadet Billy Crider informs Frank that Joel succeeded in opening him up to the Second Body: "What he [Joel] says gets you on the other side of words. Where you don't need any words.... It gets you into the Second Body.... The Second Body never speaks, and never thinks" (*AL*, 299). Corresponding to the group's metaphors of steel and sleep, the Second Body is a formula for apathetic achievement, a tool accomplishing its ends through an unthinking course of efficient action.

Diametrically opposed to the sleep-walking machine meta-phors and the nihilistic Second Body is the emotionally-charged language of Alnilam's philosophy manifested in its code words and ritualistic incantations. The overall importance of Alnilam's terminology was recognized by more than one reviewer who argued that the novel's executionary shortcomings were redeemed by its stunning poetic lyricism,[104] and the ideas of the group are linked irrevocably to its highly- ritualized language. Across the body of his work, Wittgenstein asserts that the boundaries of one's language are also the boundaries of one's world and that language

---

[104]See Arthur Waldhorn, Review of *Alnilam*, *Library Journal* 112/10 (1 June 1987): 128; and Review of *Alnilam*, *Booklist* 83/15 (1 April 1987): 1153.

is the primary idea in considering human knowledge and logic.[105] Like Dickey's favorite philosopher, Heraclitus, Joel "employs figures of speech not for prettification but as a means of exploring and adumbrating some of the more hidden aspects of reality."[106] In addition to the intrinsic appeal of Joel's practices, personality, and ideas, the semantics he employs magnify his bewitching concepts and the exclusive aura of the group.

Using the E6B Flight Computer in combination with code words, Joel energizes meaning by creating new linguistic terms and reworking traditional definitions.[107] As Harbelis explains, "The numbers on the E6B decode into another language, a special language, that only we know about" (AL, 185). Having sent messages to other bases through the mail in the form of E6B equations, the solution to a given problem provides a code word which signals a specific course of action for the entire group.[108] However, because the code words are frequently altered, an E6B message is virtually impossible to decipher. Dickey based Joel and his fascination with the E6B partially on Daniel Hoffman's portrait of Edgar Allan Poe in Poe Poe Poe Poe Poe Poe Poe.[109] According to Hoffman, Poe, like Joel, was extremely interested in puzzles and secret codes, and—as Hoffman contends—became "a self-proclaimed expert cryptogra-

---

[105]Ludwig Wittgenstein, The Wittgenstein Reader, ed. Anthony Kenny (Oxford: Blackwell, 1994).

[106]Wheelwright, Heraclitus, 94.

[107]The E6B Flight Computer is a metal object almost nine inches in length, consisting of two important parts: a circular slide rule for making quick flight calculations and a wind side for determining ground speed and wind correction angles. The slide portion of the circular slide rule face also includes quick reference material. The E6B is literally covered with numbers and numerical conversion tables relating to fuel consumption, speed conversion, time, distance, altitude, pressure, temperature, and direction.

[108]It should be remembered that Alnilam extends far beyond Peckover and continues to grow in Crux. On one of his tapes, Dickey has Shears tell Riker, in order to stop Alnilam, "you'll have to stop the mail, you'll have to stop the post offices." Series 11, tape 8.

[109]Series 11, tape 13.

pher."[110] Just as Poe enjoyed making up and breaking codes, Alnilam members take a great deal of pride in the virtually undecipherable language Joel has created in conjunction with the E6B.[111]

Dickey spent a significant amount of time creating the Alnilam language and, at one point, designated the following twelve items "Alnilam Code Words," but provided the meaning for only one: 1. censtel, 2. wheldis, 3. bau, 4. nevdar, 5. tanjim ki, 6. peëwsi, 7. llanthony, 8. cirom, 9. fear (code word for base or HQ), 10. owbes, 11. gasasop, and 12. qamwot.[112] In the book, Dickey also identifies numbers fifteen, seventeen, and twenty as relle, liades, and yakat, respectively. While the first two words remain undefined, Harbelis discloses that yakat means "destroy" (*AL*, 424). Beyond the words' linguistic meaning, Dickey drew on the Ministry of Truth in George Orwell's *1984*[113] for the psychological impact the terms would have on Alnilam members. In essence, the code words have the propagandistic effect of wiping out or subordinating traditional linguistic meaning and history in general. In Alnilam's secret language, as in that of the state in *1984*, semantics are constructions that further a particular political ideology while remaining oblivious and hostile to other usages. Joel's code language was to Dickey like the poetry of Hart Crane: "a kind of closed verbal system, bounded by its associations, which are admittedly large, but a closed system after all."[114] Furthermore, in what surely must

---

[110]Daniel Hoffman, *Poe Poe Poe Poe Poe Poe Poe* (Garden City: Doubleday, 1973) 99.

[111]Dickey also took from Hoffman's Poe a theory of imagination based on suffering: "So Poe was driven to avenge those circumstances which life made seem irreparable. His chosen means, the only one available to him, the one which he used with such pertinacity and resolution throughout his life of sufferings, was the imagination" (Hoffman, *Poe*, 326). Denied a father, just as Poe was denied a stable family, Joel lives mostly in the world of his own imagination. However, unlike Poe, he has the charismatic abilities to enforce his creative ideas on the world around him using religious, political, and psychological methods.

[112]Series 2, box 91k.

[113]Series 2, box 91g, 39.

[114]Series 2.4, box 94, folder 2, 17.

have been one of his more eccentric moods, Dickey toyed with the idea of using the Pal-ul-don language from Edgar Rice Burrough's *Tarzan the Terrible*[115] as a source for the secret codes of Alnilam.[116] In addition, Dickey attributed Joel's interest in patterns and figures to the unique and often geometrical historical ideas of W. B. Yeats. Yeats believed that "all civilization is held together by artificially created illusions"[117] and Joel, recognizing reality as a mutable construction, uses language to help invent the existence he desires. Nietzsche says, "The most extreme form of nihilism" arises from the belief that there exists "no true world," thereby resulting in a state where everything is "a perspectival appearance whose origin lies in us."[118] Nietzsche believed that such a condition serves as a catalyst for creation and, using language as a powerful tool, Joel makes his compelling world-view the perspective of everyone in Alnilam.

In addition to the code words he makes up in conjunction with the E6B, Joel extracts and modifies phrases from his nineteenth-century British literature textbook—the only book he had with him at the base and the one from which Shears quotes throughout the novel. Altogether different from code words, poetry and thinking, according to Heidegger, "are a distinctive saying in that they remain delivered over to the mystery as that which is most worthy of their thinking."[119] Whereas the code words designate certain forms of action, the poetic language of Alnilam serves as a kind of sacred scripture to energize its members. Dickey explains, "In *Alnilam* the figure of Joel Cahill has a powerful effect on people. Not only on people who love him and follow him, but

---

[115]See the Pal-ul-don dictionary in the appendix of Edgar Rice Burroughs, *Tarzan the Terrible* (New York: Ballantine, 1963): 218–20.

[116]Series 11, tape 20.

[117]William Butler Yeats, *The Collected Plays of W. B. Yeats* (London: Macmillan, 1953) 210.

[118]Friedrich Nietzsche, *The Will to Power*, trans. Walter Kaufman and R.J. Hollingdale, ed. Kaufman (New York: Random House, 1967) 15.

[119]Martin Heidegger, *On the Way to Language*, trans. Peter D. Hertz (New York: Harper & Row, 1971) 8.

also on the people who hate him but can't ignore him. Part of his power is based on language. When he has the Alnilam plotters recite the lines from Shelley about the young Charioteers drinking the wind of their own speed, the effect is hypnotic.... Part of Joel's power comes from the word, from language itself."[120] Using poetic language to amplify his aforementioned hypnotic gifts, Joel is able to stir his followers into a religious revery which serves as a call to action and a stimulant for their belief in him.

The two poets from whose work Joel specifically quotes are Percy Bysshe Shelley and James Thomson, known also by his pen-name B.V. (Bysshe Vanolis).[121] Shelley possesses with Joel a stunning gift of creative imagination in shaping the world according to his own romantic vision. In a memorable description, Santayana relates that Shelley "took the materials of the landscape and wove them into a gossamer world, a bright ethereal habitation for new-born irresponsible spirits. [He] was the musician of landscape; he traced out its unrealized suggestions; transformed the things he saw into the things he would fain have seen."[122] Suggesting Joel in another sense, James Thomson maintained that Shelley's work "glows with the solemn inspiration of prophecy."[123] Evoking ritual, hypnosis, and poetic communion, Shears explains that Shelley's lines from *Prometheus Unbound* are used "as a kind of spell. It's right here [quoting from Joel's book]: 'through incantation, each thinks he has summoned the words from some deep place in himself that only he knows. Thus the many enter into a gigantic reflex, which is like a touched muscle belonging to them all. Yet each feels it as his own'" (*AL*, 406–407). The passage of which Shears speaks, with its images of stars, flight, and dashing young men, serves as a kind of romantic anthem for the air practices Joel bestows upon his followers:

---

[120]Suarez, "An Interview with James Dickey," 129.

[121]The letters B. V. appear several times in the novel. Most notably, they are inscribed on the inner-band of the goggles Joel is wearing when he crashes.

[122]Santayana, *Three Philosophical Poets*, 58.

[123]James Thomson (B. V.), *The Speedy Extinction of Evil and Misery*, ed. William David Schaefer (Berkeley: University of California Press, 1967) 203.

The rocks are cloven, and through the purple night
I see cars drawn by rainbow-winged steeds
Which trample the dim winds: in each there stands
A wild-eyed charioteer urging their flight.
Some look behind, as fiends pursued them there,
And yet I see no shapes but the keen stars:
Others, with burning eyes, lean forth, and drink
With eager lips the wind of their own speed,
As if the thing they loved fled on before,
And now, even now, they clasped it. Their bright locks
Stream like a comet's flashing hair: they all
Sweep onward.[124]

In addition to the vivid account of flight, the lines also hint at the vague and panacean reward that comes with it: clasping "the thing they loved." With his short-lived youthful exuberance and poetic references to air and the purple field,[125] Shelley, both biographically and aesthetically, echoes the vigorous adolescent idealism and symbolism of Joel and his followers.

---

[124]Percy Bysshe Shelley, *Selected Poems, Essays, and Letters*, ed. Ellsworth Barnard (New York: Odyssey Press, 1944) 145–46.

[125]Elsewhere in *Prometheus Unbound* Shelley writes, "There was a change: the impalpable thin air/And the all-encircling sunlight were transformed,/As if the sense of love dissolved in them/Had folded itself round the spheréd world./My vision then grew clear, and I could see/Into the mysteries of the universe" (Shelley, *Selected Poems*, 165). In "The Two Spirits: An Allegory" the speaker proclaims, "Bright are the regions of the air,/And among the winds and beams/It were delight to wander there—/Night is coming!" (Shelley, *Selected Poems*, 358). In *Alnilam* the purple field is a reference to one's perspective from an airplane. In "Lines Written Among the Euganean Hills" the speakers says, "'Tis the noon of Autumn's glow,/When a soft and purple mist/Like a vaporous amethyst,/Or an air-dissolved star/Mingling light and fragrance, far/From the curved horizon's bound/To the point of Heaven's profound,/Fills the overflowing sky" (Shelley, *Selected Poems*, 70). A line from "Stanzas: Written in Dejection, Near Naples" reads, "The purple noon's transparent might" (Shelley, *Selected Poems*, 80).

Whereas Shelley's poetry functions as an inspirational romantic anthem for the cadets, James Thomson's verse reinforces the group's somber nihilism. Thomson's dark existential visions were due mostly to the death of Mathilda Weller, a young woman with whom he was much in love.[126] The Thomson poem from which the cadets directly quote is the long despairing ode, "The City of Dreadful Night."[127] The work's Weir-like landscape and general eeriness is suggestive of both Poe and the perverse fantasy magazines Joel read as a boy.[128] Thomson's use of repetition is also resembles Poe's verse; the eleven stanzas beginning with a refrain of a line-and-a-half, and the first six concluding with a short-line refrain. The repetitious, almost redundant, aspect of this section of the poem is designed to have the effect of both hypnotizing and energizing the reader, which is exactly what Joel wishes it to do. Suggesting Joel's relationship with his followers, the speaker in the poem says of the hero, "Because he seemed to walk with an intent / I followed him..."[129] and he speaks "As if large multitudes were gathered round."[130] Furthermore, as Thomson scholar and editor William David Schaefer notes, "'The City of Dreadful Night' is a

---

[126]Hannah Pelham, whose death is imminent, may have been meant to have a similar, though certainly lesser, effect on Joel.

[127]I include that section of the poem which makes use of the refrain, "No hope could have no fear." It is this portion of the work that so fascinated Joel (see appendix for text).

[128]These magazines, containing stories involving monstrous creatures and scantily-clad women, helped shape Joel's romantic and fantastic imagination. One of the authors Joel's mother, Florence Cahill, mentions to Frank is Arthur Leo Zagat (*AL*, 559), an important fantasy writer of the 1930s and 1940s. His work appeared alongside better-known science-fiction pioneers like L. Sprague de Camp in such magazines as *Argosy*, *Amazing Stories*, *Astounding Stories*, *Dime Mystery Magazine*, *Startling Stories*, and *Thrilling Wonder Stories*. Toward the end of his life, Zagat produced a novel entitled *Seven Out of Time* (Reading PA: Fantasy Press, 1949).

[129]Thomson, *The City*, 9.

[130]Ibid., 13.

pessimist's manifesto for a select group,"[131] corresponding both to Joel's nihilistic tendencies and the exclusive nature of Alnilam.

Apart from its despairing language, the guiding nihilistic symbol in the poem is the desert. Shears asserts that Alnilam thinks of the air as a "desert," the main characteristic of which is its "emptiness, the nothing of it... A huge desert that is everywhere the earth is" (*AL*, 432). The desert also serves as a metaphor for an idea of the world as a place of alienation and lack of human connection. As Dickey says in his notes for *Alnilam*, "We are lost in human communication. That is the desert."[132] An environment where emptiness and apathy reign, the desert demands the nihilistic practices specified earlier in the chapter so that Alnilam may come to reshape reality. Envisioning the emergence of a revolutionary world-view like Alnilam, Thomson had predicted, "The immaculate goodness and infallible wisdom of the new men will likewise, beyond doubt, remedy or avoid many of the sufferings to which nature now subjects us, and which we account inevitable and incurable."[133] Although Thomson and Alnilam foresee therapies for the unsatisfactory quality of existence, they share the conviction that the solution rests in stoic, nihilistic attitudes and practices rather than an active resolution to personal pain. In Dickey's hand-written manuscript of *Crux*, Harbelis speculates that the "City of Dreadful Night" might be the war, a necessary step in Alnilam's evolution towards wholeness, in which nihilism provides the formula for survival: "We'll have it [electrical power] there in the great purple field, with nihilism and music. Alnilam would be there ...[the rest of the sentence is illegible]. The City of Dreadful Night. We have to go there first. The City of Dreadful Night might be the war. That's where we take power. Superiority like nihilism, then real nihilism. Nothing. Nothing but glory. Ex Nihilo."[134] In a passage curiously suggestive of Alnilam's

---

[131]James Thomson, *The Speedy Extinction*, ed. William David Schaefer (Berkeley: University of California Press, 1967) 5.

[132]Series 2, box 86, folder 1.

[133]Thomson, *The Speedy Extinction*, 25.

[134]Series 2, box 91g.

goals and the lines from Shelley, Thomson maintained, "[The new men] will scarcely brook confinement to this petty earth of ours, but will want to roam at pleasure through the limitless universe. I think that their generous souls will be wrought to indignation by the condition and prospects of the inferior creatures."[135] With its almost overpowering bleak imagery and numbing, hypnotic repetition, "The City of Dreadful Night" constitutes a grim dirge by which the group may carry out its inhuman practices in pursuit of its universal aims.

Using poetry in its prophecy of an eventual condition achieved through nihilistic means, Joel's language takes on the qualities of traditional mystical discourse. For Michel de Certeau, the language of the mystic depicts humans as living in anticipation of a moment in time in which the mystic's subject—a prophecy or event—may either disintegrate or be brought to life: "The mystic is seized by time as by that which irrupts and transforms; hence time is for him the question of the subject seized by his other, in a present which is incessantly the surprise of a birth and a death."[136] Although Alnilam has experienced a promising beginning, its end—either through dissolution or the achievement of its goals—remains the promise which motivates it in the present.

With the beginning in the past and the conclusion uncertain, the present becomes the all-important variable upon which the mystic's powers come to bear. In the ritualized manner with which it is evoked at every meeting, Joel's language resembles what Certeau calls a "fable"—a mystical document using language in innovative ways, thereby giving the words a unique resonance:

> The mystic labour in language consists in transforming it or turning it upside down so that it inaugurates through speech, and hence in metamorphosing it into myriad 'manners of speaking.' This is the mystic science: an alteration of all existent discourses so as to turn them into

---

[135]Thomson, *The Speedy Extinction*, 26.

[136]Michel de Certeau, *The Mystic Fable*, trans. Michael B. Smith (Chicago: University of Chicago Press, 1992) 11.

'fables.' This linguistic alchemy forged for itself a set of extremely subtle rules and procedures, but these should not lead us to forget the concern which animates them and which aims to bring into language the presence of a founding speech act.[137]

In the creative establishment of fables, Certeau conceives of the mystic's language as fabricated yet always beginning—always "founding" itself: "It [the formula of the mystics] sets up fabrications of words, of 'phrases' and expressions (a language, henceforth, was something that could be produced), but within a region in which a voice that never ceased beginning could be heard."[138] In other words, because the mystic's fable—a fabrication of words and terms—is constantly caught in a self-established flux of meaning, it is always new and beginning to those who hear it, whether they be disciples or non-believers. In a state of constant creation, the mystic's language retains a spontaneous power that may be recycled indefinitely, continually fascinating converted believers in new ways.

Whereas mystical language excels in winning apostles and preserving the faith of believers, it also runs the risk, as Pierre Bourdieu observes, of fabricating to the point that it loses sight of and faith in its own principles: "The explication of their practice which can be supplied by the agents themselves, at the cost of a quasi-theoretical review of their practice, conceals from their own eyes the truth of their practical mastery as *docta ignorantia*, that is as a mode of practical knowledge which does not contain within itself the knowledge of its own principles."[139] The power of Alnilam's unusual language is undeniable, but the danger of which Bourdieu speaks becomes a reality when Shears begins to neglect its theoretical ideals in the interests of practical application. As

---

[137]Michel de Certeau, "Entretien, Mystique et psychoanalyse," *Le Bloc-Notes de la Psychoanalyse* 4 (1984): 141.

[138]Certeau, *The Mystic Fable*, 123–24.

[139]Pierre Bourdieu, *Esquisse d'une théorie de la pratique, précédé de trois études d'ethnologie kabyle* (Geneva: Droz, 1972) 202.

Bourdieu says of compelling dialects, "It is through the 'elevated style' that the status of a discourse is invoked, as is the respect due to the status."[140] This dynamic is perhaps best seen in the varying degrees of respect and deference given to Joel's Alnilam discourse as opposed to Colonel Hoccleve's military language. Possessing a spiritual and poetic element that military discourse lacks, Joel's oratory touches on the imagination and spirit of those who hear it, whereas Hoccleve's flat and dogmatic instructions merely demand to be obeyed. Echoing Foucault, Bourdieu summarizes: "Linguistic relations are always relations of power and, consequently, cannot be elucidated within the compass of linguistic analysis alone. Even the simplest linguistic exchange brings into play a complex and ramifying web of historical power relations between the speaker, endowed with a specific social authority, and an audience, which recognizes this authority to varying degrees, as well as between the groups to which they respectively belong."[141] In cases such as that of Joel—who possesses a strong language-based authority among his many other gifts—and his followers, Bourdieu believes that the relationship results in an "illusion of independence," in which the practitioners of such language—in this case, the Alnilam cadets—see themselves as "staging an artificial break" with both "normal language and normal thought."[142] In this way, language creates the group and its philosophy just as it is created by them. Although each may constitute an artificial fabrication of the other, the collective relationships are such that they display a tremendous and superior appeal when considered against conflicting ideologies. Based on Joel's practices and persona, and both created by and drawing upon a specific language, Alnilam's philosophy contains all the necessary ingredients to transform its philosophical and linguistic abstractions into vivid practical realities.

---

[140]Pierre Bourdieu, *The Political Ontology of Martin Heidegger* (Cambridge: Polity, 1991) 88.

[141]Loic J. D. Wacquant, "Towards a Reflexive Sociology: A Workshop with Pierre Bourdieu," *Sociological Theory* 7/1 (1989): 46.

[142]Certeau, *The Political Ontology*, 73.

Although the language and ideas of Alnilam have a powerful effect on the non-members who experience them, there are those—characters in the novel and critics of the book—who likely would attempt to apply Bourdieu's concept of fabrication as a means of either attacking or dismissing the group's terminology and philosophy. In the novel, Major Bruno Iannone belittles Alnilam by describing its philosophical interpretations as a whimsical kind of fantasy game: "Mostly they want to be to themselves, they want to take things in their own way, and interpret them in a way that's like, well, like make-believe" (AL, 310). Endorsing Iannone's reading in his summary of the book's plot, Henry Hart remarks, "By the end of the novel the group is debunked as a foolishly zealous cult."[143] Similar sentiments were expressed by Fred Chappell, who, reviewing the novel shortly after its publication, dismissed Joel's plans as "mere obfuscation."[144] There is, of course, a fundamental problem with these interpretations, which perhaps is best articulated in the form of a question. If Alnilam is conveniently explained away as an obscure, make-believe boys' club, why would Dickey resolve to write Crux and follow such an immature and misled cast of characters into the Pacific theater of World War II? If Dickey ultimately had denounced the group and ridiculed its cause, it seems unlikely that he would sacrifice the precious moments of his remaining years crafting a sequel.

Despite the seemingly commonsense answer that there truly is more to Alnilam than silly kids' games, the group complicates matters by subjecting readers to the same propaganda it presents to characters in the novel. In other words, seeking to present a harmless adolescent image and protect genuine information, the organization often enthusiastically applauds attacks and dismissals by characters and readers. As Shears facetiously explains, "If they call this a pipe dream, they're right. If they call it a schoolboy fantasy, they're right" (AL, 581), and, of course, Hoccleve, Iannone

---

[143]Hart, James Dickey, 675.
[144]Fred Chappell, Review of Alnilam, The State, 21 June 1987, 6-F.

and the others can go on believing it as such until their base is wrecked and Alnilam comes to dominate the war in the Pacific. Of Major Iannone's lengthy interpretations Shears remarks, "Let him keep talking... The more he explains things to himself, the farther off he is from us" (*AL*, 665). Iannone, possessing, along with Whitehall, one of the best analytical minds of anyone on the base, rationalizes Alnilam as a boys' club (*AL*, 653), but also thinks "that the same things could be said about all these so-called leaders, Napoleon and Julius Caesar. Huey Long down in Louisiana. Most of the time they don't really offer much" (*AL*, 655). Yet even Iannone is forced to confess that "about the Alnilam notion, it keeps coming back to me that something like it might work" (*AL*, 658). Ultimately, Joel's thinking is not to be dismissed as fraudulent drivel since Dickey asserted, with characteristic hyperbole but in all earnestness, "Maybe in trying to imagine Joel's thinking of it, *I* can think of it: can think of the thing to change the whole picture, and the way people take each other and their life on earth."[145] In the end, the reader must wade through both Alnilam's propaganda and various characters' interpretations of it, and make the difficult decision of choosing between the world as it is and Joel's plan for an alternative one.

Of what Joel's world would be, little has been written thus far. This is due to the fact that its complexities rely upon a firm understanding of Joel's practices and the Alnilam philosophy before it may be fully appreciated. During the composition process, Dickey struggled a great deal with the kind of existence Joel had in mind:

> The hardest thing was to decide what the *Alnilam* plot was going to lead to, what Joel told them they were doing all these destructive things in order to achieve. I read a good many works on utopias, and at one time, I had him lead his followers or disciples with a long detailed schemata of the

---

[145]Series 11, tape 28.

new society that they were going to try to found, that they were going to bring into being, but I realized that it would never have been that detailed. It was more compelling to leave the ultimate goal of the *Alnilam* plot in a kind of mystical vagueness so that they don't really know where they're going, but they're convinced through the charismatic character of their leader that he's going to create a new heaven and new earth. If they'll just follow him, they'll get there—everything's going to be different.[146]

Creating a formidable collection of details for Joel's planned society, Dickey later discarded them for the purpose of accentuating Joel's mystical charismatic appeal as a basis for faith. As he summarized elsewhere, "Suppose [Joel] had presented them with a complete plan about a new kind of government, a new kind of economics. It wouldn't have had nearly as much impact. They don't follow him in spite of the fact that he doesn't have a complete program, but *because* of it."[147] Dickey perhaps was correct in this assessment since, as Ezra Pound asserts, "Deceiving the ignorant is by some regarded as evil, but it is the demagogue's business to bolster up his position and to show that God's noblest work is the demagogue."[148] Arriving at the conclusion that Joel's singular personal characteristics are more important than his specific ideology, Dickey drastically limited the novel's information about the envisioned state.

Even though Dickey excluded from *Alnilam* many of Joel's precise plans, his notes on the imagined society provide a fuller understanding of Joel's mind and the goals of Alnilam. On a page dated 11 March 1981 and entitled "Notes on Joel's Utopia," Dickey wrote:

---

[146]Broughton, *The Writer's Mind*, 187.

[147]Truehart, "James Dickey's Celestial Navigations," F6.

[148]Pound, Ezra, "The Constant Preaching to the Mob," in *Literary Essays of Ezra Pound*, ed. T .S. Eliot (New York: New Direction, 1968) 64.

On the possibility of using Plato's ideas of defining the perfect state by defining the qualities of the perfect man, the leader, the philosopher-king, his qualities radiating outward from his personality through the body of the state: It may be that we incorporate into the story Joel's 'secret' journey, the steps or stages, the means by which the ideal man, the leader, takes control.... The extreme virtue of Joel's ideal man is something like that of the early Ernst Jünger: the effort of human beings to approximate the simplicity and soullessness of their own most perfect creations, which are forms of machinery: an effort of man to live up to or come up to his own exemplified perfectability...."[149]

Whereas I have discussed Jünger's influence at length, Dickey's use of Plato's imagined republic is also substantial and worthy of note. The main aspect Dickey takes from Kallipolis is the concept of the philosopher-kings and their practical application of lies. Socrates asks:

What about the lies in words? When and to whom is it useful, and not deserving of hatred? Isn't it useful against enemies and those of one's so-called friends who, through madness or ignorance, are attempting to do some wrong, in order to turn them away from it? The lie then becomes useful like a drug. And in the case of those stories we mentioned just now, those told because we don't know the truth about these ancient things, making the lie as much like the truth as we can, don't we also make it useful?[150]

With lying as an important guiding principle, Plato felt that a handful of philosopher-kings were best qualified to lead Kallipolis since they could both administer the republic and make theoretical decisions about what socio-political adjustments needed to be

---

[149]Series 2.3, box 83.

[150]Plato, *The Republic of Plato*, trans. Allan Bloom (New York: Basic Books, 1968) 382c6–d3.

implemented. Although the guardians and producers—those who served beneath the philosopher-kings—would be the products of superior breeding, Plato felt it still would be necessary "to make considerable use of lies and deceptions for the benefit of the ruled. We said that such things are useful as a kind of drug...."[151]

Drawing upon Plato's idealization and application of lies, Joel envisions a society where aesthetic creation and philosophical thought are the fruit of brilliant falsehoods, or a practice he called "continuous invention." Dickey explained, "Joel believes that lying exercises the creative and imaginative faculties, and, when indulged in on either an individual or group basis, raises the consciousness of the party or parties concerned."[152] In addition to echoing Hannah's sexual fantasy and Henry Hart's interpretive thesis for Dickey's life,[153] Dickey's statement is embodied by Captain Claude Faulstick's story about "the original spark," an imaginary bullet from the nose cannon of a German ME-109 airplane. As he prepares to leave his plexiglass bubble for the interior safety of the B-17 on which he serves as bombardier, Faulstick glimpses an enemy fighter heading straight for his plane and thinks he sees a bullet explode at him from the aircraft's nose cannon. Although he is not hit, a gunner in another part of the plane is shot and killed.[154] From this experience, Faulstick constructs a compelling *raison d'être*, symbolized by the spark of the bullet. Frank is powerfully moved by Faulstick's provocative description:

I get a real strange thrill, every time I think about it. It has nothing to do with God. The *ex nihilo* spark: it proved everything, it disproved everything. It couldn't be and it was. And I'm here. That's proof enough for me. The airplane that made it is gone; it just dissolved around the spark, just left that one little wink of light, so intense and

---

[151]Ibid., 459c8–c10.

[152]Series 11, tape 19.

[153]See Hart's introductory chapter in the Dickey biography (xi–xix).

[154]The circumstances of Ham Stynchcomb's death in Faulstick's plane bear a strong resemblance to Snowden's passing in Joseph Heller's *Catch-22.*

penetrating that it could cut through tungsten steel, or anything else. It's the original spark, with no meaning; just a kind of impulse, but there's no way for it not to be. It made the world, and if the world was made in any other way than that, I can't imagine it. It scares me to death to carry it around, and I don't know what I'm ever going to do with it. But I do have it. (*AL*, 204)

Despite the account's minute detail and descriptive eloquence, Whitehall later informs Frank that the ME-109 is not equipped with a nose cannon. Living up to the linguistic connotation of his name, Faulstick embroiders his war story just as Dickey and many other veterans accentuated and created wartime accounts of their own. However, in its fraudulence, the story embodies Joel's technique of "continuous invention" by affecting and raising the collective consciousness of Faulstick—the inventor—and Frank—the consumer—through a moving creative lie.

Beyond the techniques, like "continuous invention," that would stimulate the state's existence, Dickey also examined sources for its organization and political aims. One of the most influential models for these concepts is the Birch Society, an organization formed by Robert Welch in honor of John Birch—an American fundamentalist religious thinker, killed in China by Communists ten days after V-J Day in 1945. Welch believed that the "collapse of our country [the Unites States] is eminent" as a result of a "Communistic plot."[155] Like Alnilam, the Birch Society fused religious ritual with "practical" solutions in attempting to promote a new political movement. Like Joel, Robert Welch believed that his "dynamic personal leadership [could] best be expressed through an authoritarian organizational structure" and, like Shears—who speaks with a certainty and resoluteness that troubles Frank—, Welch saw his undertaking as "Messianic—to tell to all of us precisely what that 'one increased purpose' is, and to direct our

---

[155]J. Allen Broyles, *The John Birch Society: Anatomy of a Protest* (Boston: Beacon Press, 1964) 5.

'reach' in the direction that is truly 'upward.'"[156] As J. Allen Broyles remarks in his sociological study of the Birch Society, such an endeavor would be "quite an undertaking for any mortal unaided by any scripture beyond ambiguous poetry."[157] The same could be said of Joel, yet he succeeds nevertheless. Furthermore, Dickey's use of poetry in Joel's utopia, beyond its extensive functions in the Alnilam language, seems to draw on his Southern/Vanderbilt background in that the agrarians saw poetry as a powerful moral and aesthetic force for enriching individuals both within and for the greater profit of larger society.[158]

Furthering the importance of poetry in government, another source for Joel's utopia were the ideas of the influential eighteenth-century Italian thinker Giambattista Vico, one of the fathers of social science.[159] Vico believed that the positive aspects in the shaping of humanity and the birth of civilization were the result of "poetic" undertakings (the Greek meaning of "poet" is "maker"), marked by exercises in imagination and sensibility rather than process-oriented rationality. This assumption evokes Joel, whose sacred text is a nineteenth-century textbook in English literature. Furthermore, in his meditation on an "Eternal Natural Common-wealth" Vico holds that any successful utopia must have a strong sense of religion. Although Vico was thinking of Christian divine providence, his statement points to the religious aspects of Alnilam and the ways in which those tropes build a shared mystique among the members.[160]

---

[156]Ibid., 19.

[157]Ibid.

[158]See Eugene D. Genovese, *The Southern Tradition: The Achievement and Limitations of an American Conservatism* (Cambridge: Harvard University Press, 1994) 9.

[159]Series 11, tape 17.

[160]See Gambattista Vico, *The New Science of Gambattista Vico*, trans. Thomas Goddard Bergin and Max Harold Fisch (Garden City: Doubleday, 1961); and Gamabattista Vico, *The Autobiography of Gambattista Vico*, trans. Thomas Goddard Bergin and Max Harold Fisch (Ithaca: Cornell University Press, 1944).

Poetry is replaced with music in the society of Hermann Hesse's novel *Das Glasperlenspiel*, translated as *Magister Ludi*,[161] from which Dickey extracted ideas and details on a futuristic utopia. Castalia, a state based on music and mathematics, seeks to consolidate knowledge into an entity that transcends its parts. Hesse's protagonist, Knecht, is a member of the controlling elect of Castalia who, like the members of Alnilam, speak in an exclusive, elevated language. Inherent in the work of Hesse and Ernst Jünger is the idea that futuristic technology has much in common with the general concept of utopia since both usually strive for uniformity and maximum efficiency in their functions. Although technology is hardly mentioned, music also plays an important role in a more traditional perfect state, Sir Thomas More's *Utopia*.[162] In addition to its musical dimension, Utopia is an island country, physically cut off from its "depraved" neighbors, and thriving—as Alnilam does—on its difference and alienation from others. Furthermore, like Alnilam, Utopia is a patriarchy that celebrates conformity and its social violators are punished quickly and severely by the collective. As More's contemporary Machiavelli believed, it is best to be both feared and loved—or, if one must chose between the two, feared.[163]

While the general concept of utopia often implies egalitarianism, Alnilam is administered by a single leader—Joel and then Shears—and several of Dickey's sources, like Plato's Kallopolis, celebrate a dominant individual or individuals. Although he is no ruler, the protagonist of Paul Valéry's *Monsieur Teste*[164]

---

[161]Hermann Hesse, *Magister Ludi*, trans. Mervyn Savill (New York: Frederick Ungar, 1949).

[162]Sir Thomas More, *Utopia*, in *Famous Utopias* (New York: Tudor Publishing, 1937): 129–232. Dickey also consulted Thomas Campanella (*The City of the Sun*, in *Famous Utopias*, 275–317), but does not seem to have incorporated any of its unique ideas into *Alnilam*.

[163]Niccolo Machiavelli, *The Prince and the Discourses* (New York: Modern Library, 1950).

[164]Paul Valéry, *Monsieur Teste*, in *The Collected Works of Paul Valéry*, ed. Jackson Matthews, vol. 6, Bollingen series 45, (Princeton: Princeton University Press, 1956).

exhibits the singular qualities that Alnilam celebrates. Monsieur Teste is an intellectual figure who wishes to attain maximum freedom by throwing away external existence and giving himself wholly over to the vitality of consciousness. As in Joel's utopia, the ambitions and accomplishments of the detached creative mind are valued and praised over any human qualities, and the reader perceives Teste simultaneously as both an emotionless monster and an existential hero. The same might be said of King Arthur in T. H. White's *The Once and Future King*.[165] Largely a satire of Sir Thomas Malory's *Le Morte D'Arthur*, White's epic portrays Camelot as a utopia of Arthur's making which he uses as an instrument for his personal ambitions. Although the ideas that accompany White's book are drastically different from those in *Alnilam*, as a relatively typical king White's Arthur employs the manipulations and power-plays which connect him to the practices of Plato's philosopher-kings. Joel takes this dynamic and infuses it with the aesthetics of lying in identifying the leaders of Alnilam's utopia: "The highest group of all, the group that corresponds to the philosopher-kings or sages, are those who need make no sign as to whether what they say is true or whether it is fantasy. These are the master inventors and the state reveres them."[166] Administered by an oligarchy, ostensibly consisting of original Alnilam members, Joel's utopia would serve as a kind of nirvana for the imagination, where fact and truth are subordinated to the superior rewards of great creative lies.[167]

If Joel were to be supreme ruler or president of such a realm, Malcolm Shears undoubtedly would assume the role of first lieutenant or vice-president and secretary-of-state. As a master spokesman and administrator, Shears plays the part of Peter to

---

[165]T. H. White, *The Once and Future King* (New York: G. P. Putnam's Sons, 1958).

[166]Series 11, tape 19.

[167]Although lying is the guiding principle of Joel's state, Dickey specifies that there also would exist "areas of truth" which would allow for the practical functions of government and commerce. Series 11, tape 19.

Joel's Jesus. Under Shears's leadership, Alnilam moves away from Joel's idealistic air-based philosophy as it carries out Shears's practices of genuine subversion and revolution. As I have demonstrated, Joel was interested in the practicalities of making his philosophies into realities. In paraphrasing T. E. Lawrence, Dickey evoked Joel: "One remembers Lawrence's statement to the effect that the dreamers of the night are harmless, for their dream is all they want, and they recognize that this is the case, but the dreamers of the day are dangerous, for they act that their dream become fact."[168] However, a seizer of the day rather than a dreamer, Shears takes pride in embodying "the sledgehammer side of Alnilam, and not the cloud side. Let Joel Cahill look down from his cloud and see what we did, with what he set in motion. And let him keep on looking. We won't give down. Not now" (*AL*, 669). Aligning Joel with misty ether and himself with a blunt object, Shears takes pleasure in directing the "dirty work" of spreading Joel's airy gospel.

Shears's job is made easier by the presence of a clear adversary: the military. Once the cadets lose faith in the Air Corps it is easy to substitute Alnilam in its place. Sartre asserts, "The upheaval that rends a collectivity [*collective*] of individuals by the lightning stroke of common *praxis* obviously originates in a synthetic—and consequently, material—transformation, which occurs in the context of scarcity and of existing structures."[169] In the vacuum created by the military's departed authority, Alnilam asserts its own and makes the former organization its object of attack—the importance of which cannot be stressed enough. As Nietzsche says, "How good bad music and bad reasons sound when one marches against an enemy!"[170] In their consideration of Marxism, the French "new philosophers" cautioned that promises of a given future condition justified any and all means, thereby licensing

---

[168]Series 2.4, box 93, folder 10, 2.

[169]Jean-Paul Sartre, *The Philosophy of Jean-Paul Sartre*, ed. Cumming (New York: Vintage, 1965) 464.

[170]Friedrich Nietzsche, *The Portable Nietzsche*, trans. and ed. Walter Kaufman (New York: Penguin, 1954) 91.

suffering and anarchy in the present.[171] With Alnilam's promises and ambitions clearly and compellingly defined, Shears resolves to achieve those ends at all costs, ignoring the possibility that the group's worthy goals may be compromised in the process. Dickey summarized Alnilam under Shears, contending, "They [Shears and the Alnilam cadets] have created a community that has been inspired by lofty ideas but that has become inhumane, bloodthirsty, and unfeeling. They have, in short, embraced a fascism not far removed in its cold, totalitarian nature from the fascism they are being trained to combat."[172] Beyond Alnilam's role in the war, Dickey was very serious in his view that Shears's version of the group would eventually come to threaten society, and read Henri Malreux's novels concerning the Chinese Revolution for ideas on how determined, philosophy-driven people overthrow cities.[173]

Whereas Shears is a master administrator and propagandist, he functions on the premise of his own interpretation of Joel's ideas and is not without his own ambitions. As Nietzsche warns, "In every party there is one member who, by his all-too-devout pronouncement of the party principles, provokes the others to apostasy."[174] In his creation of Joel and Shears, Dickey consciously drew upon the traditional relationship of Jesus and Peter. He recounted: "Jesus is sort of a mystic and seer, but it's Peter who organizes the church out of Jesus's examples. The same way with Shears. Shears is the organization man. And he doesn't want Joel to come back, because he's got the organization himself now."[175] Joseph Campbell effectively articulates Shears's attempt to make practical Joel's philosophies in his consideration of Peter's dilemma: "A certain element of comic relief can be felt in Peter's immediate project (announced even while the vision was before his

---

[171]B. H. Lèvy, *La barbarie à visage humain* (Paris: Grasset, 1977).

[172]Ronald C. Baughman, "James Dickey's *Alnilam*: Toward a True Center Point," *James Dickey Newsletter* 10/2 (Spring 1994): 177.

[173]Series 2.3, box 91g, 38.

[174]Nietzsche, *The Portable Nietzsche*, 58.

[175]Baughman, *Voiced Connections*, 264.

eyes) to convert the ineffable into a stone foundation. Only six days before, Jesus had said to him: 'thou art Peter; and upon this work I will build my church,' [Matt 16:18] then a moment later: 'thou savorest not things that be of God, but those that be of men'" [Matt 16:23]."[176] Concentrating on the things of men, the "sledgehammer" aspect of Alnilam, Shears, like Peter, loses sight of the principles he has pledged to bring into being. Forsaking Joel's gospel through the process of implementing it, Shears comes to resemble Hoccleve and the military authority that Alnilam has replaced. In his consideration of tyrants, Campbell says of the corrupt apostle figure:

No longer referring the boons of his reign to their transcendent source, the emperor [or philosophical activist] breaks the stereoptic vision which it is his role to sustain. He is no longer the mediator between the two worlds [philosophical and practical]. Man's perspective flattens to include only the human term of the equation, and the experience of a supernal power immediately fails. The upholding idea of the community is lost. Force is all that binds it. The emperor becomes the tyrant ogre (Herod-Nimrod), the usurper from whom the world is now to be saved.[177]

Losing sight of Joel's philosophy and becoming the kind of authority figure Joel despised, Shears polymorphs into Campbell's ogre in *Crux*, flexing his power for power's sake, bereft of any idealistic purpose.

Dickey accentuates the despotic aspect of Shears's personality in his screenplay for *Alnilam*, entitled *Flying Blind.*[178] In the planned movie version, Dickey associates Shears and Hoccleve by

---

[176]Joseph Campbell, *The Hero with a Thousand Faces*, Bollingen series 17 (New York: Princeton University Press, 1949) 230n28.

[177]Ibid., 349.

[178]The screenplay originally was called *The Pathfinder*, a reference to Frank Cahill's search for knowledge of his son. Series 2.5, box 98c.

transforming their characters into lovers who make a pact to murder Joel. Also at variance with the novel, the farmer, Luther Bledsoe, claims he could hear two planes, instead of just one, when Joel crashes into the fire. During a flashback sequence, Joel warns Alnilam that there will be a Judas among them and this turns out to be Shears, who forces Joel's plane down into the fire. Sensing that Frank has discovered the truth, Shears takes him up in a Stearman for the purpose of crashing the plane and killing them both. However, once in the air, Shears's resolve fails and, instead, Frank nearly dives the plane into a lake, terrifying Shears—as he did McCaig in the book—who is suffering from an overpowering sense of guilt. When they land Frank asks to shake hands with Shears in reconciliation and proceeds to crush the bones, just as he does to Lieutenant Foy in the novel. Using Shears's lust for power as a guiding motivation, Dickey's screenplay turns *Alnilam* into a bizarre story of power, murder, and sexual lust.

In *Alnilam, Flying Blind,* and *Crux,* Shears's quest for authority taints and dehumanizes the goals of the group. The increasing apathy of the cadets as they follow Shears's orders is based on Rex Warner's *The Aerodrome,*[179] which Dickey cites as a source.[180] Originally published in 1941, *The Aerodrome* explores a fictional English society in which a military air base gradually assimilates and destroys the traditional values of a small English village. Religion, family, and love progressively give way to the cold, efficient mandates of the "Aerodrome," a kind of futuristic super air force with strict laws and expectations that invade and subordinate the private lives of its personnel. Despite its incredible technology and remarkable efficiency, the Aerodrome, like Alnilam, is an organization which ultimately suffers from its exhausting promotion of nihilism and human apathy. It is this lack of humanity which destroys the leaders of Aerodrome and gives the book's prominent characters hope for the future.

---

[179]Rex Warner, *The Aerodrome* (Oxford: Oxford University Press, 1982).
[180]Series 11, tape 27.

In addition to its overall nihilism and the demeaning leadership of Shears, *Alnilam* evokes the theme of dehumanization through the book's repeated episodes of violence and blood. Reflecting the essentials of birth, love, and death, the novel is fraught with powerful bloody episodes. One impetus for this dynamic is Djuna Barnes's *Nightwood*,[181] which, like *Alnilam*, constitutes a work of poetic prose, combining all manner of vivid images and sounds in its descriptions. The themes of music and blood, recurring ones in *Alnilam*, also appear in *Nightwood* with great frequency and the book's title, like *Alnilam*, consists of a single, mysterious word which captures the reader's imagination and curiosity. One of the bloodier sections of *Alnilam* begins with the carnage of Zack's dog fight, which precludes Frank's and Hannah's gory lovemaking. These events—scenes of bloody violence and bloody love, respectively—foreshadow Zack's needless decapitation and the general chaos of graduation day, accompanied by Billy Crider's seemingly meaningless death. Unlike the earlier bloody episodes, which essentially are life-preserving acts, the violence of graduation day, carried forth by Shears, has at its center no natural impetus.

In *Crux*, Harbelis becomes a savior of sorts, rescuing Alnilam from Shears's bloody reign. However, before considering Harbelis's redemption of Joel's ideas, it is necessary to consider the circumstances of *Alnilam*'s unfinished sequel in a fuller context. In early 1994, less than three years before his death, Dickey announced, "I'm taking notes on a new novel, which will be the one to follow *Alnilam*, called *Crux*. Alnilam is in Orion, which is a northern constellation. Crux Australis is the Southern Cross. This novel takes place below the equator, and that way I thought to cover the whole globe."[182] In *Crux*, Dickey wanted to establish a "vast tolstoyan [sic] vision of the Pacific night war,"[183] stimulated by the immediacy of battle and the continuing evolution of

---

[181]Djuna Barnes, *Nigtwood* (London: Faber and Faber, 1936).

[182]Greiner, "'The Iron of English,'" 19.

[183]Series 11, tape 18.

Alnilam. He claimed that the idea for *Crux* grew out of a sequence he originally had planned for *Alnilam* called "The Night-Fighter Chase," an air pursuit over New Guinea narrated by one of Joel's followers.[184] Once he established that he would never be able to fit all of World War II into *Alnilam,* he concluded that a sequel would be necessary. Although Dickey produced coffee-table books and attempted to write screenplays, both for the purpose of making money, one need look no further than the poor reception of *Alnilam* and the risky prospects of a sequel to perceive that his enthusiasm for *Crux* was genuine. While novels sell better than poetry, *Crux* was far from a guaranteed success, yet Dickey toiled at it nevertheless as his life wound down.

Dickey wanted his fourth published novel to demonstrate how Joel's continued influence and its varying interpretations by Shears and Harbelis affect the Pacific war, and confessed, "This would be a stupendous undertaking, but might be worth spending the rest of my life on."[185] Two of Dickey's proposed epigraphs for the book point to Joel's lingering presence, even though Dickey made it clear that he would not appear, at least physically, in the novel. Employing some adventurous spelling, he wrote out an epigraph which he attributed to Schiller:

Doch oft engriff'r ihr plötzlich wundersam,
Und der geheimnisvollen Bryst ont fuhr
Sinnvol und Leuchtend ein Gedanstrahl,
Dass wir uns staumend unsahn, nicht recht wissend,
O Wannsinn, ob ein Goot aus ihm gesprochen....[186]

Roughly translated, the passage reads, "Often, however, we experience a brilliant flash of sensibility and would look around in wonderment, not quite sure if a god had spoken from the depth of our hearts...." Suggesting Joel's pervasive influence, the statement aligns Joel's practices and philosophy—his overall sensibility—with

---

[184]Series 11, tape 10.
[185]Ibid.
[186]Series 2, box 91g.

the teachings of a divine figure. However, the second epigraph, credited to Lord Voux, indicates that the interpretive lessons of such teachings are not set in stone: "Thus do I stretch and change."[187] Foreshadowing the transformations Alnilam undergoes during the war, the phrase points to the group's increasing brutality under Shears and its possible redemption by Harbelis.

While Dickey's research for *Alnilam* gave him a head-start on the information he would need for *Crux*, the sequel contains additional sources while exhibiting a similar narrative structure. In addition to Dickey's own recollections, some of the background material on life in the Pacific theater comes from the diary of W. L. Wright, a member of the 8th Squadron, 3rd Bomber Group, who flew dozens of missions in the Pacific in 1943–1944. Although the diary contains sparse analysis of its recorded events, it is notable for its day-to-day accounts of life in the Air Corps around the time that Alnilam attempts to influence the war in the Pacific.[188] Dickey also intended to take advantage of the great Okinawa hurricane of 9 October 1945, in which he planned to have a squadron leader blown out to sea during the storm, experiencing the sensation of pure "bodily flight."[189] Also, in terms of the work's structure, Dickey hoped to repeat the innovative split-page technique he had used to couple sight-based perception with Frank's blind impressions in *Alnilam*. However, in *Crux* his plan was to apply the method to the differing impressions of a night fighter pilot and the plane's radar observer—each one blinded and sighted in his own way.[190] In his notes, Dickey proposed a "split page for [flight] interceptions," with the radar observer's reports on the left side of

---

[187]Series 11, tape 15.

[188]Series 6, box 123, folder 16.

[189]Series 11, tape 36.

[190]While the pilot has the benefit of naked vision, he is virtually blind to the presence of enemy aircraft. Conversely, the radar observer's instruments alert him to the proximity of other planes although he cannot see them visually.

the page, "running things," and the "confusion of the pilot on the right."[191]

In addition to its continuation of *Alnilam*'s themes and structure, *Crux* also demonstrates how the group becomes increasingly successful, but also inhuman, as the war goes on. One of the ways in which Alnilam continues to grow is through the notorious publicity it receives for influencing battles and shaping military policy. In his notes, Dickey explains that Shears "*wants* Alnilam investigated, because none of these [disruptive] episodes can be proven.... There is not a document that can be identified with Alnilam. But *publicity*, the media, will get it around: its reputation as a powerful underground influence will spread. All this will be exploited, be used after the war."[192] However, the group's growth would not be without its negative connotations and Dickey even proposed tying Shears in with the Ku Klux Klan, thereby demonstrating the unsavory political characteristics Alnilam takes on under his leadership. Furthermore, Shears's self-serving propaganda instincts are confirmed when Harbelis records a kill on his first mission and Shears asks him to use the distinction for the advancement of themselves and Alnilam, since "Anything we can do for Joel is good. (Pause) (Also good for us)." Shears begins the novel with the qualification, "Anything we can do for Joel is good." Yet, as the book progresses, he starts adding "—and for us," until, at the height of his power, the statement reads, "Anything we can do is good for us."[193] In the handwritten manuscript, Dickey had written the word "key" in large letters and drawn a box around the following dialogue: "Shears says, 'We don't need Joel anymore.'"[194] This moment serves as an epiphany for Harbelis, who realizes the group has forsaken its ideals and become something altogether monstrous.

---

[191]Series 2, box 91g. For an exploration of the writer and multiple narratives in *Alnilam* see Marion Hodge, "*Alnilam* and the Subversion of Story," *James Dickey Newsletter* 12/2 (Spring 1996): 2–12.

[192]Series 2, box 91g.

[193]Ibid.

[194]Ibid.

One of the ways in which Dickey had sought to resolve the problem of Shears's despotic reign involves a "revenge mission" against the Japanese in which Shears and a great many Alnilam members are killed.[195] The event that serves as the catalyst for the air raid is the beheading of two American fliers by the Japanese.[196] One of the airmen is extremely terrified, almost frantic, and the Japanese soldiers hack him to pieces, limb by limb, in the process of interrogating him. The other flier, a member of Alnilam, is extraordinarily calm and stoic throughout the ordeal, spitting into the face of the Japanese captain, who runs him through: a comparatively quick death. Dickey describes his dying moment: "It takes all his effort to raise his head—and he says, with the blood running out of his mouth, his last words: 'I know something you don't.'"[197] The flier's calm, his disregard for his own life, and his Alnilam training (which informs both his stoicism and the final sentence he utters) suggests the manner in which persecuted martyrs met their ends at various points in history. Whether admirably devout or horribly misled, the airman's faith in Alnilam sustains him in his dying moments. Although he never wrote out the sequence or even made notes on its specifics, Dickey had planned that the flier's death and its circumstances would trigger a disastrous "holocaust" during the revenge raid, resulting in the deaths of the elite Alnilam personnel.

Dickey determined that one of the survivors of the ill-fated raid would be his favorite Alnilam member, Harbelis.[198] Dickey's

---

[195]The alternative solution was that the "The Night-Fighter Chase" would involve Harbelis and Shears, with Harbelis and his pilot destroying Shears's plane.

[196]The theme of beheaded airmen is a recurrent one in Dickey's work, stemming from the fate of two fliers he knew during World War II. See, for example, "The Performance" (*WM*, 58–59), "Between Two Prisoners" (*WM*, 94–95), and *To the White Sea* (*TS*, 103–105).

[197]Series 2, box 91g, 74.

[198]Stathis Harbelis is based on Cadet Andrew Harbelis, one of Dickey's friends in primary training (Hart, *James Dickey*, 68). Like Dickey, Andrew Harbelis was held back as a result of becoming lost over the Atlantic Ocean in his

fondness for Harbelis is apparent in the first chapter of *Crux*, the only part of the book completed in its entirety, which follows his thoughts as he heads for the Far East on a troop ship. Harbelis believes in Joel's ideas rather than Shears's practical application of them, and his opinion of the latter is evident early on: "The air was his [Harbelis's], as it was Alnilam's but he did not want to do in it what Joel had done. Joel was the pilot, the only one possible; the rest, like Shears and Nielson, like Blazek even, were pilots far down the ladder; they were in the air but not of it."[199] Regarding Shears as distinctly inferior to Joel in his understanding of flight, Harbelis simply lumps him in with the other members. For him, Joel and his philosophy remain something altogether above and beyond the group and its participants. However, although he may reject Shears's interpretation and appropriation of Joel's ideas, Harbelis is not afraid to apply them in his own way. In essence, Harbelis approaches gunnery in the same manner that Joel connects with the air. As his commanding officer remarks, "'Well, Harbelis, you really got together with it. That's the best I've seen yet in eighteen classes.'"[200] Harbelis's gunnery tactics resemble Joel's flight practices in their attempt to get at the essence of the element or object in question. Elsewhere, Harbelis's NCO says, "Your pick up was first rate; you got right into the interception. You were really *in* it, part of it, controlling it, and that's what we look for."[201] In order to survive, Harbelis must *be* the enemy just as Ed Gentry merges with the hillman in *Deliverance*. Harbelis's training officer summarizes, "'Be one ahead of him. Always. Every second. Think like he does. *Be* him.' He paused at the tent flap. 'And you'll live.'"[202] In his notes, Dickey has Harbelis liken himself to "an electric bat.... This is Joel's electricity, his mystery. This is Joel's

---

PT-17 Stearman (Hart, "James Dickey," 3). In *Alnilam*'s composition process, Harbelis's first name originally was "Takis."

[199]Dickey, "Journey to the War," 217.
[200]Ibid., 220.
[201]Ibid., 227.
[202]Ibid., 228.

hunt."[203] Applying Joel's practice of merging to his own discipline, Harbelis exhibits both his allegiance to Joel's philosophy and his autonomous self-assertion in independently applying it.

In one of his endings for *Crux*, Dickey has the surviving members of Alnilam petition Harbelis to lead them, but—considering the destruction rendered by Shears—he deems it too dangerous and chooses to dissolves the group instead. Dickey described the "coda" of *Crux* as a post-war sequence at a hospital near Mount Fujiyama in which Harbelis is recovering from the burns he sustained during Shears's catastrophic revenge raid. He explained that this part of the book seeks to capture a "reawakening" of Harbelis's "sensuous life."[204] During his recuperation, he walks past a schoolhouse and a passel of Japanese children come out waving American flags at him. The use of youthful innocence in the wake of burning destruction—appearing earlier in *Alnilam* when the Bledsoe children play in the rafters of their ash-encircled house[205]—reinforces the humanistic regeneration Harbelis is undergoing. Gazing at the beautiful Japanese mountain, he experiences a deep feeling of peace similar to that of the speaker in Dickey's poem, "A View of Fujiyama after the War" (*WM*, 100–101), and ponders Alnilam and his own future. On one of his tapes, Dickey has Joel say of Alnilam, "It would never end and take many forms"[206] and, even though the group is disbanded and many of its members dead, Harbelis believes the spirit of Joel's philosophy will live on. The last lines of the handwritten manuscript suggest as much: "It [Alnilam or the idea of it] could move by itself if nobody was looking, but definitely with the wind, always. It could move with the wind; it was moving now. Rise and be with."[207] No longer a human organization, the idea of Alnilam returns to the air which gave it life and waits for that unusual

---

[203]Series 2, box 91g.

[204]Series 11, tape 11.

[205]The Bledsoe children resemble the shy young protagonists in Dickey's poem, "The Rafters" (*WM*, 26–27).

[206]Series 11, tape 36.

[207]Series 2, box 91g.

being, like Joel, who, finding it by himself, will give it words again, making it his own.

CHAPTER 3

EARTH: *TO THE WHITE SEA*

Genius resides in instinct; goodness likewise. One acts perfectly only when one acts instinctively.
—*Nietzsche,* Werke: Kritische Gesamtausgabe, *127*

If I were to tell you that the rise of any free bird / Is better/the larger the bird is, / And that I found myself one of these / Without surprise, you would understand / That this makes of air a thing that would be liberty / Enough for any world but this one, / And could see how I should have gone / Up and out of all / all of it...
—*Dickey, "Eagles" in* The Whole Motion, *431*

I am not dead, I have only become inhuman.
—*Robinson Jeffers, "Inscription for a Gravestone" in* The Selected Poetry, *480*

Despite its Japanese milieu and singular narrator/protagonist Muldrow, *To the White Sea* has close symbolic and thematic associations with each of Dickey's first two novels. As in *Deliverance*, water—in this case, the ocean—constitutes an identifying imaginative trope. In fact, Dickey originally called the book *Thalatta*, a variation of a Greek word meaning "sea."[1] The novel's conceptual similarities to *Alnilam* are equally notable. At its conclusion Muldrow's essence, like Joel Cahill's ghost, constitutes "a voice in the wind" (*TS*, 274) and, analogous to the idea of Alnilam at the end of *Crux*, Muldrow feels himself changing form and moving with the air. However, although over the course of the book Muldrow journeys across and through the elements of earth, air, water, and fire, his general sensibility remains acutely earth-based. A child of the frozen arctic wastes, Muldrow thinks of the cold of high-altitude aircraft as "the wrong cold": "The cold of high air is not real, it's not honest. Cold should be connected to the ground, even if it's at the top of a mountain" (*TS*, 20). Muldrow's strong association with the landscape, his use of and extended meditations on camouflage, make *To the White Sea* Dickey's apotheosis for the tactical practice of merging. Whereas the amalgamating actions of Ed Gentry and Joel Cahill are only symbolically apparent in his first two novels, Dickey directly explores Muldrow's poetic and literal desire "to blend in the place you're in, but with a mind to do something" (*TS*, 273).

Among the notes for his third novel, Dickey lists Muldrow's resources as "his cool," "his purpose: to get to…the sea 'with ice in it,'" "concealment," and "his ruthlessness."[2] Following a discussion of Muldrow's background and its sources, I will be examining *To the White Sea* in terms of the qualities Dickey identifies. The first and last of Muldrow's assets, his "cool" and "ruthlessness," are expressions Dickey uses in depicting Muldrow's conscienceless personality, and I will seek to illustrate how Muldrow's circumstances and Dickey's background materials mold the character into an unrepentant killer. Even so, despite Muldrow's pitiless love of bloodshed, many readers sympathize with him through much of the novel. This is due largely to his semantic appeal, which—possessing an unusual combination of stunning poetic imagery and glib common sense—seduces the reader into

---

[1] Series 2.3, box 91k.
[2] Ibid., 12.

his world view. Whereas Dickey had strongly encouraged the reader's merging with Ed Gentry, Muldrow presents substantial problems and the reader, as with the language of Joel and Alnilam, ultimately must decide whether to accept Muldrow's deadly impressions or write them off as dangerously delusional. Establishing the importance of Muldrow's discourse, I go on to demonstrate how it leads to his *Umwelt*, or self-world, which is based largely on a philosophy of latter-day Epicureanism. This is apparent both in his dialogue with the American monk and his obsessive cataloguing of equipment. Muldrow's interest in matter and space also intersects with his need to arrive at the "sea with ice in it," the spatial and material environment in which he feels most comfortable. Correspondingly, I reveal how his magnetic drive northward takes on the quality of migration as he begins associating himself with various animals through the practice of dreaming. Amid his identifications with creatures and the drive to go north, Muldrow develops and perfects his method of camouflage or "concealment," which feeds upon a dynamic of inhumanism that, in turn, makes his final transformation possible. Having waited throughout the novel, like the speaker in "Fog Envelops the Animals," to feel "Long-sought invisibility / Come forth from my solid body" (*WM*, 80), he arrives at a cumulative juncture in space, time, and place where he presumes such a metamorphosis is possible.

A scion of the frozen north and a product of the icy wastes, Muldrow is shaped—both inside and out—by the environment that surrounds him. At the beginning of the novel he explains that he grew up on the north side of "the Brooks Range, which is away from everything, facing away from the States..." (*TS*, 10). Even at this early stage, before we know much about him, Muldrow stresses the lonely autonomy of the habitat that forged him. It exists not "away from" specific places and objects, but rather "away from everything," a condition that reflects back upon the place itself—"the Brooks Range"—and the person who inhabits it: Muldrow. Significantly, Muldrow identifies his home by a geographical feature, a range of mountains, instead of evoking a principality or his national allegiance. Although Alaska is part of the United States, Muldrow characterizes his section of the Brooks Range as "facing away from the States," symbolically turning its back upon and rejecting the country that claims dominion over it.[3] Muldrow conceives of himself and his home as looking outward, northward—to an even colder and wilder environment—, as opposed to gazing inward, toward the culture and civilization of the United States.

Dickey used Barry Lopez's book, *Arctic Dreams: Imagination and Desire in a Northern Landscape*, as a major background source for both portraying Muldrow's arctic landscape and establishing his connection with Eskimos.[4] Lopez attributes his book to "two moments," one of which takes place near Muldrow's Alaskan habitat, in "the western Brooks Range of Alaska."[5] He recalls watching with lonely fascination, as Muldrow does in his youth, the herds of caribou, the wolverine, the elusive fox, and various migratory birds—all flourishing in a seemingly barren landscape, nearly devoid of people. Throughout Lopez's engaging book—a fluid arrangement of history, science, and memoir—the dynamics of desolation, beauty, alienation, and death constantly reappear, culminating in an act of homage. Asserting at the book's conclusion that "the landscape and the animals were like something found at the end of a dream,"[6] Lopez faces northward and bows to the inscrutable Arctic—a worshipful act that suggests Muldrow's repeated idealizations of his Alaskan environment.

In addition to the rich frozen wildness of Lopez's book, Dickey employed Vardis Fisher's novels *Mountain Man* and *Dark Bidwell*

---

[3]Muldrow's apathy for his country is further demonstrated by his lack of patriotism and respect for the military, both stemming from his staunch, almost radical, individuality. At one point he explains, "I had a way of doing things that was about half the Air Force's and half mine" (*TS*, 20).

[4]Series 2.3, box 91k.

[5]Barry Lopez, *Arctic Dreams: Imagination and Desire in a Northern Landscape* (New York: Charles Scribner's Sons, 1986) xvii.

[6]Ibid., 371.

as source texts for Muldrow's upbringing and personality.[7] *Mountain Man*[8] takes place in the American West, north of the Oregon Trail, during the 1840s. The story follows Sam Minard, a scout and trapper, whose pregnant Crow wife is murdered by a band of renegade Crow. Vowing revenge, Minard declares war on the entire Crow nation and much of the novel is spent describing his battles with various Black Feet and Crow, to whom he becomes known simply as "The Terror." Minard's interest in woodcraft and fighting strategies (which he compares to the tactics of various wild animals), and his single-handed attack on an enemy nation are suggestive of Muldrow, although their characters and circumstances are otherwise quite different.

More of Muldrow's character, especially his childhood development, is drawn from *Dark Bidwell's* Jed Bidwell, a boy raised in a rattler-infested Idaho gorge on the Snake River in the early 1900s. Fisher's summary of Jed's childhood development is notable for its remarkable similarity to Muldrow's:

Everything around him [Jed], for that matter, invited him to solitude or to reckless deeds. The great mountains, the untamed headstrong river, the wild animal life and the lonely blockade of winter months—he felt the power of all these, and their ruthlessness, and their savage ways. He took the spirit of them into his soul. The people whom he met, besides his own kin, were coarse in speech and thought. Sly sheepherders became his tutor, feeding his hungry imagination, suggesting deeds that he had never done. The early events of his life, often the tasks which his father gave him to do, shaped his emotions into a pattern of pride and revenge.

And so he grew, schooled by savagery. Cruelty in his life was a meaningless word. Suffering and pain he was accustomed to from his first years. The agony of a tortured

---

[7] Series 2.3, box 91k.
[8] Vardis Fisher, *Mountain Man* (New York: Morrow, 1965).

thing meant no more to him than the flow of the river or the cutting down of a tree; and he looked upon death as calmly as he looked upon life.[9]

Like Muldrow Jed is shaped by the environment in which he is raised, taking its qualities into himself—"into his soul." The morals of civilization mean nothing because they are such alien, nearly nonexistent, concepts; their only representatives are wandering sheepherders and occasional traveling settlers—themselves not very civilized.

In this vacuum of morality and collective human existence, Jed Bidwell gives himself over almost entirely to the qualities of the inhuman natural world.[10] The sheepherders who rarely visit, like Muldrow's Eskimo acquaintances, offer a weak sampling of human

---

[9]Vardis Fisher, *Dark Bidwell* (Boston: Houghton Mifflin, 1931) 151–52.

[10]Jed's and Muldrow's upbringings also mirror that of Joe Makatozi in Louis L'Amour's *Last of the Breed* (1986), a popular novel that anticipates *To the White Sea* in a number of important respects. Taking place during the 1980s Cold War, the story follows Major Joe Makatozi, an American Sioux Indian, who is captured when his experimental aircraft goes down over Siberia. Escaping from prison, he resolves to follow the path of his ancestors and cross the Bering Strait, thousands of miles to the northeast. Like Muldrow and Jed Bidwell, Makatozi's isolated wilderness upbringing has prepared him for such an undertaking. L'Amour recounts, "He had never lived on a reservation. His one white grandparent had left considerable property to the Makatozi family in the Snake River country of Idaho, most of it high country in the mountains, a land of rushing rivers, of small meadows and forest. Most of the land lay far from any highway, completely cut off in winter, isolated even in summer" (Louis L'Amour, *Last of the Breed* [New York: Bantam, 1986] 12). In order to make it to Alaska, Makatozi resolves that he, like Muldrow, "must cultivate the art of invisibility" (145). However, along the way, he becomes less interested in escape as he moves progressively closer to the ways of his ancestors: "All this—the forest, the wilderness—it is my home. With each day I find myself regressing.... I am supposed to be escaping, and to win my own battle, I must escape. Nevertheless, in many ways I'd rather stay here" (208). While Makatozi does not share Muldrow's poetic sensibility or love of killing, he exhibits a similar knack for woodcraft and survivalism during his icy northward journey. Although Dickey never cited *Last of the Breed* as a source or even admitted reading it, its strong similarities to his book are difficult to ignore.

interaction but—"coarse" and uneducated—there is nothing overly civilized about them, and their existence too depends on nature and animals. Also significant in Jed's development is the importance of the father—described by people who knew him as "a little bit out of his wits"[11]—whose reasons for coming west "remained a dark riddle,"[12] a play on his name, Dark Bidwell. Muldrow's father's basis for moving from Virginia to Alaska is equally ambiguous, even to his only son. Muldrow speculates: "He had his own reasons for being there, which he never did get around to telling me, or that I ever really understood. It may have been he got into some kind of trouble, back in Virginia or somewhere in the States, though I don't think it had anything to do with the law. But something had happened to him that made him want to be by himself, or maybe he was just that way all the time. Like I say, he never did give me the straight of it" (*TS*, 19). Echoing the eccentricity and possible madness of Jed's father, Muldrow says of his own, "The red wall was my father's only strangeness, though other people might have told you different" (*TS*, 213). While other civilized humans regard Jed's and Muldrow's fathers as peculiar or perhaps even mad, the sons—raised without the benefit of any substantial comparative references—accept their sires' behaviors as customary, allowing them to shape their own.

It is Jed Bidwell's father who, for practical reasons—the protection of crops and livestock—, encourages Jed to kill woodchucks and wipe out the snake population on their property. Yet the result of this responsibility is a nurtured love of killing in Jed—a desire to outwit and destroy the entire species of whatever animal happens to threaten him. In order to eradicate them, Jed, like Muldrow, dedicates untold hours to the study of creatures—following them, watching them, and imitating them. He shares with Muldrow the obsessive poetic love of an animal's appearance and manner. Having built a snake pit, into which he casts dozens of captive rattlesnakes, Jed sits "on the stone wall, staring with pride into his

---

[11]Ibid., 16.
[12]Ibid., 18.

venomous den. His breath would come slow and deep, and his eyes would darken, as he sensed fully their tamelessness and their power. He loved their jungle ferocity, and the lidless cunning hatred of their eyes."[13] Identifying himself with the powerful aspects of nature and its predatory creatures, Jed, like Muldrow, develops a strong inhuman and conscienceless personality from which he draws his opinions on existence: "'Some things is good,' Jed declared, 'and some things is bad. The bad things should ought-a-be killed. Human or beast, it's all the same to me.'"[14]

A dominant byproduct of Jed's and Muldrow's upbringings is their predatory inhuman ruthlessness, which resembles the indifferent environments that produced them. Possessing an animalistic poetic sensibility, Muldrow conceives of the Alaskan landscape as Robinson Jeffers portrays the coastal hills at Sovranes Creek: "This is the noblest thing I have ever seen. / No imaginable / Human presence here could do anything / But dilute the lonely self-watchful passion."[15] Because Muldrow is so irrevocably alienated from human society, Nelson Hathcock labels him the victim of a "de-evolution."[16] Yet, it is Muldrow's very *Götterdämmerung*, his downfall from the communal order of societal norms and mores, which enables him to survive as long as he does. Mindful of this dynamic, Dickey constructs a provocative scenario in which a human being's subsistence hinges on the strength and effectiveness of his apparent inhumanity.

---

[13]Fisher, *Dark Bidwell*, 177.

[14]Ibid., 210.

[15]Robinson Jeffers, "The Place for no Story," in *The Selected Poetry of Robinson Jeffers* (New York: Random House, 1937) 358.

[16]For condemnations of Muldrow's inhuman survivalism see Sandra B. Durham, "A Felt Absence: The Female in *To the White Sea*," *James Dickey Newsletter* 13/2 (Spring 1997): 2–7; Collie Owens, "Quest for the Savage Self: The Unrepressed Man in James Dickey's *To the White Sea*," *James Dickey Newsletter* 11/2 (Spring 1995): 16–24; and Richard Wiley, "The Fittest Survive, But Fit for What?" *Los Angeles Times*, 19 September 1993, Book Review 2+.

According to Dickey, Muldrow's lack of a conscience[17] is based on Xenophon's *Anabasis*,[18] the ancient historical account of 10,000 Greek soldiers who fight their way home 1,500 miles through rugged terrain and numerous barbarian hordes. Like Muldrow, the Hellenes find themselves far behind enemy lines in an alien culture. After several Greeks are beheaded—like the downed airman in Dickey's novel—while negotiating a truce, the survivors vow to use any means necessary that they might glimpse the Hellespont again. Like Muldrow, who also wishes to reach a specific geographic destination, the Greeks repeatedly commit what most twenty-first century readers would consider atrocities or war crimes. Throughout the campaign they liberally kidnap young boys and women of all ages from various villages to keep with them as unwilling sexual companions and hostages. More suggestive of *To the White Sea*, in one incident, after repulsing a contingent of Persians, the Hellenes resolve to maim and behead the bodies of the fallen in an effort to discourage the enemy's morale. This episode calls to mind both the firebombing of Tokyo, which is partly an "anti-morale" raid, and Muldrow's decapitation of the old woman. Although Muldrow clearly is amused by his handiwork, his action, like that of the Greeks, accomplishes the practical military objective of spreading fear and confusion in the enemy's homeland. Furthermore, Xenophon—the advisor of the Hellenes and narrator of the account—never hesitates to make human sacrifices of prisoners when consulting the gods on matters

---

[17]For readings that argue the novel's violently nihilistic content overpowers its fine poetic form see Joyce Pair, "'The Peace of the Pure Predator': Dickey's Energized Man in *To the White Sea*," *James Dickey Newsletter* 10/2 (Spring 1994): 15–27; Richard Martin, "Yankee on the Edge," Review of *To the White Sea*, *Far Eastern Economic Review* (28 April 1994): 41; Leon Rooke, "Sergeant Muldrow finds Transcendence," *New York Times Book Review* (19 September 1993): 14; and Gail Caldwell, "Shooting the Moon," Review of *To the White Sea*, *The Boston Globe*, 29 August 1993, B12+.

[18]Series 2.3, box 91k. Xenophon, *Xenophon's Anabasis: The March Up Country*, trans. W. H. D. Rouse (New York: New American Library, 1970).

of military strategy. Like Muldrow's path, the swath cut by the Greeks is littered with enemy corpses.[19]

Dickey also claimed that Muldrow's conscienceless demeanor was drawn in part from the personality of Ted Bundy, the famous serial killer. Like Muldrow, Bundy enjoyed manipulating his appearance for the purpose of luring his victims to him. Using crutches or placing an arm in a sling, he often asked attractive female undergraduates to help him carry books to his Volkswagen Bug, at which point he would force them into the vehicle and spirit them away to a secluded place where, having eliminated the possibility of detection, he could rape and kill them at his leisure. However, although Bundy was an ingenious predator who displayed little guilt and, like Muldrow, killed women, his similarities with Dickey's protagonist end there. With his good looks, magnetic charisma, and keen intellect, Bundy resembled Joel Cahill more than Muldrow. Whereas Bundy relied on conventions of humanity—qualities like physical attractiveness and civic virtue—as props for his premeditated crimes, Muldrow imagines his actions in natural terms, shunning society-based deceptions for the lethal instinctive cunning of rapacious beasts.[20]

Coinciding with Muldrow's developmental background and "ruthless" personality are the linguistic explanations he gives for his actions. Dickey maintained, "The hardest part of writing *To the White Sea* was to establish a tone or voice for Muldrow which would be convincing and yet distinctive to him. He's practically illiterate, but he has a highly developed personal mystique, which

---

[19]Readings that consider the novel's socio-political and cultural implications against Muldrow's conscienceless demeanor include Nelson Hathcock, "No Further Claim to Innocence: James Dickey's Revision of the American War Story," *Texas Review* 17/3–4 (Fall/Winter 1996/1997): 26–42; Ernest Suarez, "James Dickey's Literary Reputation: Romanticism and Hedonism in *To the White Sea* and *Deliverance*," *The South Carolina Review* 26/2 (Spring 1994): 141–53; and Douglas Keesey, "James Dickey's *To the White Sea*: A Critical Controversy," *James Dickey Newsletter* 10/1 (Fall 1993): 2–16.

[20]For a depiction of Ted Bundy's personality see Ann Rule, *The Stranger Beside Me* (New York: Norton, 1980).

he states as a matter of course as though anybody would understand it. Actually, nobody but he understands it."[21] Dickey strengthens the appeal of Muldrow's unique discourse early in the novel by setting it in relief against less attractive language.[22] In the book's first few pages, Muldrow's discriminating commentary appears reasonable versus the hyperbolic *Krieglust* of the colonel's fire-bombing speech: "'Fire…. We're going to put it in his eyes and up his asshole, in his wife's twat, and in his baby's diaper'" (*TS*, 1). As in *Alnilam*, military language functions as an unflattering alternative discourse to that of the protagonist. Exact, concise, and ordered, military speech contrasts with the illiterate but frequently penetrating musings of characters like Frank Cahill and Hannah Pelham—who often speak in what Dickey labeled "country surrealism."[23] Muldrow falls into this category as well, although his dream and nature dialogue also possesses the poetic lyricism of Joel and the Alnilam language, ringing with the same groping attempt to articulate sublime aspects of existence.

Beyond his negative use of military semantics, Dickey further attracts the reader to Muldrow's language by contrasting it with that of Arlen and the "Florida boy," the green airmen who approach him in the barracks. The larger of the two, Arlen, comes across as an insecure bully, flaunting his juvenile snake tattoo and badgering Muldrow with idle threats. In the face of Arlen's aggressive language ("I could bust his back with one chop" [*TS*,

---

[21]Robert Kirschten, "Interview with James Dickey," in *"Struggling for Wings": The Art of James Dickey*, ed. Kirschten (Columbia: University of South Carolina Press, 1997) 68.

[22]For examinations of the book that consider the reader's (in)ability to identify with Muldrow's dialogue see Ronald Curran, Review of *To the White Sea*, *World Literature Today* 68/4 (Autumn 1994): 809–10; and John Melmoth, "A Man in the Wilderness," *Times Literary Supplement* (11 February 1994): 21.

[23]In his notes for the part of the book he called the "Blue section," Dickey wrote, "Make some of his talk and diction sound something like that of Huckleberry Finn." Series 2.3, box 91k, 18. Dickey's determination to infuse Muldrow's language with Huck's rough combination of natural innocence and penetrating realism further underscores his attempt to make Muldrow engage our sympathies.

6]), Muldrow appears patient and forgiving, returning the money he wins from Arlen in their pinch-grip competition. He is equally tolerant of the Florida boy, who reveals his naivete and fear of combat in the numerous questions he asks, which threaten to annoy both Muldrow and the reader. In his interaction with the young airmen, Muldrow's language seems neither boastful, like Arlen's, nor unsure, like the Floridian's. Against the inadequacies of the inexperienced fliers, Dickey portrays him as a patient and mature soldier who happens to excel at his job.

Muldrow continues to attract our understanding along dialogic lines once his plane is shot down, justifying his violent actions through repeated references to the emasculating and "decapitation-happy" Japanese, who have pledged to maim and execute any American airman found in Japan. Having stressed this dynamic to the reader, Dickey uses two events in order to finally undermine Muldrow's credibility: his seemingly gratuitous decapitation of the old woman and his confessed responsibility for the pre-war death of the "Kansas girl." After inviting the reader's allegiance through the first half of the book, Muldrow performs alienating acts—both apparently committed on nothing more than a whim. *To the White Sea,* like *Deliverance,* is a first-person narrative; however, in the later novel Dickey upsets the reader's relationship with his narrator in order to make her/him examine more fully both the nature of his character and his own reading practices. Dickey plays with the idea of reader/text merging by forcing the reader either to condemn Muldrow on the basis of his actions or accept him, subordinating his destructive deeds to the aesthetic value of his philosophical vision. Through Muldrow, Dickey flirts with an aspect of the eternal debate involving art and morality: should, for example, a brilliant work of art be celebrated for its raw aesthetic genius or condemned for its unconscionable ethics if written by or about a serial killer, racist, sexist, or someone equally "immoral"? Faced with such a dilemma, the reader must determine whether to reject Muldrow and the novel on ethical grounds or to defer his indiscriminate killing in favor of his compelling artistic imagination.

Through Muldrow's poetic sensibility, rendered in sparse, penetrating language, the reader is made privy to the world he sees around him: his *Umwelt*, or self-world.[24] Muldrow's interpretive outlook is essentially Epicurean in that its foundation rests on material objects and the space in which they exist.[25] Dickey accentuates this philosophy during Muldrow's conversation with the American ascetic. As Ernest Suarez rightly deduces, "Dickey uses the scene in that Muldrow encounters the American monk to distinguish between Muldrow's naturalistic impulses and the monk's Zen Buddhism."[26] Beneath Muldrow's "naturalistic" drive—his attempt to take on attributes that will enable him to survive in Japan—rests his Epicurean sensibility, which is apparent in his emphasis on the use and function of physical matter. After he kills the Japanese swordsman, Muldrow remarks, "You're a good one.... You sure are. I can use you" (*TS*, 175), and indeed he does utilize him materially, splintering the dead swordsman's forearm and gathering the boney needles for the purpose of sewing his arctic outfit.

---

[24]For readings that praise Muldrow's and/or Dickey's poetic rendering of nature and primitive savagery see Lawrence Lieberman, "Warrior, Visionary, Natural Philosopher: James Dickey's *To the White Sea*," *The Southern Review* 33/1 (Winter 1997): 164–80; George Searles, Review of *To the White Sea*, *America* 172/14 (22 April 1995): 261; Steve Brzezinski, Review of *To the White Sea*, *The Antioch Review* 52/3 (Spring 1994): 358; Bill Hunt, "Homeward Bound," *Alaska* 60/1 (1994): 75–76; Gary Kerley, "Living, Survival are Epic Poetry in 'Sea'," Review of *To the White Sea*, *Atlanta Constitution*, 26 September 1993, N8+; Greg Johnson, "A Walk on the Dark Side," Review of *To the White Sea*, *Chicago Tribune*, 19 September 1993, 14.5; Christopher Lehmann-Haupt, "From Man to Beast of Prey," Review of *To the White Sea*, *New York Times*, 13 September 1993, C17; and Review of *To the White Sea*, *Publishers Weekly*, 240/25 (21 June 1993): 82.

[25]Muldrow's brand of Epicureanism also resembles Edmund Husserl's original idea of phenomenology: an apprehension of things themselves—the "touched" dimension of experience. See Edmund Husserl, *Cartesian Meditations: An Introduction to Phenomenology*, trans. Dorian Carnes (The Hague: Martinus Nijhoff, 1960).

[26]Ernest Suarez, "'Real God, Roll': Muldrow's Primitive Creed," *James Dickey Newsletter* 10/2 (Spring 1994): 9.

Drawing on his Epicurean world view, Muldrow discounts the American monk's philosophy because it rationalizes things into abstractions for which he has no use or interest. After the ascetic's psychological interpretation of dreams and temporality, Muldrow thinks, "I had never heard any kind of talk like this, and I tried to head it off. Not that it bothered me, but I couldn't find any way to connect with it, or get interested in it" (*TS*, 195). The monastery's rock garden functions as the epitome of such abstract uselessness, symbolizing the monks' fabricated relationship with nature. As an artificial human construction of the natural world, the rock garden is, to Muldrow, as worthless as it is uninteresting. Whereas the monks repeatedly order nature into a time-honored, formulaic arrangement, Muldrow wishes to know and assume the identity of the natural world as it truly is. While Zen practitioners flirt with the void for the purpose of enlightenment (*kensho* or *satori*, the apprehension of the authentic self), Muldrow appreciates the importance of nothingness in relationships between natural manifestations.[27] When, for example, he muses upon the shared qualities of clouds and icebergs, he concludes, "There was no reason for them to be like they were, and have the shapes that they did, except that that was the way they happened to be, for nothing" (*TS*, 18). For Muldrow, nothingness is an integral part of understanding the natural world rather than an abstract tool in the quest for an essence of the inner self.

Muldrow's contempt for the monk's impractical acquired knowledge, as opposed to his own experience-based, Epicurean understanding, is substantiated later when he thinks back on their conversation: "I thought of something I should have said to him when he was coming at me with all that religious stuff he had learned how to say. This would have been good, I thought: when he said something like, God is everywhere there is, God is in the snow, I should have come back at him and said, No, the snow is in the snow. That would have settled his hash, and it made me feel better

---

[27]Ironically, for all his vaporous preaching about the void and self-dissipation, the American monk goes out of his way to alert the Japanese military to Muldrow's presence, confirming that his interests are very much of this world.

when I realized I could have said it" (*TS*, 217). Elsewhere, Dickey himself has endorsed Muldrow's non-religious material-based mentality, asserting, "The human being does not address or learn how to live with, to love and to use, by getting away from the immediate reality of the things of this world but by diving into them."[28] Muldrow's allusion to snow and Dickey's emphasis on exploring "the immediate reality of things" also suggests Hegel's characterization of nature as frozen and non-spiritual: "In Nature, …in theological language, we have the Divine Idea momentarily excluded from the Divine Love: everywhere it shows anticipations and vestiges of intelligence, but in a frozen, petrified form, in which God may be said to be dead. Nature, in short, is the raw material of self-conscious Spirit, and being raw, it is, in its immediate form, the exact antithesis of anything spiritual."[29] Recognizing snow for what it is—a minuscule manifestation of raw nature—, Muldrow resists the monk's spiritual imposition of a divine entity upon it. For Muldrow, Dickey, and Hegel, spirituality is something humans bring to and imprint upon nature. Thus, Muldrow cannot help but abjure spiritual claims to universal enlightenment. As Richard Jefferies—one of Dickey's favorite writers—maintains, "By no course of reasoning, however tortuous, can nature and the universe be fitted to the mind. Nor can the mind be fitted to the cosmos."[30] When Muldrow compares icebergs and clouds he is glad that they are the way they are "for nothing"; abstractions only threaten to misdirect him from the natural essence he seeks to know and become.[31]

---

[28]James Dickey, foreword, in T. Crunk, *Living in the Resurrection* (New Haven: Yale University Press, 1995) x.

[29]J. N. Findlay, *The Philosophy of Hegel* (New York: Collier, 1958) 272–73.

[30]Richard Jefferies, *The Story of My Heart* (Portland ME: Mosher, 1900) 49.

[31]Another example of Muldrow's distaste for abstraction is his refusal to name the hermit's giant predatory birds. For him, what they are and what they do is all that matters: "There was another side to them, another dimension, you might say. I never put names to them. Names are chickenshit; they didn't need any names" (*TS*, 265). At one point in the composition process Dickey was determined that Muldrow too should remain nameless. His editor, Mark Jaffe, talked him out of it.

Dickey used Peter Matthiessen's collection of journals, *Nine-Headed Dragon River*, for background on Zazen, monastic practices, and the Japanese landscape.[32] Matthiessen's diaries constitute an introduction to Zazen from an American's perspective and Dickey likely drew on the "I" of Matthiessen's writings as a model for the American monk in *To the White Sea*.[33] The Zazen aim—"a silent training directed toward unification of body, mind, and spirit with the universal consciousness sometimes referred to as Oneness, Zen Mind, Buddha-nature"[34]—superficially appears to suggest the embodiment of what Muldrow ultimately attempts to achieve. Yet, his goal is to assume the being of a physical place rather than bond with a transcendent spirit—a significant distinction. Furthermore, the monastery Muldrow visits strongly resembles Matthiessen's description of Kennin-ji, a traditional Rinzai training center with several stone gardens, where "seven days a week, as in the old days, thirty-one monks arise at 4:00 A.M. for zazen.... In the afternoon the monks perform their monastery duties, followed by zazen until near midnight."[35] The nocturnal ascetics Muldrow encounters wandering in the fog appear to be functioning on a similar ritualistic schedule. In addition to Kennin-ji, Dickey drew on Mathiessen's discussions of Zen time for the American monk's conversation with Muldrow. Matthiessen's citation of Dogen Zenji, a thirteenth-century Soto master, in regard to "Being-Time"—the understanding that different beings and states exhibit varying interpretations of temporality—suggests the ascetic's discourse on dream time and real time. Finally, Matthiessen's book makes references to Hokkaido and the native inhabitants he calls "the

---

[32]Series 2.3, box 91k, 16.

[33]Matthiessen's description of a Canadian monk at one of the Japanese monasteries also suggests the American ascetic and his behavior: "The Canadian monk who showed us about seemed at once eager and ill at ease, as if voices from home in this far place might dispel the effect he had come so far to find" (Peter Matthiessen, *Nine-Headed Dragon River: Zen Journals 1969–1982* [Boston: Shambhala, 1986] 225).

[34]Ibid., 14.

[35]Ibid., 172.

remnant aborigines, or 'Hairy Ainu,' tall, blue-eyed, bearded hunter-gatherers, at one time considered a relict population of the early Cro-Magnon."[36] The tribe to which Muldrow refers as "the little bearded people, the bear people," (*TS*, 261) are probably based on the Ainu, although he makes no mention of their blue eyes or the fact that they are taller than the average Japanese.

Beyond the sequence involving the American monk, Muldrow's Epicureanism is present in his compulsive itemizing of equipment, which takes place at frequent intervals in the book. To be sure, equipment is critical in the Arctic, where a person cannot survive outside for long without the necessary tools (and the skill to use them) to provide mobility, food, and warmth. However, Muldrow's fondness for his equipment, which Dickey claimed he took from George Orwell,[37] goes beyond the simple idea of material preparation. In his notes, Dickey contends that Muldrow's things have a "talismatic quality,"[38] exemplified by their associations with aspects of nature. For example, in addition to appreciating his knife's flexibility, Muldrow is interested in the way it captures and reflects light. He is fascinated by the manner in which it can manipulate light; in addition to having the pliable capacity to curve around a bone when plunged into someone, the blade can also "bend" light, giving Muldrow a certain control of and use for nature's illuminating element. Angling his knife toward a candle inside a Japanese home, he "catches" the flame on the blade and explains with satisfaction, "That was my mark" (*TS*, 82).

In addition to his fondness for objects like the knife and compass—which gives him pleasure through its adherence to the northern magnetic pull—, Muldrow enjoys appropriating physical aspects of the challenging opponents he conquers. Hoping to gain some of the power of his most worthy adversaries, he takes some physical part of them as a way of internalizing their essence. In addition to the aforementioned bone splinters of the skilled

---

[36]Ibid., 236.
[37]Series 2.3, box 91k, 2.
[38]Ibid., 15.

Japanese swordsman, Muldrow uses the skins of the goats that gore him with their horns. He is ecstatic when the bear women present him with a shirt and pair of pants made from the hides: "These were the hides I had skinned off the goats in the woods, and I can tell you I was plenty grateful, because I wanted to have that kind of vitality and fire pass into me. I had already eaten a lot of the goats, and now to wear them, too, would be luck beyond the best of luck" (*TS*, 251). Dickey's interest in the talismatic effect of Muldrow's possessions is underscored by the fact that he read William Humphrey's *The Spawning Run*[39] in the hopes of finding a way to exhibit the "fishing mystique" in Muldrow.[40] Humphrey's first-person narrator goes into great detail in cataloguing his gear and fishing techniques as if the gear itself is essential in understanding the fish. Similarly, based on his background, Muldrow believes that the proper comprehension and mastery of an adversary or environment is partly contingent on having the appropriate implements.

In addition to its focus on gear, Humphrey's *The Spawning Run* is a literal and symbolic meditation on instinctual homecoming, in terms of both salmon and humans, and just as salmon return, through very formidable obstacles, to mate and die in their native streams, so Muldrow works his way north to the environment of his youth—the native habitat in which a defining transformation awaits him. Muldrow struggles to articulate the underpinnings of his migration, confessing "North was north, and it would stay that way. And there was the pull of something else to go with it: that other thing that was not called north but was at the same place, the thing nobody could say" (*TS*, 39). Scientifically, Muldrow's journey north is the embodiment of what biologist Hermann Schöne calls "goal orientation," a term which "includes all orientation behaviors that lead the animal to a previously determined place, near or far away. To reach distant or hidden goals an animal must employ orientation mechanisms whose

---

[39]William Humphrey, *The Spawning Run* (New York: Knopf, 1970).
[40]Series 2.3, box 91k, 23.

spatial references are not directly associated with the goal."[41] In Muldrow's case the unrelated mechanisms are those necessary in negotiating the diverse environments through which he passes during his trek toward the "goal environment."[42] Although Muldrow cannot express goal orientation as the "something else" he feels tugging at him, he recognizes aspects of it in various things. At the end of the decapitation scene with the old woman, Dickey wanted to emphasize Muldrow's "definite reluctance to leave the water-wheel: the connection of the wheel and the water, the never-ending quality of it, touches something in him; some primitive thing."[43] Although Muldrow cannot fully grasp it, the wheel's motion of eternal return suggests his own migration, which is also a return to his beginnings, through the cycle of elements, and constituting—in its relation to the point of origin and return—the circle of life.

Muldrow's migratory impulse, his goal orientation, is also animalistic in its absorption of different creatures' characteristics for the purpose of increasing its effectiveness.[44] This is something with which Dickey had experimented in his poetry. In his introduction to *The Achievement of James Dickey*, an early collection of Dickey's poems, Laurence Lieberman makes the observation: "In the earlier poems, Dickey supposed he could give

---

[41] Hermann Schöne, *Spatial Orientation: Spatial Control of Behavior in Animals and Man*, trans. Strausfeld (Princeton: Princeton University Press, 1984) 14.

[42] For readings that interpret Muldrow's journey as a mythical quest or ritualistic exercise see Lawrence Broer, "Fire and Ice in Dickey's *To the White Sea*," *Texas Review* 17/3-4 (Fall/Winter 1996/1997): 1-25; Joyce Pair, "Postmodernism and *To the White Sea*," *James Dickey Newsletter* 12/2 (Spring 1996): 19-23; and Marion Hodge, "'All that Religious Stuff He had Learned How to Say': Camouflage, Ritual, and Writing in *To the White Sea*," *James Dickey Newsletter* 11/1 (Fall 1994): 12-19.

[43] Series 2.3, box 91k, 22.

[44] For examinations of Muldrow's practice of identifying with animals see Ronald Baughman, "James Dickey's Evolving Self and the Void," *James Dickey Newsletter* 17/2 (2001): 8-13; and Steven G. Kellman, "Sergeant Muldrow's Bird's-Eye View," *Texas Review* 17/3-4 (Fall/Winter 1996/1997): 43-49.

up his human self to the animal realm. The human/animal encounter in the last poem of the series, 'Encounter in the Cage Country,' has become a medium through which his human limitations can be transcended, but in going beyond his human condition, he no longer transforms into a new, wholly other being; instead, he intensifies and deepens the human self by adding animal powers to it."[45] In addition to its similarities with some of Dickey's poetry, Muldrow's belief that animal traits are bound to his own human existence is a powerful Eskimo conviction. In *Arctic Dreams* Barry Lopez relates that Eskimos "have difficulty imagining themselves entirely removed from the world of animals. For many of them, to make this separation is analogous to cutting oneself off from light or water."[46] Drawing on Eskimo culture and his own poetic method, Dickey adds a compelling animalistic dimension to Muldrow's directional odyssey.

The main avenue by which Muldrow identifies with animals and their characteristics is dreaming. In his dream visions Muldrow exhibits a "totemic" relationship with creatures, in which the dream beast he imagines bestows its powers upon him.[47] As Suarez holds, Muldrow's transformations are not abstract or philosophical: "instead each moment represents a transcendental attempt to attain skills that will enhance his power within the natural world."[48] The alien systems through which Muldrow passes and the lack of animals he encounters on Honshu are responsible for the vivid immediacy of his dreams: "There was something about Japan that bothered me, now more than before. In all these woods, among the trees, under them, in them, and over them, there were not many birds, and I hadn't seen any animals at all. The ones in my head got stronger, though; stronger because of the

---

[45]Laurence Lieberman, "James Dickey: The Deepening of Being," in *The Achievement of James Dickey*, ed. Lieberman (Glenview: Scott, Foresman and Company, 1968) 21.

[46]Lopez, *Arctic Dreams*, 180.

[47]See Alan Bleakley, *The Animalizing Imagination: Totemism, Textuality, and Ecocriticism* (New York: St. Martin's Press, 2000) 132.

[48]Suarez, "'Real God, Roll,'" 7.

absence of the others. Luck or not, I couldn't tell you" (*TS*, 125). Muldrow's dream creatures are, in fact, fortunate for him since they strengthen his animalistic sensibility, unconsciously contributing in his practical need to survive.

Although Muldrow's dreams generally benefit him, they occasionally threaten to cloud his conscious perception of reality, resulting in dangerous situations. At one point he boasts, "I can hear as well as anything on two feet, and most of them on four. I can listen with any animal" (*TS*, 115). However, Muldrow is both envious and embarrassed when he realizes the senescent swordsman can hear better—as well as move more quickly—than he. Indeed, his underestimation of the elderly man's auditory ability and darting swordsmanship nearly costs him his life. Muldrow's miscalculation with the swordsman makes the reader dubious when he later maintains, "I could outthink any animal or bird that lived in the cold, by thinking more like he did than he could do. All I had to do was get there" (*TS*, 214). Becoming overly enamored of his *Umwelt*, Muldrow occasionally allows his dreams to become seductive abstract panaceas instead of life-enhancing catalysts. While plummeting to earth earlier in the novel, Muldrow becomes lost in the dream-like sensation of bodily flight and comes to believe, like Joel Cahill, "that a man ought to be able to fly without an airplane" (*TS*, 26). However, almost simultaneously he realizes, "But that was dangerous: I could have held on to the notion too long" (*TS*, 26) and returns to his Epicurean mind-set in time to activate his chute.

While Muldrow's dream visions have an element of danger, more often than not they are beneficial to and symbolic of his practical challenges. For example, the recurring image of deer heads, introduced at the conclusion of the train ride (*TS*, 145), which Muldrow calls "Deer Herd for Infinity,"[49] suggests his northward journey. Just as the entire herd gazes into eternity, so Muldrow concentrates all his energy and focus in one direction,

---

[49]Dickey notes that Muldrow's vision is a description of a painting of the same name by Billy Dunlap. Series 2.3, box 91k. Dunlap also made Dickey's life mask in the early 1970s.

toward a goal that is singular yet vague. The arrangement of Muldrow's unconscious world is suggestive of Paul Valéry's comments on the practicality of dreams: "Man is the separate animal, the curious living creature that is opposed to all others and rises above all others by his...*dreams!*—by the intensity, succession, and diversity of his *dreams!*—by their extraordinary effects, which may sometimes even modify his nature, and not his nature only, but that surrounding nature which he tirelessly endeavors to subjugate to his dreams."[50] In addition to applying the positive elements of his dreams to his practical actions, allowing them to shape him in the process, Muldrow permits his reveries to define and shape the environment around him. As a result, the landscape Muldrow perceives, filtered through his dreams and his *Umwelt*, is drastically different from that which is visible to most humans. Shaped by him and reflected through him, the land is something he ultimately wishes to be the same as himself—a place in which he might hide to the extent that he *becomes* the place.

In a letter to his editor, Mark Jaffe, Dickey summarized his novel:[51]

Drawing at least partly on his upbringing in northern Alaska, on the Arctic Circle side of the Brooks range, he [Muldrow] has an instinctive knowledge and mastery of camouflage, the use of color to make himself either invisible or the next thing to it. The sections of the novel are divided into episodes dealing with the color spectrum, beginning with red—the fire-bombing raid on Tokyo—and ending in white, as Muldrow reaches the northern tip of Hokkaido and sees the icebergs in the water, fulfilling what he has told someone in the first section of the novel: 'For me, the ocean is not the ocean unless it's got ice in it.'[52]

---

[50]Paul Valéry, "Note," in *Variety*, trans. Malcolm Cowley (New York: Harcourt, Brace and Company, 1927) 29.

[51]The letter is dated 19 September 1988.

[52]Bruccoli and Baughman, *Crux*, 454.

Dickey's comments on camouflage and "the color spectrum" reveal both Muldrow's interpretation of landscape and the text's underlying symbolic structure. At one point Dickey had even thought to entitle different sections of the book using the names of various colors, and early manuscripts demonstrate this practice. The black section of the novel, which also includes red, pertains to the burning and smoking descriptions of Tokyo. These colors then give way to orange as Muldrow leaves the city and dawn breaks on the Japanese countryside. Next, yellow, the balance of the roads and the countryside as he journeys north, becomes the dominant color, reflected further in the yellow glimmer of light on the knife blade. Dickey asserted that brown "centers around a grove or forest of trees, with pine needles on the ground. Everything brown."[53] This section, in which Muldrow colors his hand the same color as the landscape, overlaps with blue—the sequence at the lake where he rests and begins to "conceive of Japan as his domain."[54]

The symbolic sequence of colors concludes with white which, drawing on his upbringing, Muldrow feels is the best color for camouflage. He says of his youth in Alaska: "I got to know what lived up there in the snow, and how they lived. Some of the animals, and birds, live by being able to hide, and the others live by being able to find 'em. But being hard to see, to make out, is part of it on both sides" (*TS*, 16). Although Muldrow likens himself to both predator and prey, he has a special affinity for aggressive animals like the wolverine and hawk. Describing one of his poems, "Fog Envelops the Animals," Dickey recounts the joy invisibility brings to the predator: "'Fog Envelops the Animals' is about hunting. In the poem, fog rolls up and envelops the protagonist.... He feels himself become invisible. We all want to be invisible, at least part of the time, but most especially the hunter does.... In this case, the hunter being exactly the same color as the fog, has total concealment. As long as he can see enough to shoot, but the

---

[53]Series 2.3, box 91k, 21.
[54]Ibid.

animals can't see him, he's in heaven."[55] Muldrow exhibits a similar feeling in his preferred method of killing, which brings his oblivious antagonist directly to him. Capitalizing on the blindness of the swordsman, Muldrow explains, "I led him with sound, he came in, he came onto my knife. I held it for him, just so" (*TS*, 175). In the snow-covered expanse of an arctic environment Muldrow feels that his invisibility and camouflage come closest to reaching their potentials; in perfect harmony with his surroundings he revels in silence, whiteness, and hunting.

Although Muldrow often speaks of camouflage in mystical, inhuman expressions, his merging also operates in terms of other human beings. During the chaos of the firebombing raid on Tokyo he endeavors to blend in with the panic-stricken Japanese masses: "Through the blasts of smoke I got into the crowd, making the turn to be in their direction and slowing down to their pace, which was a kind of fast shuffle" (*TS*, 44). Seeking to lose himself in the moving multitudes, he discards his efficient running for the herd-like shuffle of the terrified crowd. Using his mind instead of his legs, Muldrow later assumes the mental perspective of a Japanese soldier who is trying to kill him, anticipating his opponent's course of action. After having used his predatory cunning to dispatch two other servicemen, Muldrow pauses: "I changed my mind around and thought with him" (*TS*, 202). Like Ed Gentry's mental identification with Stovall's perspective in *Deliverance*, Muldrow thinks with his antagonist in order to survive—merging with the other for the purpose of its annihilation.[56]

---

[55]James Dickey, *Self-Interviews*, ed. Barbara and James Reiss (New York: Doubleday, 1970) 111.

[56]Unlike Ed, however, Muldrow uses merging in order to get into the problem-solving area of his *own* mind: "Driving along on the dregs of my gas, I tried my best to get back into my feelings and thoughts on the log train, where everything seemed so easy. Then, I could project forward and back, and get involved in the landscape of my own head" (*TS*, 217). With landscape as a metaphor for the mental topography of others and himself, Muldrow believes he can get to the essential being of his own thoughts and others', just as he becomes the embodiment of his physical surroundings.

In addition to Ed's and Muldrow's shared method of mind-merging, both are also significantly transformed by their immediate surroundings. Just as Ed is shaped by the river, becoming fluid and shifty in relation to his circumstances, Muldrow is influenced mentally by the camouflage he takes on from his various environments. Rubbing soot into his face during the bombing of Tokyo, he feels a change taking place: "As the color of my face disappeared and went to another color, there was something inside me that changed, too. It moved, and then sat still. In my mind there was a shape I couldn't exactly make out, but it seemed to be in a crouch, pulled up into itself and ready, and that was the feeling I got from the soot, the stronger the more I put on" (*TS*, 47). Putting on a physical aspect of his immediate environment triggers a response from deep inside Muldrow's consciousness. In addition to its general suggestion of his predatory nature, "the shape" inside him is strongly suggestive of what Eskimos call the *angakoq*, a being of immense power and ardor, whom Barry Lopez characterizes as "an intermediary of darkness."[57] The *angakoq* possesses the gift of *qaumaneq*:

> The inexplicable searchlight that enables him to see in the dark, literally and metaphorically. He reaches for the throat of darkness; that is the primitive, as primitive as an explosion of blood. Out hunting, in the welter of gore, of impetuous shooting, that heady mixture of joy and violence, sometimes it is possible for an outsider to feel the edge of the primitive. Unbridled, it is frightening. It also defeats starvation. And in its enthusiasm for the concrete

---

[57]Lopez, *Arctic Dreams*, 217. Strengthening *To the White Sea*'s connection to Eskimo myth, Muldrow's buddy, Tornarssuk, takes his name from a supernatural being in Eskimo legend who bestows power upon those he deems worthy. In most stories *Tôrnârssuk* serves as an attendant helper, much like an assisting Greek god, to a mortal. Although Muldrow's friend does not appear to possess any divine powers, he is present when Muldrow witnesses the sublime heart of the calving glacier. In Eskimo myth *Tôrnârssuk* often is associated with *Kokogiaq*, a great multi-legged bear.

events of life, it can defeat what weighs against the heart and soul.[58]

In the face of seemingly insurmountable odds, Muldrow summons the *angakoq* which banishes his trepidation and accentuates his predatory confidence as he crouches in the shadows of burning buildings, waiting for the right victim. Further suggestive of the *angakoq*'s presence, although Muldrow's black face makes him resemble the soot-smeared Japanese civilians, he identifies—not with them—but something, not someone, less distinct: "I was not like them, I say again; like something else" (*TS*, 47).

   Muldrow's successful use of camouflage in and around Tokyo helps him to arrive at his conscious strategy for reaching Hokkaido. After fleeing from some civilian men and hiding behind a wall, he thinks of the lynx and muses at great length on the prospect of surviving through his utilization of color:

> You need the color of the place you're in. Even in the big rush of good feeling, when the colors came over me and I felt like I could be any of them, any time of the day or night: when I felt like I could lie down in green or yellow, in purple or red, in the moonlight or the sunrise, and I could stay until I got ready to get up and go on, and nobody would know, or fall out of any of them, like a hawk: fall on somebody's back, or right into his face like a blaze of light flashing through him, or doing anything I wanted, I knew that it was only part of the truth, only part of the truth that would be, from here on. There would be lots of colors between me here and the snow fields there, between me and the ocean and the bergs, and there was not any way I could take advantage of everything between the place I was now—this wall—and where I was trying to get to. But there would be long stretches—there were bound to be long stretches—where the color was more or less the same, and

---

[58]Ibid., 217–18.

if that was true, I could find some way to tap in on it, take advantage of it, make it work for me. If there were colors in Japan, if there were colors in the world, I could go with them, be what they were. I could, damn it: I sure could. When I came on a long stretch of color—stayed in it for a day, maybe—I would try to make the best way to do it for the next day. (*TS*, 72–73)

Having already instinctually exercised his gift for concealment, Muldrow rationalizes it as a long-term practice of survival—a progressive method that can both deliver him to Hokkaido and bring him closer to the transformation he seeks.

As a result of Muldrow's oblique statements and allusions, his specific understanding of camouflage—and what it leads to—remains partially buried. As in the concept of the ghost in the machine in *Alnilam*, in which Joel has ostensibly come out on the other side of the machinery he idealizes, Muldrow's philosophy of camouflage takes him to the other side of visibility, and he even evokes a ghost when speaking about it:

To be invisible and still know what was going on, that was something. I wondered what it would be like to be a ghost. When I started thinking about camouflage, like I say, I knew what I wanted to do—no, what I *had* to do. It was going to be the way.... There ought to be places between me and the mountains and the snow fields where I could more or less pick the colors, and take them on, at least in some way. If I took my time—and I had plenty of it—I should be able to fit the color of some of my situations—hillsides, fields, woods—and tune to them by color. Maybe this wouldn't always work, and maybe I wouldn't always be able to do it, but I planned to try. It was worth it, worth a lot. It might be worth everything. (*TS*, 101)

Muldrow's assertions that he "*has*" to practice concealment and that it "might be worth everything" point to the defining metamorphosis toward which he is gravitating. Like the migratory impulse of the salmon, Muldrow's drive becomes something he lacks the power to alter: an unavoidable destiny he does not and cannot resist.

Like Joel Cahill's arrival on the other side of the machine, Muldrow's transition puts him beyond human existence and more fully into the place that surrounds him. Dickey explains:

> Muldrow wants to achieve the perfect camouflage. He believes that the perfect camouflage will enable him to cease to exist and merge with the landscape. The only thing that will give him away is his eyes. When he closes them, he thinks he can become the place. He is covered with his own blood and swan feathers when he goes out into the snow and attempts to become a landscape of snow and cold and desolation, an environment that he's always loved so much. Perhaps he's killed. It may be that death itself is the perfect camouflage. I'll leave that for the reader.[59]

Although the speeding bullets complicate the exact nature of Muldrow's ultimate fate, he fully believes that his shift into a place has the power to save him, transferring his essence to a non-human area of existence:

> From watching the animals and birds up on the muskeg, on the tundra, and on the Brooks, I've always believed that if camouflage is good enough, if it is right *exactly*, the bird or the animal will not just be invisible, it won't be there. When the rattlesnake did something so that my eyes—which can see what the others can't—couldn't pick it up, I knew I was right. My hand on the bare place on the slope, there in

---

[59]Suarez, "An Interview with James Dickey: Poet and Novelist," 130.

Japan, was like that. Like that or just about, it was almost somewhere else, or just not. (*TS*, 112)

At the conclusion of the novel, when Muldrow feels a bullet pass through him without touching him, we are either witness to the surreal impressions of a dying man or the moment of meta-morphosis in which he sheds his humanity and assumes the iden-tity of his surroundings—literally becoming "somewhere else" or "just not."[60]

Muldrow's final transformation, whether into death or a place, also rescues him from the barren solipsism of his human existence. No longer constituting a destructive and alienated self, Muldrow becomes part of the "all" that constitutes a natural environment. Such a shift suggests David Abram's use of Edmund Husserl's defense of phenomenology against the accusation of solipsism: "The field of appearances, while still a thoroughly subjective realm, was now seen to be inhabited by *multiple* subjectivities; the phenomenal field was no longer the isolate haunt of a solitary ego, but a collective landscape, constituted by other experiencing subjects as well as by oneself."[61] Constituting a connective part of a collective place, Muldrow rejoices at being "everywhere in it" (*TS*, 275). Furthermore, Abrams maintains that the premise of his philosophical and ecological book, *The Spell of the Sensuous*, asserts that "we are human only in contact, and conviviality, with what is not human,"[62] and Muldrow appears to establish the ultimate "contact," to the point that his human form no longer exists.

---

[60]Although Dickey never wrote a screenplay for *To the White Sea*, he often recorded ideas for it. At the conclusion of the film, he wanted to portray Muldrow's would-be killers as not knowing "where he is. They don't know what's happened. What has happened is that he's a place. One of the posse picks up Muldrow's red knife out of the snow and looks at it uncomprehendingly, and then they go on walking around, as the camera pulls back, and that's the end" (Ernest Suarez, "An Interview with James Dickey: Poet and Novelist," *Texas Review* 17/3–4 [Fall/Winter 1996/1997]: 131).

[61]David Abram, *The Spell of the Sensuous : Perception and Language in a More-Than-Human World* (New York: Pantheon, 1996) 37.

[62]Ibid., ix.

Although Muldrow's final transformation marks the literal death of his human existence, there are hints of his departure from the human world throughout the novel. While riding on the train and imagining various animals, he recounts, "The chute had saved my life, but this was better—better, believe me, there are better things than life" (*TS*, 144). Meditating upon the qualities of inhuman creatures, Muldrow belittles the importance of his own mortal existence, for, in becoming an inhuman place, he feels that he will have achieved a higher level of being. As Sartre says, "Let no one reproach us with capriciously creating a being of this kind; when by a further movement of thought the being and absolute absence of this totality are hypostasized as transcendence beyond the world, it takes on the name of God."[63] Having moved "beyond" the human world and into the planet's very essence, Muldrow becomes part of the inhuman order of things, which many people identify as God. And losing his human life along the way is a small price since "One who lives the life of the universe cannot be much concerned for his own."[64]

In addition to dream animals, the most powerful expressions of Muldrow's inhumanism are linked to manifestations of ice. At one point Dickey had even thought to use an epigraph concerning icebergs from *Arctic Dreams*: "I looked up at the icebergs. They so embodied the land. Austere. Implacable. Harsh but not antagonistic. Creatures of pale light."[65] Like the icebergs, Muldrow wishes to "embody the land" and his cold, inhuman harshness is part of what makes that possible. Although he is responsible for many deaths, Muldrow does not kill in inimical rage, but rather revels in his own existence—solitary and white, he, too, is a creature of pale light. Muldrow's inhumanism is also captured in another manifestation of ice. While paddling from Honshu to Hokkaido, he remembers witnessing the pure blue heart of a calving glacier:

---

[63]Jean-Paul Sartre, *The Philosophy of Jean-Paul Sartre*, ed. Cumming (New York: Vintage, 1965) 171–72.

[64]George Santayana, *Three Philosophical Poets* (Cambridge: Harvard University Press, 1945) 56.

[65]Lopez, *Arctic Dreams*, 224–25.

I had seen it, and would see it again, the real pure thing, the pure color. Believe me when I tell you that when the glacier calves off there is something that you don't get with every day.... Well, where I was heading I couldn't get enough of remembering it, the pure blue: the pure more-than-blue... It was the most intense, and the most pure, it was—well, you could say—secret, the best of it, the heart of ice, the heart you never had any idea was there, and when you saw it, knew had to be there. (*TS*, 231–32)

In *Arctic Dreams*, Barry Lopez speaks of a Lakota woman, Elaine Jahner, who holds that the religion of hunting peoples relies on the idea that "a spiritual landscape exists within the physical landscape...occasionally one sees something fleeting in the land, a moment when line, color, and movement intensify and something sacred is revealed, leading one to believe that there is another realm of reality corresponding to the physical one but different."[66] In the icebergs and the blue heart of the glacier Muldrow glimpses cold inhuman embodiments of the natural world that promise another reality. His identification with them simultaneously reminds him of something in himself and increases his desire to become part of their natural essence.

After leaving the bearded bear people, Muldrow exclaims, "I felt young, young and on top of the whole situation, to go on up north, to go *into* it" (*TS*, 157), and the final step of his inhuman evolution centers around his connection with the old hermit's great birds. More than his imaginary dream creatures, the flying predators demonstrate the bestial abilities and visionary perception he wishes to attain: "I began to transfer my feelings—or soul, or spirit, or whatever you want to call it—to them, because they did more than any other creatures for the wish I had that was most like me: not only the need to attack but to fall on something from above" (*TS*, 265). However, more than their diving attacks, Muldrow admires their vision, which fascinates him because it is

---

[66]Ibid., 245.

superior to that of any human. He reflects, "The hawk's view, which was beyond any man's. It was being able to see what you don't. It was being able to see into the snowbank, into the stone. To see beyond what any human, any man who has ever been born, could see. Like I tell you, out of the snowdrift, into the snowdrift, into the stone" (*TS*, 271). Nietzsche conceives of the average human as being "deeply immersed in illusion and dream images; their eyes glance only over the surface of things and see 'forms'; their sensation nowhere leads to truth, but contents itself with receiving stimuli and, as it were, with playing a game of touch on the back of things."[67] Muldrow admires the hawks because they see beyond surfaces and *into* the hearts of things. Possessing an inhuman visionary power, the birds apprehend the essence in all things; something Muldrow achieves only rarely, as when he glimpses the heart of the calving glacier.

Having arrived at the inhuman sensibility necessary for his transformation, Muldrow waits for the appropriate time: "All the time I'd been in Japan, all the time I'd been living, this seemed to be the truth of the thing: you can get to the perfect blend if you know exactly how to do it, and if the time is right" (*TS*, 272). Reaching at the northern tip of Hokkaido and developing his understanding of the birds, he has nothing left to accomplish as a human being. In a letter to Richard Roth,[68] Dickey explained that in the film version he envisioned Muldrow disappearing amid a heavy gust of snow while the Japanese posse fires at him.[69] Like the speaker in "Fog Envelops the Animals," Muldrow feels that "Soundlessly whiteness is eating / My visible self alive. / I shall enter this world like the dead, / Floating through tree trunks on currents / And streams of untouchable pureness" (*WM*, 80). Although he may literally be killed by the bullets, Muldrow believes with

---

[67]Friedrich Nietzsche, "On Truth and Falsity in an Extra-Moral Sense," in In *Early Greek Philosophy and Other Essays*, vol. 2 of *The Complete Works of Friedrich Nietzsche*, trans. M. A. Mügge, ed. Oscar Levy (New York: Russell & Russell, 1964) 175.

[68]The letter is dated 23 July 1996.

[69]Bruccoli and Baughman, *Crux*, 509.

Lucretius that, "The minds of living things and the light fabric of their spirits are neither birthless nor deathless."[70] Dead or transformed, he feels himself flowing out of his human existence and into the grand being of another. Whether or not the metamorphosis actually takes place, Muldrow's *Umwelt* can only believe that it has; in his dream of reality it is real enough.

---

[70]Lucretius, *On the Nature of the Universe*, trans. R. E. Latham (Harmondsworth: Penguin, 1951) 108.

CHAPTER 4

FIRE: UNPUBLISHED FICTIONAL FRAGMENTS AND SCREENPLAYS

They [the early fictional works] never did anything but show me what I couldn't do and didn't want to try to do.
—Dickey in Suarez, "An Interview with James Dickey: Poet as Novelist," 142

I just can't shake the film makers off me. They want original scripts.
— Dickey circa 1977, in Baughman, Voiced Connections, *163*

In calling this chapter "Fire" I mean to suggest the rough embers I found, half-completed and half-abandoned, among Dickey's papers at Emory University. These embers, many of them unknown and undiscussed,[1] are the miscellaneous remainders of Dickey's creative fire and constitute the final element of his fictive corpus. By necessity, because of the nature of the work (the fact that it is unpublished), the format of this chapter calls for the summary, as well as analysis, of the texts in question, which break

---

[1]Nearly all of Dickey's unpublished fiction was undiscussed and largely unknown until the publication of Hart's biography which summarized portions of it.

off into two basic categories: pre-*Deliverance* fiction and screen-plays.[2] The former category consists of an unfinished novel manuscript and four more or less completed short stories. The latter group is made up of three completed screenplays and the prospectuses for five others. I do not discuss here the screenplays for *Deliverance* and *Call of the Wild.* The screenplay for *Deliverance* was published in 1982[3] and there are several essays that consider it in relation to the novel.[4] *Call of the Wild*—a made-for-television movie which aired on NBC 19 May 1976—is a relatively straight-forward adaptation of Jack London's characters and ideas, and as such is not—apart from the distinctive nuances of his writing—the imaginative creation of Dickey. Also undiscussed here are the novels or short stories for which Dickey prepared only a page or less of very general notes[5] and the screenplay for *To the White Sea.*[6] Though interesting to examine, many of Dickey's fictional ideas never went any further than the notebook or cassette tape where they were recorded, and Dickey was famous for both spontaneously making up fictional ideas and informing people that he was working on projects which in fact did not, or never would, exist. Finally, although there are significant similarities between much of

---

[2]At one point Dickey had contemplated publishing his screenplays in a single volume under the title *Escaped Shadows.*

[3]See entry in works cited.

[4]See Ernest Suarez, "*Deliverance*: Dickey's Original Screenplay," *The Southern Quarterly* 33/2–3 (Winter–Spring 1995): 161–69; Linda Ruth Williams, "Blood Brothers," *Sight & Sound* 4 (September 1994): 16–19; James J. Griffith, "Damned if You Do, and Damned if You Don't: James Dickey's *Deliverance*," *Post Script* 5 (Spring/Summer 1986): 47–59; and R. Barton Palmer, "Narration, Text, Intertext: The Two Versions of *Deliverance*," *James Dickey Newsletter* 2/2 (Spring 1986): 2–10.

[5]For Dickey's early notes reflecting his fictional ideas see *Striking In* (in the works cited). Editor Gordon Van Ness's introductory comments on Dickey's notebooks are also quite helpful.

[6]Although he provided ideas and recommendations, Dickey never wrote a screenplay for his final published novel. The original screenplay for *To the White Sea* was adapted by David Peoples (who also wrote notable screenplays for *Blade Runner* [1982] and *Unforgiven* [1992]) and his wife Janet. After Joel and Ethan Coen obtained the rights to the movie, they developed a screenplay of their own.

Dickey's unpublished fiction and the three published novels, I have resisted the temptation to assimilate them into the "merging" thesis which is the foundation of my readings in the first three chapters. Clever critics are often successful in making any text they select fit into a theoretical blueprint they have appropriated or created. But these unpublished pieces—so varied in their subjects and concerns, and often separated by several decades—resist affected unification and, being reluctant to lock them into an enforced pattern, I have resolved to discuss each on its own terms.

Dickey's most notable work of early fiction is his manuscript novel *The Casting*, for which he began making notes in 1952.[7] As Van Ness discloses in his introduction to Dickey's notebooks, the novel's title comes "from Sir Walter Baldwin Spencer and Francis J. Gillen's anthropological study *The Native Tribes of Central Australia*." [8] The *Casting*'s first chapter begins with Julian Glass's description of his girlfriend's father, Dr. Arrington, shooting a suction-tipped arrow at a gold-fish aquarium. More than simply nervous, Julian—a young man of twenty-odd years—suffers from acute anxiety in the presence of Dr. Arrington, described as a man of "epic ugliness,"[9] and his daughter, Sara, who is critical of her father's whimsical habits. The novel's strange opening scene is explained by Julian's and Arrington's shared, though affected, interest in "cheap toys," which maintains an uneasy relationship of which Sara is the center. Although Julian is of a very sensitive nature, his extreme nervousness is explained largely by the fact that he is expected to propose to Sara, and Dickey arranged the arrow imagery to suggest the contest of suitors in *The Odyssey*—although in this case the struggle is between father and suitor. Possessing a fine artistic sensibility despite his youth, Julian relates his thoughts

---

[7]Elements of *The Casting* were fused into a novel with another title, *The Entrance to the Honeycomb*. Dickey sent a manuscript of the work to Doubleday in 1953, but Emory does not have it.

[8]James Dickey, *Striking In: The Early Notebooks of James Dickey*, ed. Gordon Van Ness (Columbia: University of Missouri Press, 1996) 7.

[9]Series 2, box 91, 3.

to the reader in an often strained, learned voice intermingled with a nervous innocence. His contemplative and impressionistic descriptions of a suburban setting are very similar to those at the beginning of James Agee's *A Death in the Family*.[10] Despite the almost overpowering tension in the initial scene, we also learn that Mrs. Arrington, a florist, like Florence Cahill in *Alnilam*, is very fond of Julian. The chapter concludes with Julian lifting weights and contemplating its importance as a hegemonic act of pure will. Dickey makes it clear that, at this point in the novel, Julian is capable only of contemplating will power and not exercising it.

In chapter 2 Julian describes the summers he spent with his uncle, from whom he has inherited a sizeable amount of money. Estranged from his father, Julian's relationships with other men—especially Dr. Arrington—are difficult for him. During a flashback sequence, Julian's father tells him how embarrassed he is after Julian plays poorly in a football game. Weeping alone in the locker room, Julian's nose begins to bleed, an incident that anticipates Hannah Pelham's sexually-triggered nosebleed in *Alnilam*.

In the section of the manuscript Dickey called "The Birthday Scene," Julian presents Sara with an engagement ring and the family rejoices while the idiot handyman, George, a kind of disfigured Orpheus, plays his harp. Dr. Arrington gives Julian a lecture on "the dangers of individuality"[11] and proclaims that success comes only to those who follow the crowd. They decide to play horseshoes and Julian is victorious, which he interprets as a reification of his superior world view. Later, Julian and Sara drive out into the country, hike up a mountain, and enter a cemetery where Sara's ancestors are buried. In this macabre setting Sara wants very much to make love but Julian refuses. Although his sister teasingly suggests that he may be sexually attracted to men, Julian later develops a powerful, though violent, physical attraction for another

---

[10]James Agee, *A Death in the Family* (New York: McDowell, Obolensky, 1957). Agee's masterpiece had not yet been published at the time Dickey was working on *The Casting*.

[11]Series 2, box 91.

woman, Laverne Coachman. His lack of sexual interest in Sara seems more a result of her physical unattractiveness.

Julian's unwillingness to consummate his relationship with Sara foils their engagement, and he goes to see his old high school friend Jack Herlong, who is a football coach. They meet at a watermelon stand near the school and plan to do something together in the near future. The next chapter opens with Julian lifting weights and then shaving his chest. Julian's weight training symbolizes his formidable, though currently repressed, will power and foreshadows his climactic battle with Taz Light-horn, a dark abusive figure. Julian admires himself in the mirror, describing his "cat-like face"[12] and crew-cut, before driving out to the Pickerel Club, a member-based lake and bar. Like Frank Cahill's pool in *Alnilam*, the facility is about to close for the year and it is the last weekend of swimming. Julian, who is becoming increasingly voyeuristic as the novel progresses, watches Laverne Coachman and Taz Light-horn play in the pool. After Taz departs, Julian has a few beers with Laverne and her friend Theodora Jakes. They talk about Taz, with whom Laverne is involved. She confesses that he is fond of beating her which seems to prick Julian's interest. Not surprisingly, Taz is a tenebrous figure with black hair and a falcon tattooed on his right bicep. Mirroring Julian's engagement to Sara, Taz has given Laverne a silver ring which is meant to resemble a coiled snake with green eyes.

Dickey called the next chapter "The Buffalo Hunters (The Effigies)," in which Jack and Theodora, and Julian and Laverne begin double-dating on a regular basis. Laverne, who is physical and outgoing, fascinates Julian in contrast to Sara, who speaks in fictional metaphors and strikes him as possessing a contemplative "oriental" quality. On the couples' third night out they go to the fairgrounds, where they linger after closing time. Having the abandoned park to themselves, they ride in a boat through a yawning devil's mouth and into a tunnel of love. The symbolic implication here is that Julian recovers Laverne and himself, both

---

[12]Ibid.

of them abused and damaged, like Orpheus traveling to Hades for
Eurydice. The boat stops in the tunnel near a Roman scene of a
woman impaled on a centurion's spear, which Laverne regards
"with delighted fascination"[13] and later appears in Julian's dream.
As they come out of the tunnel, the boat drifts up against a
concrete barrier and they engage in foreplay which fails to excite
Julian.

In the following chapter Julian has a dream in which he attains
complete dominance over a masked female dancer whose self is
defined only by her acquiescence to him. Gyrating erotically, the
masked female figure brings Julian's dream-persona into a frenzy,
which culminates in his whipping the succubus, who "shudders,
moaning gratefully."[14] Dickey also proposed a split column
technique—as in *Alnilam*—for this chapter, revealing that he had
conceived of the radical method as early as 1952. Through Julian's
conscious and unconscious actions it becomes apparent that his
sexual arousal is partially contingent upon physical abuse. Perhaps
consciously realizing this or simply acting on his voyeuristic
compulsion, he goes to a park near Laverne's apartment and, like
the protagonist in "The Fiend" (*WM*, 231–34), climbs a tree that
stands next to her window. He witnesses Taz whipping Laverne
with a belt and experiences another nosebleed. His voyeuristic
participation, coupled with his very real blood, leads to "the surge
of an uncommon energy, a spring of belief, almost an assumption,
into a kind of life I had thought impossible to me."[15] Later, Julian
confronts Taz about his activities with Laverne, grapples with him,
and bests him in a hand-to-hand struggle. Part of the tension at the
book's conclusion revolves around whether or not Julian has saved
Laverne from an abusive relationship or merely replaced Taz in the
role of brutal lover. Julian's development over the course of the
novel tends to suggest the latter.

---

[13]Ibid.
[14]Ibid.
[15]Ibid.

The focus of much of Dickey's early fiction is on the problem of human relationships, often accompanied by the protagonist's inability to separate sex and violence, and fact and fantasy. In the *Casting*, Julian overcomes his voyeuristic impotence in order to bring his sadistic fantasies to life. In essence, he has forsaken an imaginative mania for one that is real and threatens to destroy another human being. Dickey's psycho-suburban setting, forced classical allusions, and largely contrived semantics result in a lurid and complex work which utterly lacks the vivid immediacy of his published novels. However, the shortcomings of his early fiction were not lost on Dickey, who, years later, maintained it "never did anything but show me what I couldn't do and didn't want to try to do."[16] Fragmentary and overly labored, *The Casting* showed Dickey that he had little aptitude for the social and psychological themes of suburban fiction. In order to find his fictional voice, he would strip down society, reduce his casts of characters, and hint at the lurking presence of natural manifestations. He would simplify his materials and plunge more deeply into what remained.

Perhaps the best surviving piece of Dickey's early unpublished fiction is "The Eye of the Fire," which is a well-constructed short story in near-publishable form.[17] Although it is not clear when the twenty-one page manuscript was typed, Dickey was making notes for the story under various titles as early as 1952. Anticipating *Crux* and many of his poems, "The Eye of the Fire" deals with American fliers in the Pacific Theater during World War II. The first section of the story begins with two fliers named Nettles and White arriving as replacements at the base of the 649th Night Fighter Squadron. New to the war, they are described as anxious and dramatic in their behavior: White is overly boastful and Nettles a withdrawn pariah. After flying several patrols (White is a pilot and Nettles, like Dickey, a radar observer), the men take their leave in

---

[16]Ernest Suarez, "An Interview with James Dickey," *Contemporary Literature* 31/2 (Summer 1990): 142.

[17]At the time that this book went to press, "The Eye of the Fire" was forthcoming in the literary journal, *Oxford American*.

Manilla, which has just been liberated from the Japanese. Dickey does a fine job of capturing the feel of the city, "liberated and full to the throat with flies, black marketers, pimps no more than three or four years old ('Pom-pom, Joe?') and the uncontrollable flutter of lust, like the onset of fear, amid the reeling and pocked walls of its streets."[18]

In the story's third section, back at the 649th, Nettles learns that Laster, Nettles's roommate, and another man have wrecked their plane on an island still held by the Japanese. The following section records the squadron's first offensive operation using napalm. Nettles has a violently sexual reaction when the bombs explode, firing his guns into the flames and ejaculating as White pilots the plane away from the target. After the raid, when White helps him take off his parachute, he notices "a long stain resembling salt or rime on the upper part of one leg of Nettles' flying suit."[19] The severe trauma Nettles experiences is suggestive of the more contemplative guilt felt by the speaker in Dickey's poem, "The Firebombing." In the fifth section, White finishes building the officer's club and the fliers begin congregating there. Nettles confesses to Thornton Hawley, an older fatherly man who gives the boys advice, that he has burning glass in his eye and that "there's someone's bed in it, that I made, by God."[20]

In the sixth section Nettles thinks back to his childhood and remembers Elaine Shields, a woman of twenty-four with whom he was infatuated at the age of twelve. She often walked and swam with him at the beach, and always rinsed-off afterwards in an outdoor shower. Early one morning after their swim, Nettles, with the aid of a mirror, sees her bathing against the fiery brilliance of the rising sun. Speechless at the sight, he continues to watch and when Elaine sees him he flees in shame. In the next section, Nettles goes outside the officer's club where he sits down and, wracked by his guilt, sexual and otherwise, begins to rant: "I put her there, by God. Glass and fire. That's where I made her bed, a red-hot spike

---

[18]Series 2.4, box 93, folder 7, 6.
[19]Ibid., 13.
[20]Ibid., 15.

through her nipples, and her blowing and screaming and begging me. I saw it, I did it, I was there. I told them where to put her bed."[21] Nettles ineffectually tries to start a fire and the other fliers take him to his tent and put him to bed. Liggins, the commanding officer, attributes his behavior to his roommate's crash and probable death. In section eight the squadron learns that the two downed fliers are, in fact, dead, Nettles's roommate by beheading. Thus, "The Eye of the Fire" is important for its early examination of a recurrent theme—decapitation—that haunted Dickey and surfaced in various works throughout his career. In a section that anticipates Shears's revenge raid in *Crux,* the air command promises to send a B-24 to bomb the responsible Japanese if they can get a volunteer P-61 to fly in low and show them where to hit the island. Nettles opts for the mission along with Liggins. In the last section we learn that the raid is a huge success and that Nettles and Liggins have become companions. Meanwhile, White, insecure and not so boastful, is upset for having missed out on the action.

The dynamics of sex, violence, and guilt in "The Eye of the Fire" also inform "Sennacherib,"[22] a four-page narrative composed in the early fifties. Unique among Dickey's fiction, it is the first-person account of a maid who has an abusive affair with a school teacher named Sorley Pettilo. The narrator tells the story to Mrs. Wingham, a friend of Mrs. Harbelis, for whom the narrator works, and refers to both women as "Pleasure Seekers," the meaning of which is unclear. Through the narrator's rough colloquial dialogue we are able to ascertain that Sorley had seduced and manipulated her for the purpose of acting out a sexual fantasy of his own making. While his wife is out of town for a month, he takes the narrator to a bar nearly every night. Sorley, evidently a history or classics teacher, indoctrinates her with tales of ancient civilizations and conquests. The night before his wife's return, he proclaims that he wishes to leave his wife for her.

---

[21]Ibid., 17–18.
[22]Sennacherib was an ancient Assyrian king noted for his bloody battles.

Once his wife is back home however, Sorley bides his time before arranging for them to get a hotel room. Since the narrator knows "all them names he taught me, and knew how he wanted me to act,"[23] Sorley is now ready to direct his drama. In his fantasy he plays the role of the victorious King Sennacherib while the speaker is a captured Elamite maiden. Vowing that the narrator will "welcome the king's bed when I get through with you,"[24] Sorley strips her, binds her to the bed with his tie, and proceeds to spank her with his belt. Once Sorley has exhausted his passion the narrator asks to be "the bride of Sennacherib," in reply to which he begins to weep, untying her and holding her close to him. As the speaker explains, "I knew right then he wouldn't never marry me; it was too much for him. I could stand it better than he could."[25] And the narrator evidently can handle it; after concluding the story she simply moves on to a discussion of her new employer and a complimentary description of Mrs. Wingham's house. Yet, the narrator's crisp dismissal of the account also raises the possibility that the story, like Hannah Pelham's in *Alnilam*, may be designed simply to tantalize Mrs. Wingham, who is a "Pleasure Seeker." Although the term remains unexplained, it may be a reference to her hunger for erotic stories and thereby constitute a sexualized equivalent to Joel's practice of "continuous invention," in which an individual's consciousness is titillated through the power of fabricated narratives.

"Through the Loft," a short story about an estranged father and son, also foreshadows *Alnilam*. As in the novel, the father figure, Ira Block, has never laid eyes on his son Roy North, a World War II veteran who has resolved to confront his natural father. Block, of Jewish descent, had lived in the South managing hardware stores, but, after impregnating Roy's mother, had come to New York and gotten into advertising. Roy comes to see him in the big building where his office is located. Although, like Frank Cahill, Ira has never seen so much as a photograph of his own son,

---

[23]Series 2, box 95, folder 13, 3.
[24]Ibid.
[25]Ibid., 4.

he has often tried to imagine him. While tedious and somewhat stupid, Roy, like Joel, is also indolent and arrogant, distant in his personal strength. When the two meet, Roy's behavior is off-putting to Ira, who is both intimidated by and proud of his son's demeanor.

Roy proceeds to tell him why he has come, which stems from an American plane crashing into a sugar mill in the war. The first person to arrive at the crash site, Roy climbs up and through the loft of the mill in order to get down into the wrecked plane. The pilot dies while they wait for help and the other three fliers in the craft are already dead. Incidentally, many of the pilot's symptoms—facial wounds, missing teeth, probable internal bleeding—are similar to those from which Joel suffers after his wreck. Presumably this incident, which underscores the fragility of life, has caused Roy to seek out his origins. Block, though, will have nothing of it when Roy belligerently asks him for a loan to get a garage started. Rejected by both his father and step-father, a drunkard who never took responsibility for his son, Roy smiles "cruelly," walking out of the building as the story ends. Having nearly connected when Roy tells the story of the downed pilot, the two are alienated once more after Roy combatively asks for financial assistance. The imaginary bond Block contemplates disappears as he realizes that he is conversing with a total stranger. This has important implications for *Alnilam* in which Frank never has the opportunity to speak with Joel and is constantly surprised at the things he learns about him. As a result, and fueled by the things the Alnilam members say about Joel, Frank idealizes his son to an extent that empowers the Alnilam group and endangers the base.

Dickey's interest in the aesthetics of sexual encounters involving spankings[26]—Taz and Laverne in the *Casting*, Sorley and

---

[26]Hart asserts that Dickey's obsession with paddling stemmed from the hazing he underwent as a freshman at Clemson. Although Dickey's roommate claimed he was paddled, Dickey vehemently denied that he was ever subject to such a ritual (Henry Hart, *James Dickey: The World as a Lie* [New York: Picador

the narrator in "Sennacherib," Ed and Martha in the Jacques de Spoelberch manuscript of *Deliverance*, and Joel/Frank and Hannah Pelham in *Alnilam*—is reflected in an untitled, six-page work I shall refer to as "The Ring of Girls."[27] Unlike the others, however, there is no male presence in the story, aligning it more closely with *Alnilam*'s fictional prison-beating which Hannah Pelham recounts to Joel (and later to Frank) in order to arouse him sexually. As in Hannah's story, the action in "The Ring of Girls" stems from an authority conflict between women. Shirley, an assertive and invidious young woman, has in some way caused trouble for a powerful club or clique at a girls' school. As Mirabell, referred to as "the president," explains to her, "You've already ruined it [the club]. Thornton [presumably the principal] took away our charter this morning. None of us likes that, Shirley."[28]

Having conveniently lured Shirley out to a house in the country, the president gives her three opportunities to apologize before having the ring of young women close in, pin her to a bed, and disrobe her. Mirabell and then "a big black-headed girl" proceed to slap her bottom repeatedly with "a small thin dog-whip." One of the interesting dynamics of the story is how Dickey describes the change in Shirley's demeanor from truculent resistance to outraged embarrassment, in the first moments of the spanking, to crushed submission at the end. This episode suggests the narrative of Hannah Pelham, a tough foul-mouthed young woman, although she owes her willing submission to Joel—to his charisma, his psychological power—and not to the characters in the fictional story she relates.

In both "The Ring of Girls" and *Alnilam* Dickey is interested in the interaction between physical actions and psychological control, and it is significant that Hannah comes to enjoy both the slide-rule spankings and her own made-up story to a substantial degree. Like

---

USA, 2000] 53–55). Whether or not Dickey was actually spanked, Hart claims that he later subjected various lovers to role-playing paddlings (457).

[27]The work is untitled and the first sentence reads, "The ring of girls closed silently behind her." Series 2, box 96, folder 12, 1.

[28]Series 2, box 96, folder 12, 1.

Temple Drake in Faulkner's *Sanctuary*,[29] she becomes complicit to a significant extent in the physical and psychological drama to which she is victim. Although Shirley has not yet been "initiated" to the extent Hannah and Temple are, the implication is that she soon will be. As Mirabell promises her, "We're going to keep you here, naked, for three days. Anytime you do or say anything we don't like, you go back on that bed. You understand?"[30] As an anticipation of Hannah's narrative and the hegemonic influence of cliques, "The Ring of Girls" is an important precursor to *Alnilam.*

Considered together, Dickey's early fiction is important mostly for the tentative styles and ideas he experimented with in finding his voice, a number of which would surface again in *Alnilam.* After the publication of *Deliverance*, Dickey began working in earnest on the story that eventually would become *Alnilam.* Although he no longer dabbled in experimental novels and short stories, the success of the film version of *Deliverance* opened his eyes to the kind of money he could make writing screenplays. The movie's success also led opportunistic agents to encourage his screenplay writing, even when the ideas were less than promising. As Dickey said in 1977, "I just can't shake the film makers off me. They want original scripts,"[31] and he did in fact spend significant amounts of time on screenplays, producing three original ones, excluding *Call of the Wild,* and five other prospectuses.

In the late 1970s Dickey spent a considerable quantity of time composing a 141-page screenplay entitled *Gene Bullard*.[32] The project, existing in several drafts, was undertaken in conjunction with Charles Fries, an executive producer then working with Metro Goldwin Mayer. The movie opens in Elijay, Georgia, "a small southern city-scape. It is an unappetizing-looking town, a typical

---

[29]William Faulkner, *Sanctuary* (New York: J. Cape and H. Smith, 1931).

[30]Series 2, box 96, folder 12, 6.

[31]Ronald C. Baughman, ed., *The Voiced Connections of James Dickey: Interviews and Conversations* (Columbia: University of South Carolina Press, 1989) 163.

[32]Dickey had conceived of *Gene Bullard* as early as 1974—its title then was *Crownfire*—but did not work on it in earnest for another two years.

southern industrial village, with [sic] fairly shabby whitewashed storefronts, a lot of glass and cheap furniture in the shop-windows, and we COME-IN [this is a camera direction] on these."[33] After the camera drifts over and around several townspeople, it cuts to Gene Bullard,[34] "leaning against a 'meter-maid' type of vehicle" and making out a parking ticket. Dickey describes Bullard as "a good-looking fellow, of the curly-headed country type."[35] The camera then catches the sun striking off of his sheriff's badge. Gene was a local sports star in high school and one of the locals challenges him to use his famous basketball pick move against him, claiming he can stop it. Gene fetches his basketball and performs the maneuver against two locals, shooting the ball into a wire garbage can. The locals compliment his feat and recount his exceptional high school career. Yet, unlike Updike's Harry "Rabbit" Angstrom,[36] Bullard does not live in the glories of the past and his basketball exhibitions are more for the amusement of the townspeople than any personal desire to show off. The camera then cuts to a softball game and a pitcher with a "hard, gum-chewing, cracker, mill-girl, determined face."[37] This is Beth Culcashure, whom Dickey hoped would be played by Karen Black.[38] The screenplay continues to cut to different scenes, introducing the two other main characters and the

---

[33]Series 2.5, box 99, 1.

[34]In the screenplay Dickey lists James Caan as Gene Bullard (Series 2.5, box 99, 7). Caan is perhaps best known for his role as the dying football player Brian Piccolo in *Brian's Song* (1971). However, he also appeared as the eldest Corleone son in *The God Father* (1972), for which he received an Academy Award nomination for Best Supporting Actor. Among his other films are *Freebie and the Bean* (1974) and *Rollerball* (1974).

[35]Series 2.5, box 99, 2.

[36]John Updike, *Rabbit, Run* (New York: Alfred A. Knopf, 1960).

[37]Series 2.5, box 99, 9.

[38]Black became an actress of note after *Easy Rider* (1969), in which she worked with Peter Fonda, Dennis Hopper, and Jack Nicholson. She would appear with Nicholson the following year in *Five Easy Pieces* (1970) for which she received an Academy Award nomination. Among her other movies are *The Great Gatsby* (1974) and Alfred Hitchcock's last film, *The Family Plot* (1976).

people Dickey hoped would play them: Ernest Borgnine[39] as the villainous Makens, and Janet Hawkins as Lila, the harp player.

The action of the movie begins with Gene driving out to the cotton mill where Beth works. In the course of their conversation we learn that Beth wishes to marry Gene but that he has reservations; it is obvious that they have been involved for some time. The plot then shifts to a more general sequence of events: the first night of the town fair gets underway and there is a lot of Appalachian music and Southern arts and crafts; all of the main characters are present. During the fair, Lila—the harp player who is also a religious fanatic—is named the Chenille Queen and Jimbo—one of Makens' cronies—the best dancer. The town tradition is for them to go out that evening, which they do. Lila brings Jimbo back to her trailer where she introduces him to her eight-foot-long rattlesnake, hoping that her snake-handling faith will help bring Jimbo to God; they end up in bed together. The screenplay then cuts back to Makens who is plotting to steal the mill payroll with the help of his goons. Next, there is a somewhat humorous sequence in which a journalist from Atlanta comes to Elijay to do a story on country life. He is given a tour of the area by a town councilman who takes him to a church picnic and tells him a tall-tale concerning a man-eating beast called the Buddyro. Later that night the town councilman arranges to have a big dog, made up like the hound of the Baskervilles, with powder and fake wings, jump down out of a tree and chase the stricken journalist. From this scene we cut to Lila's trailer, where it is surprising to find Lila and Gene naked together in bed. After Gene leaves, Lila summons

---

[39]Borgnine's film career took off in 1953 when he won the role of Sergeant "Fatso" Judson in *From Here To Eternity* (1953). That memorable part led to numerous supporting roles in a steady string of dramas and westerns. Borgnine was able to avoid type casting in 1955 by landing the part of Marty Piletti, a sensitive butcher, in *Marty*, for which he won an Academy Award. Throughout the 50s and early 60s, Borgnine gave memorable performances in films such as *The Catered Affair* (1956) with Bette Davis, *The Vikings* (1958) and *Barabbas* (1962). Later notable films include *The Dirty Dozen* (1967), *The Wild Bunch* (1969), *The Poseidon Adventure* (1972) and *Emperor of the North Pole* (1973).

her snake which slithers its way onto the bed, sliding up between her legs and breasts to her open mouth which receives its head.

By this point in the screenplay, it becomes apparent that the film's meandering plot needs some refining. The anecdotal scenes, responsibly composed and interesting to read, lack sufficient relevance to the central dramatic action: Makens' robbery of the cotton mill payroll. Yet, the screenplay continues on its whimsical course, describing next a basketball game in which Joby—Gene's high school teammate and also Lila's brother, now working with Makens—and Bullard challenge Floyd, a local store clerk, and Beth. At one point in the game Beth, who happens to be a superb female athlete, blocks Gene's famous shot, which shames him but earns his respect. In the next scene the robbery finally takes place in which Makens carries away the mill payroll and also kidnaps Mr. Lundeen—the factory manager—, his wife, and son. At a stoplight Corbett—Gene's high-strung deputy—sees the Lundeens in a car with Makens and, thinking it strange, pulls them over. Makens proceeds to gun down Corbett with his .45. After the car speeds away, a crow and then several crows alight next to Corbett's blood-soaked body and begin circling it in hungry anticipation. When Gene sees Corbett's body he contemplates it solemnly and then, in a ritualistic manner suggestive of many Dickey poems, touches him with the tips of his fingers and then licks the blood from them, whispering, "This'll give me the power to stand against those sons of bitches. They can't stand against me. After this, nobody can."[40]

Having glimpsed Joby with Makens at the fair, Gene perambulates to Lila's trailer in order to establish the whereabouts of her brother. Joby, who has helped Makens find a hiding place, has stopped by to see his sister and, when Bullard arrives, hides in the bedroom. When he overhears that Gene and Lila are lovers Joby rushes forward and sucker-punches Gene before taking off in his vehicle. A car-chase ensues in which Gene overtakes Joby, who loses control and crashes horribly in a burst of flames. Pinned inside the car, Joby is literally burned alive while he begs for Gene

---

[40]Series 2.5, box 99, 103.

to shoot him, which he finally does out of mercy. Meanwhile, believing he needs another hostage, Makens sends his goon Leon to abduct Lila. Claiming she can't find her shoes, she gives Leon a flashlight and asks him to help her locate them; Leon is struck by the serpent and stumbles out of the trailer, dying in venomous agony. Acting on a tip from Beth—who used to date Joby and knows his favorite haunts—, Gene and Beth go to the old sharecropper's place where Makens is hiding out. As they fight through the underbrush they discover the bodies of the Lundeens, which have been mutilated by Makens: the son, Andy, has been decapitated and the head has been placed in a tree crotch, a cigar dangling from the slightly parted lips. Failing to find Makens at the sharecropper house, Beth and Gene go back to town. In the meantime, Makens, blaming the deaths of Joby and Leon on Bullard, has resolved to kill Gene. Combing the town for him, he runs across Gene in his meter-maid vehicle and another car chase ensues which carries the men out into the country. Gene runs out of gas and Makens gets out of his car, preparing to kill him. At this point Beth, who has followed them, rams her Jeep into Makens's car which erupts into flames, catching the surrounding woods on fire. Through the fire Makens sees Gene and fires at him, but Gene employs his basketball move, using a pine tree as a pick, and vanishes into the flames. As Makens looks for him in vain, Gene steps up behind him and shoots him in the back of the head, execution style. In the wake of all this Gene and Beth are married.

Although it is steeped in sensationalism and cliche, *Gene Bullard* has a number of affinities with tropes from Dickey's other fiction, most notably the setting, which is reminiscent of Aintry in *Deliverance*. In fact, Gene's last name is the same as that of the Aintry sheriff in Dickey's first novel. Though younger than the Bullard of *Deliverance*, Gene has the same easy-going, "good-ol'-boy" demeanor of his precursor, who wishes to avoid disquieting controversies so that his seemingly pastoral town may die peacefully. Gene enjoys the simple drama of writing parking tickets and initially is overmatched when he finds out that he has a dangerous killer stalking his town. Just as the elder Bullard has

Deputy Queen to fuel his suspicions, Gene's deputy, Corbett, is extraordinarily mistrustful and high-strung. On the first night of the town fair he observes Makens' group and offers some prophetic remarks on their criminal appearance, and it is this very power of observation that gets him killed when he sees the Lundeens with Makens and decides to pull them over.

Dickey's portrayal of rural Georgia life is very positive, even to the point of bucolic sentimentality. The journalist from Atlanta, like the figure in Dickey's coffee-table book *Wayfarer*, is impressed by the rich culture—music, sewing, storytelling—and powerful sense of community in Elijay. The locals jest with each other and discuss humorous local legends like Gene's jumpshot and the existence of the Buddyro. The industrial mill, instead of homogenizing the town, has more or less been assimilated into its culture. The screenplay also possesses competing portrayals of two traditional Southern female types: Lila, the seemingly virginal religious woman, and Beth, a wonderful specimen of fearless, back-talking white trash. Dickey undermines Lila's religious faith by illustrating how she has come to associate it with sex: her willingness to sleep with Jimbo and Gene, and the overpowering symbolic presence of her eight-foot rattlesnake. Even Gene, despite his myopic literalness, recognizes Lila's hypocrisy and chastises her for it when trying to ascertain Joby's whereabouts. When she tells him it's none of his business he replies heatedly: "Don't tell me what my business is. I've screwed you so many times—you and your goddamned religion and your white dresses that you think make you look like the Virgin Mary, and your crazy snakes—now you tell me where your brother is. People are being killed and kidnaped all over the place, I don't give a damn that I've screwed you so many times that if you've had so many of my pricks sticking out of you as I've stuck in you, you'd look like a porcupine."[41] An important dynamic of Lila's character is to what extent she is perverted by religion and to what degree she uses the myth of Southern womanhood to further her private sexual pleasure.

---

[41]Ibid., 114.

Through Lila, as he does with the speaker in "May Day Sermon" (*WM*, 287–96), Dickey criticizes the effects of zealous religion and conservative tropes on the women who are forced to live by them.

A more healthy feminine existence belongs to Beth Culclashure who says what she wants and does as she pleases. Beth's last name—Culclashure[42]—was also Hannah's last name in early versions of *Alnilam* and Dickey even uses the same line in both works to describe the two women: "Rougher than a night in jail in South Georgia."[43] Though Beth is not dying and Hannah is no athlete, the women are essentially the same character. Dickey celebrates Beth as a woman of action: she pitches softballs, stuffs Gene's jumpshot, and saves his life by ramming her Jeep into Makens' car. In the last part of the screenplay she basically makes a man of Gene, telling him how to confront Makens and urging him to be puissant. Gene's decision to marry her over Lila at the end underscores his appreciation of her individualistic resourcefulness over the illusory nature of Lila's pedestaled, though decadent, demeanor.

The last important character is Makens, a natural killer. The word "killer" immediately calls to mind Muldrow, but—apart from the high body count—there is little similarity between them. Muldrow's sensibility is primitive, intermixed with elements of mysticism; Makens's is dramatic—he sees himself as a great villain in the narrative of life. More than once when greeting one of his stooges, Makens exclaims, "Well met," a reference to Shakespearean dialogue. Makens also is pleased when the Lundeen boy calls him a "master criminal," underscoring the fact that he perceives himself as an artistic villain, a man of creative genius, designing and carrying out complex plots. There is also an unlikely connection between Makens and Lewis Medlock, whom Dickey

---

[42]Culclashure was the maiden name of Paula Goff, Dickey's long-time literary assistant. The backgrounds of Beth and Hannah are based partly on Goff's life.

[43]Ibid., 13.

describes as an obsessive enthusiast.[44] Dickey says of Makens, "His eyes glitter with the same paranoid look of the enthusiast, whether he is committing murder or engaged in festivity. It is all the same with him. There are people like this, and we all know them."[45] Makens is the character Lewis might have been had he channeled his formidable will power into a career of criminal intrigue and constant murder, instead of weightlifting and archery. With the possible exception of the rapists in *Deliverance*, Makens is the only definitively evil character Dickey created in his fiction.

In a personal note dated 6 February 1981 Dickey pondered the idea of turning the script of *Gene Bullard* into a novel.[46] Although he never actively pursued the transition, Dickey—while finishing *Gene Bullard*—was composing another full-length screenplay entitled *The Sentence*. The 136-page work was completed in 1979 in conjunction with Malcolm Stuart, a producer at Charles Fries Productions, and is the story of Stanley Hollis, "a professor of physics at a small southern university."[47] Stanley is middle-aged and not very well-known in his field, but he has very far-ranging interests, from literature and poetry to music and hypnosis. We witness his broad learning in an early scene which takes place in a lecture hall. He is talking about the reality of the ocean and makes a qualification between the sea without and the sea within. Whereas the sea without is reducible to hydrodynamic equations, the sea within is only articulated through art, and he reads part of a poem by Matthew Arnold. The next scene takes place in a student's apartment where a party is going on. One of the students proposes a "generational experiment" in which Stanley—who has never consumed recreational drugs—smokes as much marijuana (the narcotic of the younger generation) as possible, while a female student named Lou Ann drinks as much liquor (the narcotic of

---

[44]When the Atlantans discuss the burial of the hillman in *Deliverance*, Lewis bears a countenance of "humorous conspirational craftiness, his look of calculated pleasure, his enthusiast's look" (*DL*, 126).

[45]Ibid., 29.

[46]Series 2.5, box 99, folder 10.

[47]Series 2.5, box 99e, 1.

Stanley's generation) as she can. After answering some questions about how they feel, Lou Ann asks Stanley to give her a ride home. Stanley begins experiencing powerful hallucinations as he drives and becomes mesmerized by the patterns he sees in the headlights of an approaching car. A head-on collision ensues in which Lou Ann and the other driver are killed. Stanley is convicted of involuntary manslaughter and sentenced to six years at the state facility near Firebreak Mountain.

Stanley's cell-mate at the prison is a black man named Cleveland Hawkins, with whom he strikes up an enduring friendship. Later, when Stanley makes a satirical remark about folding laundry, he is sent to the warden, Mr. Strasser, who offers him a job in the prison library with the understanding that he will try and ferret out how drugs are getting into the prison. Stanley refuses this offer since he does not wish to betray any of the prisoners and the warden places him in indefinite solitary confinement. When Stanley is let out of solitary he returns to the cell he shares with Cleveland. One day during the exercise period the big prison bully Crosscut takes an orange from a prisoner with whom Stanley is talking. When Stanley protests Crosscut strikes him to the ground with a blood-drawing backhand before he is restrained by the guards. Rising, Stanley pulls a button from his shirt and, looking at Crosscut, begins swinging it back and forth slowly while talking softly. He succeeds in hypnotizing Crosscut and then proceeds to humiliate him, making him peck at the ground and crow as if he were a chicken. In the next scene the warden asks Stanley if he would like to teach some classes which Stanley agrees to do. Although he clashes with Strasser on a number of issues, he explains to Cleveland that "there's infinite energy in...the learning process. Everything new you learn, you become somebody else. Better than you were. You know more, and you know deeper. Life opens up. And it opens down. And it widens out. Because of it, you *live* more. And that's got to matter."[48] Stanley begins teaching the inmates the fundamental principles of

---

[48]Ibid., 71.

physics using simple metaphors and examples: he defines space, for example, by holding his hands out in front of him and telling them that space is what lies between them. A lecture on the sun, the stars, and the universe—which the prisoners are able to follow—grows out of his simple illustration. As the inmates learn more they begin to trust him and even Crosscut comes and asks him about the kind of "magic" he had practiced on him. Stanley's status in the prison community continues to grow with the prisoners as well as Strasser. He even puts on a production of *Waiting for Godot* with the roles of Vladimir and Estragon ironically played by two men on death row, and Dickey humorously includes the play's dialogue about being hanged: "Hmm. It'd give us an erection."[49] Later on, the death row inmates perform Gilbert and Sullivan songs, much to the amusement of the prison population.

One day as Stanley and Crosscut take out the garbage, Stanley asks him if he remembers anything from when he was hypnotized, asserting that time may change in hypnotic states, and that the disappeared self may go to a place in the past or future. Responding "like a man who has received the word of God,"[50] Crosscut says that wherever he was there was fire all around him. In the next scene Malley—a racist gung-ho prison guard—tells Crosscut he'd "pimp his own mother,"[51] to which Crosscut responds by strangling him to death. Crosscut, with whom Stanley has formed a close bond, is dispatched in the electric chair which saddens and angers Stanley. After Stanley repairs Strasser's television so that he can watch the Super Bowl, the warden offers to do a favor for him. Stanley asks that he be allowed to channel more power into his classroom/laboratory so that he might conduct better experiments. He asks for this in the hopes that he can foil the death of Danny, a death row inmate who is scheduled to go to the chair. Making a number of calculations and figures, Stanley is able to determine the current he needs and explains to Cleveland, "The figures have spoken. The averages have come out. No more death. The elements

---

[49]Ibid., 92.
[50]Ibid., 99.
[51]Ibid., 102.

are with us. God is with us. The cold is with us."[52] Using an electrical current, Stanley is able to burn a hole in the electric fence and make the cell doors swing open. As chaos ensues, the death row inmates and a number of other prisoners escape through the fence. During the chaotic melee, a guard shoots and kills Stanley, who is not trying to escape. The screenplay concludes with Cleveland provoking a strike at the prison.

Stanley, like Dickey, is an academic figure and several of his pedagogical remarks come from Dickey's own lectures; however—like so many of Dickey's other fictional protagonists—he has strong similarities with Joel Cahill. Chief among these is his arcane approach to science, which makes many of his achievements have the appearance of magic. He also possesses the gift of putting complex ideas in simple, though unorthodox, terms. His unusual qualities earn the trust of his fellow inmates, who learn from him and are influenced by him, culminating in a destructive act of defiance, suggestive of Alnilam's chaotic revolt at Peckover.[53] Underlying the action in the Sentence is the basic principle that knowledge is power. Energized, like the cadets in Alnilam, by the teachings of an appropriate martyr the inmates are equipped with a convenient catalyst to exercise the principles they have learned.

Although Dicky had composed lengthy screenplays for both projects, Gene Bullard and the Sentence failed to attract interested directors and production companies. Recognizing their shortcomings—namely, their overly imaginative use of generic and sensationalistic characters, plots, and milieus—Dickey resolved that his next screenplay would be more thoroughly researched and realistic. Studying the Gold Rush and drawing upon his television adaptation of Call of the Wild, he planned that his new project would constitute a work of historical fiction, as well as a snowy thriller. Klondike, as the 119-page screenplay came to be called, follows the gold-motivated expedition of two men, Delmore Schwartz and Victor, into the turn-of-the-century Yukon Territory.

---

[52]Ibid., 128.

[53]Dickey also drew on the central event in Ben Greer's first novel Slammer (New York: Atheneum, 1975) for Cleveland's instigation of the riot.

Encountering each other while on business in Seattle, Victor—a romantic from Charleston, South Carolina—quickly falls under the charismatic spell of Delmore, a Jewish New Yorker based largely on the poet of the same name. Together, they buy equipment and make their way north aboard the *Humboldt*, a reference to Saul Bellow's Pulitzer Prize-winning novel, *Humboldt's Gift*,[54] in which Delmore Schwartz appears as the dead, though lingering, Von Humboldt Fleischer.

Delmore's and Victor's obvious inexperience on the boat and catastrophic disembarkment is set in relief against the calm efficiency of Jesse, a veteran prospector. Losing a portion of their supplies during their tortuous wade/swim from the boat to the shore, Victor and Delmore collapse in exhaustion before heading inland. Before they depart, however, Delmore hires Native Americans to help shoulder their gear. Dickey hoped that Delmore's interchange with the indigenous people would underscore the dynamics of his character: "What some of the other prospectors, such as Jesse, construe as self-indulgent foolishness or even weakheadedness, the Indians see as a sign of favor, of grace, of being one [of] the 'touched,' or chosen."[55] Indeed, by turns, Delmore and Victor are unrealistically impractical and admirably idealistic. On the trail to Sheep Camp they suffer a number of setbacks together and begin forming the psychological bond necessary for their survival. The men are also brought together by the arrival of snow, which Victor has never seen and Delmore believes is magical. Dickey explains, "For these two it is like coming into a new world of purity and silence together."[56]

Arriving at Sheep Camp, Delmore and Victor prepare for their ascent toward the Chilkoot Pass. The idealism of the former is emphasized again when he sees Jesse put down a sick horse and berates him at length. What Jesse believes is a logical and humane action appears brutal and needless to Delmore, who is unable to compromise under any circumstances "the uniqueness and

---

[54]Saul Bellow, *Humboldt's Gift* (New York: Viking Press, 1975).
[55]Series 2.5, box 99, 43.
[56]Ibid., 47.

preciousness of life."[57] When they arrive at the base of the pass, they encounter Hugh Wallace, a transportation specialist who is impressed by Victor's mastery of the sliderule and offers him a job. Out of loyalty to Delmore he refuses and the incident brings them closer together. After their arduous ascent of the Chilkoot Pass, the men descend to Lake Lindeman where they set up a base-camp. The two resolve to float down to Lake Bennett, and Victor designs a boat which the two of them construct over a lengthy period of time. After two white-water sequences, which nearly destroy their boat, the men arrive at Dawson City where they spend large amounts of time searching for an available claim. The two men eventually buy into Jesse's claim and leave Dawson City for the mine. Along the way Jesse explains to Delmore the importance of being "practical and non-dreaming,"[58] which Delmore shrugs off. Making slow progress at the mine, Victor resolves to construct a machine to assist in the digging. Their bad luck continues and eventually the machine explodes, killing Delmore and Jesse. Ironically, the dig in which the men are killed yields a small amount of gold. The story concludes with Victor selling the claim.

Not surprisingly, Delmore's charisma and poetic imagination align him with Joel Cahill. He says of his Talmudic training, "The rabbis can teach you how to *prove* anything; it doesn't matter whether it's true or not. That's the last thing that matters."[59] As in Joel's utopia, the skill and drama of a related event take precedence over relative truth and falsity. As he did with Joel, Dickey wanted to emphasize Delmore's "isolation, his role-playing, and the people in literature and history and philosophy with whom he identifies."[60] However, his romantic idealizations fail to account for the harsh realities of the Yukon. The impractical yearnings of Delmore and Victor are offset by the practical experience of Jesse. Like Muldrow he is a master organizer; Dickey explains that on the ship "his

---

[57]Ibid., 51.
[58]Ibid., 99.
[59]Ibid., 73.
[60]Ibid.

equipment is packed, solid and safe and completely arranged."[61] During the boat sequence, Dickey wanted to illustrate the "child-like and naive"[62] qualities of prospectors, and Jesse—a serious adventurer—is the antithesis of this. Finally, Just as Delmore suggests Joel Cahill in his charismatic mysticism, Victor resembles Stanley Hollis in his mastery of the sliderule. As reapplied manifestations of other Dickey characters, Victor and Delmore lack many distinctive qualities of their own, a condition that weakens the screenplay as a whole.

Dickey was also unable to distance himself from Joel Cahill in several of the short film summaries he developed. In his prospectus for "The Spell" Dickey describes the project as an exploration of "the intersection between politics and religion, especially as it evidences itself in the South."[63] The protagonist, thirty-two-year-old Joshua Daniels, appears out of nowhere at a rural Southern church in the village of Wedgefield. Joshua becomes minister of the small congregation and we learn by degrees "that he is a spell-binder, that is, he can cast the spell over the people, over his congregations, and over just about anybody he chooses to cast it upon."[64] He lives in a room at the house of Hannah Crewes, a local widow who takes in boarders, and we learn about Joshua's theological views from his conversations with her. For example, he asserts, "I really belong to all religions. I believe in the religion of the Lord as He created the living earth and I don't believe that people should be bound down in little groups."[65] Joshua's obsessive desire to unify all people under a single idea spills over into politics as his evangelical fame spreads throughout the country.

Joshua eventually wins a big election, possibly for governor or president, on a bizarre fundamentalist/anti-Semitic/euthanasia ticket. He somehow gains the popular support of voters, who chant for him in a "ritualistic" and "fanatical" manner. Joshua also

---

[61]Ibid., 33.
[62]Ibid., 35.
[63]Series 2.5, box 99e, 1.
[64]Ibid., 2.
[65]Ibid., 3.

experiences voices and visions on a regular basis, but it is implied
that he is either insane or is hearing the voice of the devil. In one of
his visions an alligator appears in his bedroom and sings "Racing
with the Moon" in the voice of Vaughn Monroe.[66] The main
platform of Joshua's political program is mandatory euthanasia for
all citizens over the age of sixty-five. Using a convincing
fundamentalist theology of his own making, Joshua discusses the
advantages "of sending the human soul to God before it is
humiliated by a crippled and seniled body."[67] At the age of sixty-
five, "men and women have earned the right to glory" and are
given leave to accept their eternal reward.

Like much of Dickey's other fiction, "The Spell" contains
themes that eventually appear in *Alnilam*. Chief among these is the
nature of despotic power and how masses may be manipulated by a
compelling figure, like Josh or Joel Cahill, with sufficient charisma.
Like Joel, Joshua—in the process of employing his spell—uses a
great deal of mystical poetry, particularly haiku, in his sermons.
Josh's followers being "fanatics," Dickey also exhibits how largely
subjective ideas—fundamentalist theology, anti-Semitism, euthanasia—triumph over reason if the cultural conditions are
appropriate for the right leader. Just as Dickey hints that Joel may
have been partially perverse, Joshua's visions have the
characteristics of delusional hallucinations but also provide him
with ideas that increase his power and popularity. As with Joel, the
reader is affected by Joshua's charisma yet repelled by many of his
principles. However, with his particularly unsavory agendas of
anti-Semitism and ageism, Joshua constitutes a far more repulsive
figure than Joel Cahill.

---

[66]Vaughn Monroe was a popular singer of the 1940s who had a number of
nicknames alluding to his deep voice: "The Voice with Hairs on Its Chest" and
"Old Leather Tonsils" are but two. Among his hits are "There! I've Said It
Again," "Let It Snow! Let It Snow! Let It Snow!," "Ballerina," and "Riders in the
Sky." The last song signaled Monroe's attempt at moving into Hollywood's
singing-cowboy genre and he starred in two westerns in the early fifties: *The
Singing Guns* and *The Toughest Man in Arizona*.

[67]Series 2.3, box 106, folder 23.

Dickey also used Joel's qualities to shape the nameless protagonist of "The Buzzer, " a single-page film prospectus. An outstanding basketball player, the main character is also a "natural player," suggesting Joel's prodigious and in-born mastery of flying. Further echoing Joel, the protagonist excels at basketball but simultaneously considers it and its accompanying qualities "beneath him." Sensitive and withdrawn, his favorite subject is philosophy and Dickey planned that much of the film would involve "people trying to break through his reserve and 'make a human being of him.'"[68] Cold, aloof, and incredibly talented, the star hoopster is disgusted by the mob-like vulgarity of college basketball. Striking back in a manner suggestive of Alnilam's subversive graduation-day melee, he ruins his team's chance to win a national championship by throwing "the ball down, and [walking] off the court as the buzzer sounds."[69] Thus, his final act as an athlete is a repudiating negation of everything for which competitive sports stand.

Although it too centers around an athlete, no such nihilistic despair informs "The Olympian," a four-page screenplay prospectus containing bits of dialogue for imagined scenes. "The Olympian"—surely the mildest and least promising of Dickey's screenplay ideas—was co-conceived by Dickey and Tom Huey[70] in 1978 and concerns an aging math teacher's dream of running in the Olympics.[71] The teacher, George McPherson, is talking to a group of students after school one day when a boy offers to show him a karate move he had just learned. The boy unintentionally delivers a devastating kick to George's abdomen, rupturing his pancreas which brings on a form of diabetes. As a result of his new

---

[68]Series 2.5, box 98a.

[69]Ibid.

[70]North Carolina poet (1950–).

[71]Dickey's brother Tom had once failed to make the Olympic team in the 400 meters and, even at the age of fifty-three, Dickey still entertained fantasies about running in the summer games. Hart maintains Dickey told one lover, "I keep thinkin'…that if I get back into trainin', I could be an Olympic runner even now" (Hart, *James Dickey*, 570).

condition George must eat something every fifteen minutes and exercise a great deal. Some time later George is talking to the track coach after school one day and the coach, on a whim, asks him to run his fastest 400 meters. George does it and the coach is astonished to find that the time is about two seconds off that of world-class runners. At the coach's insistence, George begins running in local competitions and eventually works his way up to national meets, finishing second in an AAU event which qualifies him for the Olympic trials. At the trials George finishes third, earning himself a spot on the team.

The last part of the film takes place at the Olympics, where George—the oldest sprinter in Olympic history—rooms with a young runner named Dennis who spends all his time carousing. George is more or less alienated from most of the athletes by his age, which is advantageous in that it allows him to focus on his training. Among the people he encounters are Tanya, a Russian athlete who wants to defect, and the heavy favorite in the 400, an unnamed Haitian who jokes with George and warns him, "I put the voodoo on you."[72] Not surprisingly, George wins his race, coming from behind in the obligatory sports-movie fashion. The film concludes with his farewells to Dennis and Tanya.

Although "The Olympian" appears to have nothing in common with Dickey's other fictional projects, it does contain themes that appear elsewhere in his work. Chief among these is the screenplay's preoccupation with diabetes[73] which haunted Dickey throughout his life. George suffers from the disease but, in a strange sense, is also empowered by it. His form of the disease forces him to eat almost continuously, which dramatically speeds up his metabolism, increases his energy level, and forces him to exercise a great deal. The implication is that George could not have attained his world-class level of performance without the "aid" of the disease. Another recurring theme in Dickey's poetry is the aging athlete.[74] Combining the wisdom of his years with the pure vigor of

[72]Series 2.5, 99d, 2.
[73]See, for example, the first section of his poem "Diabetes" (*WM*, 299–300).
[74]See, for example, "The Sprinter at Forty" (*WM*, 27–29).

athleticism, George becomes for Dickey an enviable ideal man. In effect, George lives out every aging athlete's dream by returning to his sport, not "as good," but better than he ever was before. George's age and profession are also significant in that much of Dickey's work is concerned with the relationship between men and boys and teachers and students. This important trope finds expression in *Alnilam* and *The Sentence*, as well as a number of the poems.[75] As an adult and a teacher, George has the knowledge and experience which Dennis—in his frivolous debauchery—and the Haitian runner—in his overconfidence—lack. A father and teacher figure, George has an authority which empowers him in his relations with others.

If "The Olympian" is a departure from Dickey's other screenplays, "The Breath"—a three-page prospectus—is representative of fictional themes from the collective body of his work. The protagonist, Quentin Dodson, is an imaginative voyeur, more interested in observing and playing at life than participating in its realities. A wealthy eccentric, Dodson booby-traps his house as the first step in staging a drama of survival, based on Richard Connell's "The Most Dangerous Game." Dodson then visits a seedy bar where he feigns inebriation and brags to the criminal clientele about his immense wealth. Not surprisingly, an opportunistic man from the bar, Garth, later appears at Dodson's house and becomes locked inside. Using the intercom, Dodson informs Garth that he will award him $35,000 if he can stay alive for the next six hours. Dodson and Garth then select primitive weapons to use in stalking each other. Dodson's allusion to his weapon, a blow gun, suggests the screenplay's title: "I propose to kill you with my breath."[76] Dickey explained that the actual hunt would "comprise the main body of the film"[77] and during the sequence it becomes apparent that Dodson "is cat-and-mousing with his quarry to a perverse and

---

[75]See especially "Mangham" (*WM,* 226–28) and Dickey's many poems about his sons.

[76]Series 2.5, box 98a, 1.

[77]Ibid, 2.

perverted degree."[78] In the screenplay's climactic scene, the two confront each other and Doson prepares to fire his dart at Garth. Instead, he lowers the weapon and offers Garth the $35,000, explaining that he "never wanted to kill anyone; he only wanted the *game* of life and death."[79] Garth proceeds to stab Dodson and take the money, only to find that he is permanently trapped in the house.

In his pariah-like voyeurism and perversity, Quentin Dodson resembles Julian Glass from the *Casting*. Unable to connect meaningfully with other people, each feeds off the realities of others while constructing fantasy worlds of their own. Dickey takes the immediate survivalism of *Deliverance* and *To the White Sea* and infuses it with the sado-masochistic voyeurism of his abandoned first novel. Dodson's menagerie of conflict also suggests *Alnilam's* utopia of lies, in which the imagination creates false scenarios that possess the capacity for greater meaning than reality. Of course, the problem is that Garth does not accept the fabricated nature of the event. Much like Muldrow, he is unable to grasp experience as abstraction. Ironically, however, his murder of Dodson transforms the life-and-death game into a reality. Having literally destroyed his means of escaping the fantasy construction, he is now permanently locked in the house.

Near the end of his life, in addition to the unfinished *Crux*, Dickey had ideas for at least two other novels after the publication of *To the White Sea*. In a letter to Mark Jaffe[80] Dickey outlined the general plots for *Lanyon's Stair* and *The Rising of Alphecca*, both of which draw from the practical and philosophical ideas that went into *Alnilam*. *Lanyon's Stair* takes place at an artists' colony in Cornwall and is concerned with two main characters: Rabun, "a middle-aged American poet,"[81] and Peter Lanyon, "a young sculptor" who also has a passion for flying gliders. Dickey

---

[78]Ibid.

[79]Ibid.

[80]The letter is dated 7 June 1994.

[81]Matthew J. Bruccoli and Judith S. Baughman, eds., *Crux: The Letters of James Dickey* (New York: Knopf, 1999) 497.

insinuated that the relationship of the two men would be the catalyst for the story, but did not give any information on specific scenes and dialogue.

The second book idea which he also envisioned as a film, *The Rising of Alphecca*, involves a retired widower who studies and masters celestial navigation before taking a job on a freighter headed out to sea. Dickey explains that, "A mutiny is involved, which depends on which star comes up, at what time."[82] Although further notes for *Lanyon's Stair* have not surfaced, Dickey developed a screenplay prospectus for the *Rising of Alphecca* under a slightly different title: *The Rising of Alna'ir*. Both of the proper nouns in the titles are references to a single star,[83] but—apart from aesthetic sensibility or mere whimsy—it is unclear as to why Dickey selected one name over the other. In any event, Alna'ir or Alphecca—which is in fact the more common name—is in the southern hemisphere and serves as a popular star for celestial navigation. This plays an important part in the screenplay, in which a navigator must obtain an accurate "sight" on the star in order to save a lost ship and its crew. The senescent navigator, Ralph, develops an interest in celestial during the first years of his retirement. Purchasing a sextant and some books, he—like Dickey—completes a certified correspondence course in celestial navigation.

Ralph begins frequenting the water-front area of San Diego and makes friends with several of the sea-faring professionals he encounters. From one of these men he learns of a ship that needs a navigator, and excitedly takes the job, feeling "the last surge of adventure possible in his life."[84] The ship, the *Jocasta*, breaks port and for the first few days Ralph's duties are performed with exceptional skill, earning the respect of the crew and Captain Scott. However, the ship is bound for Java and, unknown to Ralph and Captain Scott, several of the crew are wanted there for various

---

[82]Ibid.

[83]The word Alphecca is derived from the Arabic phrase "Al Na'ir al Fakkah," which means "The Bright One of the Dish."

[84]Series 2.5, box 99d, 1.

crimes. While the reader is left wondering if a mutiny may take place, a vicious storm moves in on the *Jocasta* during which Ralph loses the ship's position and makes a bad miscalculation, almost driving the *Jocasta* into a reef. Presumably unable to make radio contact, the ship remains lost at sea for several days before the clouds break and Ralph gets a fix on a star, which is Alphecca rising in the evening sky. The screenplay ends with the crew wondering whether or not Ralph has made the correct calculation, "whether there is land ahead, or only the endless sea."[85]

Like most of Dickey's tentative cinematic projects, the *Rising of Alphecca* corresponds with ideas in *Alnilam*. Ralph's almost obsessive interest in the celestial is similar to that of Captain Whitehall, who uses his sextant to save his flight group as they are running out of fuel over the Pacific ocean. Dickey implies that Whitehall's knowledge of the celestial also gives him greater insight into Joel's ideas, which are partially based on the symbolic implications of astronomy and physics. As it does for Whitehall and Joel in *Alnilam*, the sextant locates Ralph, giving him a kind of mastery over the natural environment—only in the *Rising of Alphecca* it is an environment of water instead of air.

In one of his notebooks Dickey jotted out a six-page fragmentary script called *Clementine*, a kind of generic Western which concludes with a gun fight, but the plot is too fragmented and convoluted for there to be any benefit in recording it here.[86] Like the majority of Dickey's film ideas it remains both incomplete and unproduced. Considered together, the chief benefit of Dickey's screenplays rests in the instances in which they correspond with and indirectly comment upon themes from his published work. In their aim and value, they resemble Dickey's coffee-table books: objects of casual entertainment, created largely for monetary profit. Dickey had proven the impressive power of his visual imagination with the screenplay for *Deliverance*, but he never again was able to harness the cinematic drama which made an outstanding novel

---

[85]Ibid., 2.
[86]Series 2.7, box 106, notebook 22.

into an equally impressive film. Fueled by the promise of recapturing *Deliverance*'s financial success, he half-heartedly developed new screenplays which garnered equally tepid responses from producers. Seen in this light, these embers are more ash than flame, interesting for the themes they share with the published novels, but of a distinctively lesser order—the low-burning coals of Dickey's formidable creative fire.

CONCLUSION

ELEMENTS

Though less consciously organized, Dickey novels, like Faulkner's Yoknapatawpha cycle or John Dos Passos's *U.S.A.*, constitute a sequence of shared meditations on centralized aspects of existence. While the concerns of Faulkner and Dos Passos are largely socio-historical, Dickey explores the relationships between unique human beings and diverse elemental manifestations. Although it is tempting to view Dickey's three novels as a modern epic sequence, their deep exploration of (in)human participation with nature, at culture's expense, sets them apart from both modernist social concerns and the postmodern sense of cultural doubt, paradox, and collapse.[1]

Attempting to avoid a diachronic reading of the novels, I have tried to interpret each work as the "vehicle for an implicit theory of language or of other semiotic systems."[2] Dickey's verbal and thematic theory, the practice of merging, is remarkable for the multifaceted and layered manner in which it functions, involving protagonist and environment and reader and text. Just as Ed

---

[1]Whereas Dickey's fiction remains largely unconcerned with societal issues, it does resemble postmodernism in its dismissal of the totalizing idea of reason. Like Jean-François Lyotard and others, Dickey's protagonists come to believe that there exists no ultimate form of reasoning, only reasons.

[2]Jonathon Culler, *Structuralist Poetics: Structuralism, Linguistics, and the Study of Literature* (Ithaca: Cornell University Press, 1975) 98.

Gentry, Joel Cahill, and Muldrow assume the essence of their respective environments, the reader is subtly enticed to become part of the text while retaining cognitive independence—as Muldrow says, "To blend in the place you're in, but with a mind to do something" (TS, 273).

The chapter on Dickey's unpublished fiction does not actively pursue the merging thesis and having attempted to summarize the works at the expense of extended analysis, I offer my findings with some humility. The aborted short stories and novel from the 1950s are important both for their testaments of Dickey's fictional development and their similarities to *Alnilam*. The early fiction's preoccupation with war, perversity, creative lying, and father-son relationships all resurface in Dickey's favorite novel. The screenplays, too, are significant for their exploration of themes that appear elsewhere in Dickey's fiction. Considered on their own however, they appear labored and often sensational, the products of a half-interested creator. Like Faulkner and James Agee before him, Dickey was seduced into the Hollywood money trap. Attracted by the prospect of another hit film, he periodically cranked out projects for which he had little real artistic motivation or interest.

The fictional fragments notwithstanding, the real binding power of Dickey's published novels rests in their intense and absolute dedication to the protagonist and his unique affinity for the element that surrounds him. The deep and intimate levels of meaning that are the fruit of this practice also beckon the reader to the text. Seeking to deliver his protagonists into the elements and the reader into the text, Dickey tests the sublime boundaries of words and strains to come as close as humanly possible to the essence of inhuman existence.

APPENDIX[1]

As I came through the desert thus it was,
As I came through the desert: All was black,
In heaven no single star, on earth no track;
A brooding hush without a stir or note,
The air so thick it clotted in my throat;
And thus for hours; then some enormous things
Swooped past with savage cries and clanking wings:
But I strode on austere;
No hope could have no fear.
As I came through the desert thus it was,
As I came through the desert: Eyes of fire
Glared at me throbbing with a starved desire;
The hoarse and heavy and carnivorous breath
Was hot upon me from deep jaws of death;
Sharp claws, swift talons, fleshless fingers cold
Plucked at me from the bushes, tried to hold:
But I strode on austere;
No hope could have no fear.
As I came through the desert thus it was,
As I came through the desert: Lo you, there,
That hillock burning with a brazen glare;
Those myriad dusky flames with points a-glow
Which writhed and hissed and darted to and fro;
A Sabbath of the Serpents, heaped pell-mell
For Devil's roll-call and some *fêête* of Hell:
Yet I strode on austere;
No hope could have no fear.

---

[1] From James Thomson, (B. V.), *The City of Dreadful Night* (Portland ME: Mosher, 1909) 13–16.

As I came through the desert thus it was,
As I came through the desert: Meteors ran
And crossed their javelins on the black sky-span;
The zenith opened to a gulf of flame,

The dreadful thunderbolts jarred earth's fixed frame:
The ground all heaved in waves of fire that surged
And weltered round me sole there unsubmerged:
Yet I strode on austere;
No hope could have no fear.
As I came through the desert thus it was,
As I came through the desert: Air once more,
And I was close upon a wild sea-shore;
Enormous cliffs arose on either hand,
The deep tide thundered up a league-broad strand;
White foambelts seethed there, wan spray swept and flew;
The sky broke, moon and stars and clouds and blue:
And I strode on austere;
No hope could have no fear.
As I came through the desert thus it was,
As I came through the desert: On the left
The sun arose and crowned a broad crag-cleft;
There stopped and burned out black, except a rim,
A bleeding eyeless socket, red and dim;
Whereon the moon fell suddenly south-west,
And stood above the right-hand cliffs at rest:
Still I strode on austere;
No hope could have no fear.
As I came through the desert thus it was,
As I came through the desert: From the right
A shape came slowly with a ruddy light;
A woman with a red lamp in her hand,
Bareheaded and barefooted on that strand;
O desolation moving with such grace!
O anguish with such beauty in thy face.
I fell as on my bier,
Hope travailed with such fear.
As I came through the desert thus it was,
As I came through the desert: I was twain,
Two selves distinct that cannot join again;
One stood apart and knew but could not stir,
And watched the other stark in swoon and her;

And she came on, and never turned aside,
Between such sun and moon and roaring tide:

And as she came more near
My soul grew mad with fear.
As I came through the desert thus it was,
As I came through the desert: Hell is mild
And piteous matched with that accursèèd wild;
A large black sign was on her breast that bowed,
A broad black band ran down her snow-white shroud;
That lamp she held was her own burning heart,
Whose blood-drops trickled step by step apart;
The mystery was clear;
Mad rage had swallowed fear.
As I came through the desert thus it was,
As I came through the desert: By the sea
She knelt and bent above that senseless me;
Those lamp-drops fell upon my white brow there,
She tried to cleanse them with her tears and hair;
She murmured words of pity, love, and woe,
She heeded not the level rushing flow:
And mad with rage and fear,
I stood stonebound so near.

As I came through the desert thus it was,
As I came through the desert: When the tide
Swept up to her there kneeling by my side,
She clasped that corpse-like me, and they were borne
Away, and this vile me was left forlorn;
I know the whole sea cannot quench that heart,
Or cleanse that brow, or wash those two apart:
They love; their doom is drear,
Yet they nor hope nor fear;
But I, what do I here?

BIBLIOGRAPHY

In regard to primary and secondary sources, I list those works from which I quote in my consideration of Dickey's fiction. As a result, several of Dickey's works and a substantial number of scholarly articles about him are not included. For more comprehensive bibliographies see *James Dickey: A Selected Bibliography* (by Matthew J. Bruccoli and Judith Baughman), *Outbelieving Existence* (by Gordon Van Ness), and *The James Dickey Newsletter*, which endeavors to maintain an ongoing catalogue of primary and secondary works. Information from Dickey's unpublished material is cited in appropriate footnotes.

Works by James Dickey

Alnilam. New York: Doubleday, 1987.
Babel to Byzantium: Poets & Poetry Now. New York: Farrar, Straus and Giroux, 1968.
Deliverance. Boston: Houghton Mifflin, 1970.
Deliverance. Screenplay. Carbondale: Southern Illinois University Press, 1982.
Foreword. In Adrien Stoutenburg. *Land of Superior Mirages*, iii–v. Baltimore: Johns Hopkins Press, 1986.
Foreword. In T. Crunk. *Living in the Resurrection*, ix–xi. New Haven: Yale University Press, 1995.
Foreword. In *The Complete Short Stories of Thomas Wolfe*, edited by Francis E. Skipp, ix-xv. New York: Scribners, 1987.
"How to Enjoy Poetry." International Paper Company, 1982.
"Journey to the War." In *The James Dickey Reader*, edited by Henry Hart, 212–28. New York: Touchstone, 1999.
"Lightnings: Or *Visuals*." *James Dickey Newsletter* 8/2 (Spring 1992): 2-12.
Night Hurdling. Columbia: Bruccoli Clark, 1983.

Self-Interviews. Edited by Barbara and James Reiss. New York: Doubleday, 1970.

"Small Visions from a Timeless Place: The South as One Poet has Known It."
     Playboy 21/10 (October 1974): 152–54, 220–21.

Sorties. New York: Doubleday, 1971.

Southern Light. Birmingham: Oxmoor House, 1991.

Striking In: The Early Notebooks of James Dickey. Edited by Gordon Van Ness.
     Columbia: University of Missouri Press, 1996.

"The Imagination as Glory." In *The Imagination as Glory: The Poetry of James
     Dickey,* edited by Bruce Weigl and T.R. Hummer, 166–73. Urbana:
     University of Illinois Press, 1984.

"The Total Act." In *The Seamless Web,* by Stanley Burnshaw, vii–x. New York:
     George Braziller, 1991.

The Whole Motion: Collected Poems, 1945–1992. Hanover: Wesleyan University
     Press, 1992.

To the White Sea. Boston: Houghton Mifflin, 1993.

"Vale of Soul-making." Commencement Address. *USC Magazine* (Winter 1968):
     7–9.

Wayfarer: A Voice from the Southern Mountains. Birmingham: Oxmoor House,
     1988.

Secondary Sources

Abram, David. *The Spell of the Sensuous: Perception and Language in a More-
     Than-Human World.* New York: Pantheon, 1996.

Arnett, David L. "James Dickey: Poetry and Fiction." Ph.D. dissertation, Tulane
     University, 1973.

Bachelard, Gaston. *The Poetics of Space.* New York: Orion, 1964.

Bakhtin, Mikhail. *Éstetika slovesnogo tvor_estva.* Moscow: Iskusstvo, 1979.

———. *The Dialogic Imagination.* Translated by Caryl Emerson and Michael
     Holquist. Edited by Michael Holquist. Austin: University of Texas Press,
     1981.

Barthes, Roland. *S/Z.* Translated by Richard Miller. New York: Hill and Wang,
     1974.

Baughman, Ronald C. "James Dickey's *Alnilam*: Toward a True Center Point."
     James Dickey Newsletter 10/2 (Spring 1994): 173–79.

———, editor. "James Dickey at Drury College." *James Dickey Newsletter* 5/1 (Fall
     1988): 16–25.

———. "The Poetry of James Dickey: Variations on Estrangement." Ph.D.
     dissertation, University of South Carolina, 1975.

———, editor. *The Voiced Connections of James Dickey: Interviews and
     Conversations.* Columbia: University of South Carolina Press, 1989.

Benn, Gottfried. *Primal Vision.* Edited by E. B. Ashton. New York: New Directions, 1971.

Bourdieu, Pierre. *Esquisse d'une théorie de la pratique, précédé de trois études d'ethnologie kabyle.* Geneva: Droz, 1972.

———. *Outline of a Theory of Practice.* Cambridge: Cambridge University Press, 1977.

———. *The Logic of Practice.* Cambridge: Polity, 1990.

———. *The Political Ontology of Martin Heidegger.* Cambridge: Polity, 1991.

Broer, Lawrence. "Fire and Ice in Dickey's *To the White Sea.*" *Texas Review* 17/3–4 (Fall/Winter 1996/1997): 1–25.

Brooke, Jocelyn. *The Image of a Drawn Sword.* New York: Knopf, 1951.

Broughton, Ira. "James Dickey." In *The Writer's Mind: Interviews with American Authors Volume II,* edited by Ira Broughton, 163–90. Fayetteville: University of Arkansas Press, 1990.

Broyles, J. Allen. *The John Birch Society: Anatomy of a Protest.* Boston: Beacon Press, 1964.

Bruccoli, Matthew J., and Judith S. Baughman, editors. *Crux: The Letters of James Dickey.* New York: Knopf, 1999.

Burnham, Robert, Jr. *Burnham's Celestial Handbook.* Volume 2. New York: Dover, 1966.

Butterworth, Keen. "The Savage Mind: James Dickey's *Deliverance.*" *Southern Literary Journal* 28/2 (Spring 1996): 69–79.

Butts, Leonard C. "Nature in the Selected Works of Four Contemporary American Novelists." Ph.D. dissertation, University of Tennessee, 1979.

Calhoun, Richard J. "After a Long Silence: James Dickey as South Carolina Writer." *South Carolina Review* 9/1 (November 1976): 12-20.

Campbell, Joseph. *The Hero with a Thousand Faces.* Bollingen Series 17. New York: Princeton University Press, 1949.

Carrigan, Henry L. Review of *Crux: The Letters of James Dickey. Library Journal* 124/17 (15 October 1999): 70.

Certeau, Michel de. "Entretien, Mystique et psychoanalyse." *Le Bloc-Notes de la Psychoanalyse* 4 (1984): 136–61.

———. *The Mystic Fable.* Translated by Michael B. Smith. Chicago: University of Chicago Press, 1992.

———. *The Practice of Everyday Life.* Translated by Steven Rendall. Berkeley: University of California Press, 1984.

Chappell, Fred. "'Not as a Leaf': Southern Poetry and the Innovations of Tradition." *Georgia Review* 51/3 (Fall 1997): 477–89.

———. Review of *Alnilam. The State* (21 June 1987): 6-F.

Conroy, Pat. James Dickey Tribute. The Horseshoe, University of South Carolina, Columbia. 27 January 1997.

Covel, Robert. "'A Starry Place': The Energized Man in Dickey's *Alnilam*." *The James Dickey Newsletter* 5/2 (1989): 5–17.

Culler, Jonathon. *Structuralist Poetics: Structuralism, Linguistics, and the Study of Literature*. Ithaca: Cornell University Press, 1975.

Dickey, Christopher. *Summer of Deliverance: A Memoir of Father and Son*. New York: Simon and Schuster, 1998.

Edmundson, Mark. "James Dickey: Learning from Others." *Raritan* 15/3 (Winter 1996): 47–63.

Findlay, J. N. *The Philosophy of Hegel*. New York: Collier, 1958.

Fisher, Vardis. *Dark Bidwell*. Boston: Houghton Mifflin, 1931.

Fitter, Chris. *Poetry, Space, Landscape: Toward a New Theory*. Cambridge: Cambridge University Press, 1995.

Foucault, Michel. *Discipline and Punish*. Harmondsworth: Penguin, 1991.

Frazer, James. *The Golden Bough: A Study in Magic and Religion*. Hertfordshire: Wordsworth, 1993.

Gadamer, Hans-Georg. *Truth and Method*. New York: Continuum, 1975.

Galilei, Galileo. *Discoveries and Opinions of Galileo*. Translated by Stillman Drake. New York: Doubleday, 1957.

Greiner, Donald J. "Robert Frost, James Dickey, and the Lure of Non-Human Otherness." In *His "Incalculable" Influence on Others: Essays on Robert Frost in Our Time*, edited by Earl J. Wilcox, 65–70. Victoria (Canada): University of Victoria Press, 1994.

———. "'The Iron of English': An Interview with James Dickey." *South Carolina Review* 25/2 (Spring 1994): 9–20.

Guinn, Matthew. "The Neo-Romantic in the Natural World: Naturalism in James Dickey's Poetry." *South Atlantic Review* 62/1 (Winter 1997): 87–100.

Habermas, Jürgen. *The Theory of Communicative Action*. Volume 1. Boston: Beacon Press, 1984.

Hart, Henry. "James Dickey and World War II—History into Story." *James Dickey Newsletter* 14/2 (Spring 1998): 2–8.

———. *James Dickey: The World as a Lie*. New York: Picador USA, 2000.

Hathcock, Nelson. "No Further Claim to Innocence: James Dickey's Revision of the American War Story." *Texas Review* 17/3–4 (Fall/Winter 1996/1997): 26–42.

Heidegger, Martin. *Being and Time*. Translated by John Macquarrie and Edward Robinson. New York: Harper & Row, 1962.

———. *Die Selbstbehauptung der deutschen Universität*. Breslau: Korn, 1934.

———. *Discourse on Thinking*. Translated by John M. Anderson and E. Hans Freund. New York: Harper & Row, 1966.

———. *On the Way to Language*. Translated by Peter D. Hertz. New York: Harper & Row, 1971.

Herendeen, Wyman. *From Landscape to Literature: The River and the Myth of Geography*. Pittsburgh: Duquesne University Press, 1986.

Hodge, Marion. "*Alnilam* and the Subversion of Story." *James Dickey Newsletter* 12/2 (Spring 1996): 2–12.

Hoffman, Daniel. *Poe Poe Poe Poe Poe Poe Poe*. Garden City: Doubleday, 1973.

Jameson, Frederic. "The Great American Hunter, or Ideological Contents in the Novel." *College English* 34 (November 1972): 180–97.

Jammer, Max. *Concepts of Space: The History of Theories of Space in Physics*. Cambridge: Harvard University Press, 1954.

Jarrell, Randall. "Poets, Critics, and Readers." In *Kipling, Auden & Co.: Essays and Reviews 1935-1964*, 305–18. New York: Farrar, Straus and Giroux, 1980.

Jefferies, Richard. *The Story of My Heart*. Portland ME: Mosher, 1900.

Jeffers, Robinson. *The Selected Poetry of Robinson Jeffers*. New York: Random House, 1937.

Jung, C. G. "Psychology and Literature." In *Modern Man in Search of a Soul*, translated by W. S. Dell and Cary F. Baynes, 152–72. New York: Harcourt, Brace, and Company, 1933.

Jünger, Ernst. *An der Zeitmauer*. Stuttgart: Klett, 1959.

Kahn, Charles H. *Anaximander and the Origins of Greek Cosmology*. Philadelphia: Centrum Philadelphia, 1982.

Keats, John. *The Complete Poetical Works and Letters of John Keats*. Edited by Horace E. Scudder. Boston: Houghton Mifflin, 1899.

Kirschten, Robert. "Interview with James Dickey." In *"Struggling for Wings": The Art of James Dickey*, edited by Kirschten, 65–77. Columbia: University of South Carolina Press, 1997.

———. *James Dickey and the Gentle Ecstacy of Earth*. Baton Rouge: Louisiana State University Press, 1988.

Koestler, Arthur. *The Yogi and the Commissar*. New York: Macmillan, 1945.

L'Amour, Louis. *Last of the Breed*. New York: Bantam, 1986.

Lieberman, Laurence. "James Dickey: The Deepening of Being." In *The Achievement of James Dickey*, edited by Lieberman, 1–21. Glenview: Scott, Foresman and Company, 1968.

———. "Warrior, Visionary, Natural Philosopher: James Dickey's *To the White Sea*." *The Southern Review* 33/1 (Winter 1997): 164–80.

Lopez, Barry. *Arctic Dreams: Imagination and Desire in a Northern Landscape*. New York: Charles Scribner's Sons, 1986.

Lucretius. *On the Nature of the Universe*. Translated by R. E. Latham. Harmondsworth: Penguin, 1951.

Matthiessen, Peter. *Nine-Headed Dragon River: Zen Journals 1969–1982*. Boston: Shambhala, 1986.

McClatchey, J. D. Review of *Crux: The Letters of James Dickey* and *The James Dickey Reader. New York Times on the Web.* 19 December 1999. 1 January 2000<<www.nytimes.com/books/99/12/19/reviews/991219.19mcclact.html >>.

Nietzsche, Friedrich. *Basic Writings of Nietzsche.* Edited by Walter Kaufman. New York: Modern Library, 1968.

———. "On Truth and Falsity in an Extra-Moral Sense." In *Early Greek Philosophy and Other Essays,* 171–92. Volume 2 of *The Complete Works of Friedrich Nietzsche.* Translated by M. A. Mügge. Edited by Oscar Levy. New York: Russell & Russell, 1964.

———. *The Portable Nietzsche.* Translated and edited by Walter Kaufman. New York: Penguin, 1954.

———. *The Will to Power.* Translated by Walter Kaufman and R. J. Hollingdale. Edited by Kaufman. New York: Random House, 1967.

———. *Werke: Kritische Gesamtausgabe.* Berlin: de Gruyter, 1967.

Peckham, Joel B., Jr. "James Dickey and the Narrative Mode of Transmission: The Sheep Child's Other Realm." *The Mississippi Quarterly* 52/2 (Spring 1999): 239–57.

Plato. *The Republic of Plato.* Translated by Allan Bloom. New York: Basic Books, 1968.

Pound, Ezra. "The Constant Preaching to the Mob." In *Literary Essays of Ezra Pound,* edited by T. S. Eliot, 64–65. New York: New Directions, 1968.

Review of *Alnilam. Publishers Weekly* 233/10 (11 March 1988): 51.

Review of *Crux: The Letters of James Dickey. Publishers Weekly* 246/43 (25 October 1999): 65.

Rilke, Rainer Maria. "Concerning Landscape." In *Where Silence Reigns,* translated by G. Craig Houston, 1–5. New York: New Directions, 1978.

———. *New Poems.* Translated by J. B. Leishman. New York: New Directions, 1964.

Roethke, Theodore. "The Longing." In *The Collected Poems of Theodore Roethke,* 181–83. New York: Doubleday, 1966.

Rooke, Leon. "Sergeant Muldrow finds Transcendence." *New York Times Book Review* (19 September 1993): 14.

Sagan, Carl. *Broca's Brain: Reflections on the Romance of Science.* Random House, 1979.

Saint Exupéry, Antoine de. *Night Flight.* New York: Harcourt Brace Jovanovich, 1932.

Santayana, George. *The Life of Reason.* New York: Scribner's, 1932.

———. *Three Philosophical Poets.* Cambridge: Harvard University Press, 1945.

Sartre, Jean-Paul. *The Philosophy of Jean-Paul Sartre.* Edited by Robert Denoon Cumming. New York: Vintage, 1965.

Schöne, Hermann. *Spatial Orientation: Spatial Control of Behavior in Animals and Man.* Translated by Camilla Strausfeld. Princeton: Princeton University Press, 1984.

Shelley, Percy Bysshe. *Selected Poems, Essays, and Letters.* Edited by Ellsworth Barnard. New York: Odyssey Press, 1944.

Soja, Edward W. *Postmodern Geographies: The Reassertion of Space in Critical Social Theory.* New York: Verso, 1989.

Spencer, Susan A. "James Dickey's American Cain." *College Language Association Journal* 36/3 (March 1993): 291–306.

Spender, Stephen. *Collected Poems, 1928–1953.* New York: Random House, 1955.

Stansky, Peter and William Abraham. *Journey to the Frontier.* Boston: Little, Brown and Company, 1966.

Suarez, Ernest. "An Interview with James Dickey." *Contemporary Literature* 31/2 (Summer 1990): 117–32.

———. "An Interview with James Dickey: Poet and Novelist." *Texas Review* 17/3–4 (Fall/Winter 1996/1997): 128–43.

———. *James Dickey and the Politics of Canon: Assessing the Savage Ideal.* Columbia: University of Missouri Press, 1993.

———. "'Real God, Roll': Muldrow's Primitive Creed." *James Dickey Newsletter* 10/2 (Spring 1994): 3–14.

Sullivan, Rosemary. "Surfacing and Deliverance." *Canadian Literature* 8 (1976): 6–20.

Thomson, James, (B.V.). *The City of Dreadful Night.* Portland ME: Mosher, 1909.

———. *The Speedy Extinction of Evil and Misery.* Edited by William David Schaefer. Berkeley: University of California Press, 1967.

Truehart, Charles. "James Dickey's Celestial Navigations." *Washington Post,* 24 May 1987, F1+.

Tschachler, Heinz. "'Un principe d'insuffisance': Dickey's Dialogue with Bataille." *Mosaic* 20/3 (Summer 1987): 81–93.

Valéry, Paul. "Note." In *Variety,* translated by Malcolm Cowley, 27–53. New York: Harcourt, Brace and Company, 1927.

———. "On Poe's 'Eureka'" In *Variety,* translated by Malcolm Cowley, 121–46. New York: Harcourt, Brace and Company, 1927.

Van Ness, Gordon. "'The Whole Situation was Mine': James Dickey's Fictional Protagonists and the Ethic of Survival." *James Dickey Newsletter* 10/1 (Fall 1993): 17–23.

Wacquant, Loic J.D. "Towards a Reflexive Sociology: A Workshop with Pierre Bourdieu." *Sociological Theory* 7/1 (1989): 26–63.

Warren, Robert Penn. "Why Do We Read Fiction?" In *New and Selected Essays,* 55–66. New York: Random House, 1989.

Wheelwright, Philip. *Heraclitus.* New York: Atheneum, 1974.

Yeats, William Butler. *The Collected Plays of W. B. Yeats.* London: Macmillan, 1953.

INDEX